Taming Intuition

The success of democratic governance hinges on an electorate's ability to reward elected officials who act faithfully and punish those who do not. Yet there is considerable variation among voters in their ability to objectively evaluate representatives' performance. In this book the authors develop a theoretical model, the Intuitionist Model of Political Reasoning, which posits that this variation across voters is the result of individual differences in the predisposition to reflect on and to override partisan impulses. Individuals differ in partisan intuitions resulting from the strength of their attachments to parties, as well as the degree to which they are willing to engage in the cognitively taxing process of evaluating those intuitions. The balance of these forces – the strength of intuitions and the willingness to second-guess one's self – determines the extent to which individuals update their assessments of political parties and elected officials in a rational manner.

Kevin Arceneaux is Professor of Political Science, Faculty Affiliate with the Institute for Public Affairs, and Director of the Behavioral Foundations Lab at Temple University. He studies political psychology and political communication, focusing on how the interaction between political messages and people's political predispositions shapes attitudes and behavior. He is coauthor of *Changing Minds or Changing Channels* (2013), which investigates the influence of ideologically slanted news programming and received the 2014 Goldsmith Book Prize from Harvard University. His work has also been published in *American Political Science Review, American Journal of Politics*, and elsewhere.

Ryan J. Vander Wielen is Associate Professor of Political Science and (by courtesy) Economics, and Faculty Affiliate with the Behavioral Foundations Lab at Temple University. His teaching and research interests are in the areas of American political institutions, political behavior, quantitative methodology, and formal modeling. His work has been published in *The American Journal of Political Science, British Journal of Political Science, Legislative Studies Quarterly, Political Analysis, Public Choice*, and elsewhere. He is also the coauthor of *Politics over Process* (forthcoming), *The American Congress* (Cambridge University Press, 2015), and *The American Congress Reader* (Cambridge University Press, 2009).

Taming Intuition

How Reflection Minimizes Partisan Reasoning and Promotes Democratic Accountability

KEVIN ARCENEAUX

Temple University

RYAN J. VANDER WIELEN

Temple University

CAMBRIDGE
UNIVERSITY PRESS

CAMBRIDGE
UNIVERSITY PRESS

University Printing House, Cambridge CB2 8BS, United Kingdom

One Liberty Plaza, 20th Floor, New York, NY 10006, USA

477 Williamstown Road, Port Melbourne, VIC 3207, Australia

4843/24, 2nd Floor, Ansari Road, Daryaganj, Delhi – 110002, India

79 Anson Road, #06-04/06, Singapore 079906

Cambridge University Press is part of the University of Cambridge.

It furthers the University's mission by disseminating knowledge in the pursuit of education, learning, and research at the highest international levels of excellence.

www.cambridge.org
Information on this title: www.cambridge.org/9781108415101
DOI: 10.1017/9781108227643

First published 2017

Printed in the United States of America by Sheridan Books, Inc.

A catalogue record for this publication is available from the British Library.

ISBN 978-1-108-41510-1 Hardback
ISBN 978-1-108-40031-2 Paperback

Contents

Figures

Tables

Preface and Acknowledgments

This project began with a lighthearted discussion over dinner as a simple and relatively narrow idea about whether partisan identities lead people to respond more emotionally to politics. As we talked about it more, we decided that we had the kernel of an idea that could become a research note. With these modest ambitions, we set out to learn more about the psychology of information processing and stepped into the rich literature that lies at the intersection of neuroscience, economics, and psychology. We quickly realized a grander ambition and saw the potential to fuse two theoretical traditions that provide disparate, and often conflictual, foundations for the study of political attitudes and behavior: rational choice and social psychology. Both of these traditions give different conceptions of the role that partisan identities play in shaping political decisions and, more crucially, different conceptions of whether voters are up to the task of self-governance. The rational choice framework presupposes that citizens make decisions in line with their values and hold politicians accountable when they fail to serve as faithful delegates. In contrast, social psychological accounts suggest that citizens are incapable of getting beyond their partisan biases and hold politicians from the opposing party to a far different standard than they do politicians from their own party.

Of course, we are not the first to tackle the ambitious task of merging rational choice and social psychological approaches to study political phenomena. We are indebted to scholars, such as Cheryl Boudreau, Dennis Chong, Eric Dickson, Skip Lupia, Mathew McCubbins, Rose McDermott, Becky Morton, and Jon Woon, who have blazed the path before us, showing the way. To the extent we offer something useful, it is because we were fortunate to build on the foundation that they created. We see our contribution as better incorporating psychological motivations into the model of how people arrive at political decisions, and in doing so, introducing a different way to think about rationality in political science. This project also builds on our previous separate streams of research. Arceneaux's previous work invokes a more rudimentary version of the Intuitionist Model of Political Reasoning than we present in this book, and his work with Martin Johnson starts with the idea that individual differences in psychological motivations have behavioral implications. Vander Wielen's previous work rests firmly on a rational choice framework to explain the strategic behavior of political elites. These models are often prefaced on the assumption that elite behavior is a reflection of a rational electorate, and as we discovered over our dinner conversation, this assumption did not always sit well with him. Together we discovered, and seek to explain in the pages that follow, that rationality can be thought of as a continuum, and where people fall on that continuum for any given issue is, at least in part, a function of their willingness to second-guess their gut reactions – that is, to be *reflective*.

No research project is done in isolation. We are indebted to many people who gave us feedback, advice, and encouragement along the way. We thank Lene Aarøe, Chris Achen, Quinn Albaugh, Chloé Bakalar, Adam Berinsky, John Bullock, Dan Butler, Chuck Cameron, Brandice Canes-Wrone, Devin Caughey, Tom Clark, Eric Crahan, Jamie Druckman, Michele Epstein, Patrick Fournier, Guy Grossman, Danny Hayes, Dan Hopkins, Corrine McConnaughy, Michael Bang Petersen, Markus Prior, Eldar Shafir, Rune Slothuus, Stuart Soroka, Rachel Stein, Alex Theodoridis, Nick Valentino, Ali Valenzuela, Lynn Vavreck, and Chris Wlezien. We would also like to thank participants at various workshops where we received valuable comments about the book: Aarhus University Department of Political Science, Behavioral Models of Politics Conference at Duke University, Center for the Study of Democratic Politics at Princeton University, Centre for the Study of Democratic Citizenship at McGill University, George Washington University Department of Political Science, Massachusetts Institute for Technology Department of Political Science, University of California at Riverside Political Behavior Conference, University of Michigan Survey Research Center, and University of Texas at Austin Political Communication Lecture Series. This book was markedly improved by the trenchant comments we received from three anonymous reviewers, who clearly devoted considerable energy to reading and reflecting on our work. We are deeply grateful to Dan Butler for granting us access to the The American Panel Survey at Washington University in St. Louis. We also thank Nick Anspach, Colin Emrich, Claire Gothreau, and Jay Jennings for research assistance. This book as it stands now is decidedly stronger as a result of the contributions of these colleagues. We could not have done it without their help. Yet to the extent that it could be better – as is most certainly the case – we hold ourselves responsible.

We also wish to thank the Center for the Study of Democratic Politics at Princeton University, which granted Arceneaux a year long research fellowship during his sabbatical that proved invaluable for completing this project. It also provided an intellectually stimulating environment that helped hone and sharpen our theoretical model and the book's overarching argument. Arceneaux is especially grateful to his fellow fellows, Chloé, Rachael, and Tom, who gave him needed inspiration and diversions. He is also deeply indebted to Michele Epstein for sharing her thoughts on the project from her perspective as a trained psychologist, as well as for her generosity and her administrative acumen. She made the entire year a delightful and productive one.

Finally, we thank our partners, Juliet and Samantha, for providing us with moral support, perspective, and love. It would not be an exaggeration to say that without them, we could not have written this book. Beyond engaging us in conversations that helped us think about our research in new and beneficial ways, they also ground us in ways that give us the confidence to tackle ambitious questions and the perspective needed to do so.

Democratic Accountability and the "Rational" Citizen

Democracy is the theory that the common people know what they want, and deserve to get it good and hard.

                       – Henry Louis Mencken (1916, 19)

For all of its praise as an ideal form of government, democracy provokes a lot of scorn in practice. In its pure and ideal form, democracy is premised on a simple idea: the people govern themselves. Enshrined in this idea is the principle that socially binding decisions should reflect the will of the people. In the United States and most other advanced industrial societies, rule by the people is a widely accepted, uncontroversial political creed. It is an idea so fundamental and self-evident that democracy, at least in the abstract is as much a virtue as kindness or patience. Like so many other things, however, what seems great in the abstract is usually less so in practice. As Henry Louis Mencken's wry opening quote illustrates, despite democracy's broad appeal, there is a great deal of pessimism surrounding the notion that people are actually capable of self-government.

Much of this pessimism derives from the translation of democratic ideals into real-world institutions. In its ideal form, democracy achieves rule by the people quite simply by giving all the adult citizens in a society the right to vote directly on matters of public policy. Seen as unwieldy if not impossible to re-create in large-scale societies, the democratic governments that took shape in the nineteenth century relied on republican institutions in which a smaller group of individuals chosen through election would make decisions on behalf of the people. Republican institutions generate democratic outcomes insofar as elected policy makers make decisions that faithfully represent the wishes of the constituents who elected them. Benjamin Franklin (2003/1787, 398) offered a succinct explanation of the people's role in an electoral democracy during the convention that drafted the US Constitution and created the first modern electoral democracy. He said, "In free governments, the rulers are the servants and the people their superiors and sovereigns."[1] Restated in academic parlance, Franklin's view of electoral democracy designates the people as the "principals" and their elected representatives as their "agents." The principal-agent arrangement is a common element of industrialized societies where people must rely on others to accomplish their tasks. Any time we take our clothes to the dry cleaner or our car to the mechanic, we enter into a principal-agent arrangement. All works out well if the agent independently shares the principal's goals, because the agent wants to do what the principal wants done. However, this is not always the case. For instance, when we take our clothes to the dry cleaner and our car to the mechanic, our goal is to get our clothes clean and our car fixed. Yet the dry cleaner and the mechanic want our money, not necessarily for our clothes to be clean and our car repaired. So, we have to find a way to make dry cleaners and mechanics accountable for the services they provide such that they are rewarded for rendering good service and punished for rendering poor service. Therein lies the so-called *principal-agent problem*.

In the context of electoral democracy, the principal-agent problem involves the concern that elected representatives may not be faithful to the will of the people, that they may shirk their responsibilities by pursuing policies and programs that are contrary to public opinion. Given the skills needed to campaign and appeal to a broad group of people, elections generally ensure that representatives are going to have greater social prestige and privilege than the average citizen (Manin, 1997). Consequently, one cannot simply assume that the preferences of elected representatives will match the preferences of the larger electorate. This simple fact means that republican institutions reflect democratic principles insofar as citizens hold elected representatives accountable for their decisions. Short of resorting to tar and feathers, elections offer the only reliable mechanism for ordinary citizens to hold elected officials accountable for their actions. From the principle-agent perspective, people exercise *democratic accountability* when they use elections as a way to put in place representatives who follow the will of the people and remove those who do not.

The principal-agent framework was born in economics at a time when economists widely assumed that people arrive at decisions through dispassionate and calculated reasoning. In a word, people are "rational." Consequently, this idealized model of democratic accountability also assumes that citizens behave rationally. What constitutes "behaving rationally" varies from scholar to scholar, but at a minimum the principal-agent model of democratic accountability presumes that citizens behave in accordance with three principles. First, citizens form policy preferences that are internally consistent and connected to an ideological worldview. Second, citizens base their evaluations of elected representatives on the policy decisions that they make as well as how those policies perform. Third, citizens vote for office holders who make policy decisions that are consistent with citizens' preferences (Lenz, 2012) and generate positive outcomes (Ferejohn, 1986; Key, 1966), and they vote against those who do not.

For better or worse, students of democratic politics have settled on the principal-agent framework as a normative benchmark by which to judge the health of democratic accountability, and by extension the degree to which representative political institutions reflect the will of the people. It is the gap between this idealized model of democratic citizenship and the behavior of actual citizens that gives rise to much of the current-day consternation over democracy in practice. At the risk of oversimplification, and no doubt at the cost of minimizing nuance, we categorize the various takes on the functioning of democratic accountability in the United States into two loose camps: the optimists and the pessimists. The debate exposes the fault line between scholars who approach the study of politics from the vantage point of economic theories and those who do so from the perspective of psychological theories. Those who take an economic approach are more sympathetic to the assumption that people behave in fundamentally rational ways (Chong, 2013), while those who take a psychological approach point to substantial empirical evidence that people's reasoning is clouded and distorted by all sorts of biases and constraints (e.g., Kahneman, 2011) that make it difficult (if not impossible) for many individuals to arrive at their political preferences and make political decisions through dispassionate and calculated reasoning (e.g., Lodge and Taber, 2013).

Because political parties organize electoral politics and fundamentally structure the choices that citizens make, they lie at the center of this debate. Pessimistic accounts of democratic accountability identify citizens' emotional attachments to political parties as an especially problematic source of bias that fuels *motivated reasoning*, while optimistic accounts paint party attachments as a useful guide or *heuristic*. From the optimistic perspective, people choose to affiliate with the political party that most closely represents their policy preferences, which helps them make political decisions more efficiently. Rather than spending time and energy developing an encyclopedic knowledge of public policy, people can look to the policy positions taken by partisan elites and adopt the ones that their party takes (Lupia, 1994). At the same time, people continue to evaluate how well their party's policies achieve their preferences and interests, and they are willing to switch party allegiances if their party lets them down (Fiorina, 1981). From the pessimistic perspective, party attachments – whether they are initially rooted in policy preferences or not – become a social identity that causes people to root for their party like they would for a sports team. As a result, partisan attachments motivate people to maintain a positive view of their party at the expense of ensuring that their party advocates political policies that are aligned with their interests. If the pessimists are right, elected representatives can count on constituents who share their party affiliation to support them irrespective of whether they choose policies that are consistent with their constituents' underlying preferences and interests (Cohen, 2003), undermining the central tenets of democratic accountability.

Ultimately, this dispute is about whether the act of thinking helps people make good political decisions. The classical economic models that underlie many optimistic accounts presume that people think the way computers process information – according to dispassionate optimization algorithms. In contrast, the psychological models of motivated reasoning that populate most pessimistic accounts equate thinking with a form of mental gymnastics that helps people rationalize the things they want to believe. In this book we take a different approach to thinking about thinking. We draw on insights from the behavioral revolution in the decision sciences, which fuses economic and psychological traditions, to start with a more accurate view of how the human mind works and, in the end, provides a new perspective on rationality. Human decision making does not begin and end with thinking, which is a conscious act. It begins with the unconscious mind pointing the way by quickly and effortlessly formulating an emotionally charged gut reaction or *intuition*. Sometimes our intuitions point us in the right direction, and sometimes they do not. When they do, we do not need to rely much on thinking to make a decision. Yet when our intuitions point in the wrong direction, thinking can help. It is not guaranteed to help, however – after all, if we are strongly motivated to do what our intuitions suggest, we can simply rationalize those intuitions rather than reflect on the best course of action.

This book is about the role that *reflection* plays in political decision making. In the pages that follow, we adopt a very specific definition for the word reflection. It occurs when people use thought to critically evaluate their intuitions and override their intuitions when they point in the wrong direction. As the title of our book indicates, we think that reflection tames people's intuitions. Human intuition is an incredibly powerful resource that helps us make many complex decisions quickly and efficiently. Nonetheless, our intuitions are not perfect, and, left unchecked, they can sometimes lead us astray. Reflection is that check. In democratic politics, our intuition is to side with the political party we like the best. When elected officials affiliated with our party take actions that are consistent with our ideological preferences, our intuition points us in the right direction. When they do not – when they choose policies that fail, when they take positions that are inconsistent with our values, or worse, when they are corrupt – our intuition leads us astray. It is in these instances that our intuition encourages us to behave like motivated reasoners who continue to support candidates and elected officials despite the evidence indicating that we should not. It is in these instances when a heavy dose of reflection is needed to counter our worst instincts and help us behave rationally.

We offer an updated model of political reasoning that formalizes the interplay between intuition and thought. In doing so, we improve on extant models of political decision making in several ways. We provide an explanation for where people's partisan motivations come from as well as why people vary in the degree to which they behave like motivated reasoners. Extant models of motivated reasoning surmise that people's motivations vary (cf. Kunda, 1990) but do not explain why. In addition, our model elaborates how people differ with respect to the way in which they process political information, rather than assuming that people evaluate information in a uniform way. Consequently, it offers insight into why people, when confronted with the same facts, put more weight on some facts than on others as well as why people who are highly attentive to and knowledgeable about politics do not consistently behave in ways that most of us would consider rational or reasonable. Finally, our model provides a positive role for thinking. Without a doubt, many voters use thought – to the extent that they think at all – to rationalize their decisions

(Lodge and Taber, 2013), but some do not, and we can predict the type of voter who tends to be more reflective and, as a result, more rational.

Our model demonstrates that neither the optimists nor the pessimists are entirely correct. We find that reflection minimizes partisan reasoning and promotes democratic accountability. Because the propensity to be reflective varies across individuals and contexts, partisan identities can indeed cloud people's judgments and undermine democratic accountability in the process, but they do not do so in every context or for every person. These findings put us in neither the optimists' nor the pessimists' camp. Rather, we consider ourselves to be realists who see conditional applicability of *both* of these competing schools of thought. Whether people can live up to the standard set by the textbook model of democratic accountability depends on who they are and the circumstances they confront. We find ourselves in agreement with Hobbes – the stuffed tiger in the comic strip *Calvin and Hobbes* penned by Bill Watterson, not the seventeenth-century political philosopher – who said, "The problem with people is that they're only human."[2] The function of democracy depends on humans, and while it is true that humans are inherently fallible, it is false to presume that citizens are equally incapable of navigating the demands placed on them within a democracy. Our contribution is to offer an explanation for why some people are better at doing that than others.

1.1 DO PARTISAN ATTACHMENTS UNDERMINE DEMOCRATIC ACCOUNTABILITY?

Before we say more about our take, we believe that it is important to elaborate what all the fuss is about. Much ink has been spilled over whether political parties undermine citizen rationality and democratic accountability because they occupy the organizational core of electoral democracy. As E. E. Schattschneider (1942, 1) put it, "The political parties created democracy and modern democracy is unthinkable save in terms of the parties." This assertion is certainly the case in the United States, which led the movement toward electoral democracy in the modern era and serves as the empirical testing ground for our theoretical model. Although the framers of the US Constitution did not envision the rise of political parties and, in fact, thought that republican institutions would guard against groups based on particular interests, or "factions" (e.g., bankers, farmers, etc.), dominating political decisions (Madison, 2003/1787), it did not take long for various factions to forge stable alliances in the first US Congress and to congeal into political parties that organized legislative action (Hoadley, 1986) and ultimately electoral politics (Aldrich, 1995). The two major political parties in the United States organize and reduce the choices before voters (as do parties in other countries). Citizens do not merely choose among candidates in an election; they choose among candidates affiliated with the Democratic and Republican parties. As a result, many people develop attachments to the political parties, as they reliably support one party over another from election to election, and come to see themselves as democrats and republicans.[3] Pessimism greeted the emergence of political parties from the start. In his farewell address, President George Washington considered what he called "the spirit of party" to be "the worst enemy" of electoral democracy in large part because he believed that "[t]his spirit, unfortunately, is inseparable from our nature, having its roots in the strongest passions of the human mind" (Washington, 1796).

In contrast, optimists do not see partisan affiliations as inherently problematic. Many optimistic accounts begin with the assumption that citizens possess rationally formed preferences about political issues. Drawing on Anthony Downs's (1957) highly influential formalized account of the textbook model of democracy, preferences are typically defined as a rank ordering of likes and dislikes, which are "... stable, consistent, informed, and connected to abstract principles and values" (Chong and Druckman, 2007, 103). In the domain of politics, "abstract principles and values" can be thought of as a political ideology that is summarized along a single dimension where those who fall toward the left end prefer government regulation of the economy and those who fall toward the right end prefer less government regulation. Armed with rationally formed preferences, citizens choose the candidate who takes policy positions closest to their preferred ideological position and demonstrates a record (when in office) of generating policy outcomes that fall closest to their preferred outcomes. Because candidates affiliate with political parties, it is only natural for citizens to develop preferences about which political party to support. Yet, like policy preferences, people connect their party preferences to their ideological worldview and update their evaluation of the political parties in light of the outcomes that their policies produce when they control the government (e.g., Fiorina, 1981; Franklin and Jackson, 1983; Weinschenk, 2010). The extent to which people continue to support the same party from election to election is simply an artifact of stability in the political parties' relative positions and performance (Key, 1966; Fiorina, 1981). Consequently, party attachments do not undermine democratic accountability, because a reversal in fortunes or marked shift in issue positions would bring about swift changes in party attachments or, at the very least, how people vote.

Many pessimists take issue with the assumption that citizens possess meaningful preferences on the vast majority of political issues. This line of inquiry was set in motion by a quartet of researchers at the University of Michigan who provided a social psychological account of voting behavior in their tome, *The American Voter* (Campbell et al., 1960). Their portrait of the electorate found that most citizens simply have a diffuse sense of what they like and dislike when it comes to matters of politics instead of possessing a stable, consistent, and informed rank order of policy alternatives. That is, people have *attitudes* about politics, which are summaries of likes and dislikes, rather than preferences that impose order on likes and dislikes (Bartels, 2003). Outside a few issues that are of personal relevance, most people have a rather shallow understanding of the issues that lie at the center of political debates among elites (Bishop, 2004; Converse, 1964). Consequently, it is possible to sway many people's opinions with arbitrary shifts in language and clever, but misleading, rhetorical devices (e.g., Bartels, 2003; Jacobs and Shapiro, 2000; Nelson, Clawson, and Oxley, 1997), or shifts in media coverage that bring one set of considerations, say terrorism and crime, to the fore over others (McCombs and Shaw, 1972; Zaller, 1992).

In response to the criticism that most ordinary Americans lack coherently organized political preferences, one strand of research within the optimist camp contends that people can use contextual cues, such as the source of a political message, to form political attitudes that are consistent with their values and behave as if they held meaningful preferences (Lupia, 1994; Lupia and McCubbins, 1998; Popkin, 1994). These contextual cues act as helpful heuristics that constitute a rational strategy to reduce one's effort to remain informed about politics while arriving at the same decisions that one would if one were fully informed. From this perspective, party affiliation serves as a useful heuristic, since it gives people a simple decision rule. People, according to this account, can adopt the policy positions taken by prominent members of their party and reject those taken by members of the opposing party, and in doing so, they can develop a preference ordering without the fuss of thinking too much about it (Druckman, 2001; Levendusky, 2010; Zaller, 1992).

Pessimists share George Washington's view that party attachments are grounded in an atavistic "spirit," leading them to take a less sanguine view of heuristics. Pointing to an influential strand of research in psychology on decision making, they note that heuristics do not always serve as effective shortcuts and can often lead people to make mistakes (for an accessible summary of this literature, see Kahneman, 2011). In the domain of politics, pessimists see the political party as an unreliable heuristic. The problem begins with the reality that many people gravitate to a political party early in life and come to see their attachment to their party as an element of their personal identity (Campbell et al., 1960). Some people are democrats or republicans in the same way that they are Catholics, Californians, or Cubs fans. They are members of a group, and their identity with that group takes on a life of its own. To the extent that partisans bring their political attitudes in line with the positions taken by their party as an expression of group solidarity, they cede considerable decision-making power to political leaders (Dickson and Scheve, 2006; Lenz, 2012). It puts the party in the catbird seat when it comes to picking and choosing what issue positions partisans should adopt. As a result, parties act as an effective heuristic insofar as party leaders take positions that are consistent with their followers' values. If they do not, people's partisan identities will lead them astray (Cohen, 2003).

A parallel strand of research undertaken by optimists dismisses concerns about the consistency of citizens' issue preferences by focusing on how people respond to evidence of policy performance. They point to considerable evidence that shifts in aggregate public opinion, including party attachments, reflect actual events, such as international conflicts and economic outcomes (e.g., Brace and Hinckley, 1991; Conover, Feldman, and Knight, 1986; Durr, 1993; MacKuen, Erikson, and Stimson, 1989; Page and Shapiro, 1992). Electoral outcomes also reflect economic performance, with incumbents enjoying reelection in good times and being kicked to the curb in bad times (see Fair, 2009). Shifts in public opinion, in turn, correlate with policy making (Stimson, MacKuen, and Erikson, 1995), and public opinion responds to shifts in policy (Wlezien, 1995). The relationship between the public and their elected officials is akin to the relationship between a thermostat and a furnace. When the public wants more liberal policies, it gets them and then responds by reducing its demands for liberal policies. As a result, even if people fail to hold coherent preferences connected to their values, they seem capable of holding elected officials accountable for the outcomes that their policies produce.

As should be familiar by now in this scholarly tennis match, pessimists are not convinced. The influence of partisan identities extends beyond political attitudes, they contend. Partisan attachments cause people to adopt a distorted party-affirming view of reality. After all, people are quite capable of rationalizing away inconvenient facts in the realm of politics (cf. Lodge and Taber, 2013). Partisans do not always follow the trail of the cold, hard facts. They judge the economy as doing better when their party is in power than they do when the other party is at the wheel (Bartels, 2002). Even when events – such as times of war and calamity – constrain people's ability to believe whatever they wish about reality, their partisan identities still cause them to accept the obvious but interpret facts in ways that are favorable to their party (Bisgaard, 2015; Gaines et al., 2007). These biases do not go away by aggregating people's opinions or voting decisions (Althaus, 2003; Bartels, 1996; Duch, Palmer, and Anderson, 2000; Nir, 2011). These findings, viewed in a pessimistic light, call into question whether we can accurately interpret the correlation between aggregate opinion and political outcomes as evidence of democratic accountability at work in the American system. After all, if the signal is biased, so too is the output. As a result, shifts in party control of government may have less to do with voters acting like a "rational god of vengeance and reward" (Key, 1964, 567) than with a perverse expression of random shocks and irrelevant events (Achen and Bartels, 2016; Healy, Malhotra, and Mo, 2010).

1.2 OUR TAKE: PEOPLE ARE DIFFERENT

As we have already said, we count ourselves as realists. To loosely paraphrase former US Secretary of Defense Donald Rumsfeld, a democratic system operates with the people as they exist, not as we might want or wish they did.[4] As realists, we believe that in order to understand the relationship between partisanship and democratic accountability, we should begin with a more descriptively accurate theory of how people reason about politics. Our attempt to construct such a theory begins with a simple premise: people process information in fundamentally different ways, and these differences shape whether people behave as motivated partisan reasoners or as reasonable and objective citizens.

We recognize that we are not the first to note that people are different. After all, democracy is premised on the notion that people can resolve their political differences peacefully through democratic institutions. Our point is that people's differences are not simply about having different views on how the world should work. People do not just want different things; they also go about making up their minds about what they want in different ways. The foundational models that kindled the optimists-pessimists divide presume that people arrive at decisions in the same way. The progenitor of optimistic accounts characterized citizens as thoughtful agents who rationally incorporate new information into their political evaluations (Downs, 1957), while the progenitors of pessimistic accounts portrayed citizens as largely unthinking dolts who irrationally cling to their partisan and group identities (Campbell et al., 1960).

Even newer and more sophisticated models of political attitude formation continue to presume that people arrive at decisions in the same way. The widely accepted Receive-Accept-Sample model (Zaller, 1992), for instance, assumes that when people need to form an opinion about a political issue, they simply average over the positively and negatively charged considerations related to that issue that happen to be at the top of their conscious mind. Whether the considerations at the top of people's minds are largely consistent with their political worldview depends on how attentive people are to media coverage, with more knowledgeable or "sophisticated" individuals being better at keeping their political attitudes in line with their political worldview. What differentiates individuals is not how they process information but how motivated they are to be informed about politics. The John Q. Public model (Lodge and Taber, 2013), which offers the most contemporary model of motivated reasoning in political science, departs from the Receive-Accept-Sample model's emphasis on conscious memory-based processing. Instead, it focuses on how the unconscious mind spontaneously forms opinions that feel right – those in line with one's partisan attachment, for instance – and subsequently biases conscious judgments. Although the John Q. Public model is more consistent with current neuroscience theories of how the mind works than the Receive-Accept-Sample model, it also assumes that people's unconsciously formed intuitions guide decisions to the same extent, with the only thing differentiating people from one another being the content of their intuitions.

In contrast, we explicitly incorporate differences in people's willingness to think and be thoughtful in how they process information and deal with their intuitions. In doing so, we draw on a wealth of research in psychology on *individual differences*, which posits that individuals vary from one another in terms of their fundamental psychological needs and, as a result, respond to the same environment in different ways (e.g., Cohen, Stotland, and Wolfe, 1955; Kruglanski, 1989). To help place our contribution in context, it is useful to reflect on Kurt Lewin's (1935) "grand truism" (Kihlstrom, 2013) that all behavior is the product of a simple model,

$$B = f(P, E). \tag{1.1}$$

In Lewin's formulation, what people believe and do, B, is a function of predispositions that reflect all the causal factors that lie within the individual, P, and all the causal factors that lie outside of the individual in the external environment, E. Predispositions are, essentially "... defaults that, absent new information or conscious overriding, govern" people's responses to the external environment (Hibbing, Smith, and Alford, 2013, 25). We join the rising chorus of political psychologists (e.g., Alford, Funk, and Hibbing, 2005; Dawes and Fowler, 2009; Jost et al., 2003; Oxley et al., 2008) who recognize that P varies across individuals and interacts with E to generate differences in beliefs and behavior.[5] Of course, theories of motivated partisan reasoning conceptualize party identification as a predisposition that varies across individuals. Some people are democrats, some are republicans, and the remaining few are neither. Pessimistic accounts are concerned that motivated reasoning causes partisan predispositions to interact with the political environment in perverse ways. For instance, democrats and republicans systematically interpret external information from the environment – economic outcomes, social friction, international events, and so on – to be evidence for the correctness of their party's platform and governing decisions. We certainly agree that party identification should be thought of as a predisposition that varies across individuals (cf. Settle, Dawes, and Fowler, 2009). Our point of departure is to note that people also possess predispositions with respect to the way in which they process information (e.g., Cohen, Stotland, and Wolfe, 1955; Kruglanski, 1989; Stanovich and West, 2000) and that individual differences in information processing generate individual differences in the role that partisan identities play in decision making. By considering individual differences in information processing, we also adopt a different approach toward rationality than the one that currently animates the debate between optimists and pessimists.

1.3 REFLECTION MAKES RATIONALITY POSSIBLE

We build our theory on a more descriptively accurate model of the human mind that has emerged from decades of research in psychology and neuroscience. Rather than being a single-purpose machine in which conscious, cold, and calculated thought reigns supreme, the human mind consists of two information-processing pathways (Stanovich and West, 2000). One pathway works below the surface outside of conscious awareness, automatically categorizing incoming information with emotional content. Its qualities are that it works quickly, efficiently, and constantly. The other pathway is the one we are most familiar with; it is the conscious part of the mind, which is responsible for what we call "thinking" or the deliberate act of constructing reasons (or sometimes rationalizations) for particular courses of action.

The two pathways work in parallel, and much of what happens on the unconscious, automatic level rarely rises to the level of conscious awareness. However, that doesn't mean that what happens outside of conscious awareness has little effect on our attitudes or behavior. In fact, accumulating evidence suggests that the automatic part of our mind plays an extremely important role in constructing our attitudes and directing our behavior by furnishing us with intuitions about what is the right thing to believe and do. When the conscious part of our mind gets involved – say, when one is answering questions on a survey – it generally starts with an intuition generated, unbeknownst to us, by the automatic part of our mind.

The conceptualization of rationality that arises from the two-pathways (or *dual-process*) model of the mind is less about cold calculation and more about critical reflection. Reflection involves using conscious reason to override intuitions when they lead to incorrect or suboptimal decisions. In order to behave in ways that are consistent with the classical model of rationality, individuals must possess the capacity to second-guess themselves. Importantly, people differ in their capacity to do so, creating individual differences in the propensity to behave rationally (Stanovich, 2009). Individual differences in reflection, not simply differences in raw intelligence or social identities, are responsible for people's willingness to entertain thoughts and actions that are contrary to their gut reactions. This view of rationality has revolutionized the study of economic behavior, where scholars have observed many departures from classical models of rationality (cf. Kahneman, 2011). For instance, people tend to be more preoccupied with avoiding losses than they are with realizing gains. In many facets of human life, this proclivity serves us well (Kelman, 2011). Yet when asked by economists to evaluate which sorts of risks they should take, people's intuitive loss aversion often leads them to make suboptimal choices, such as the willingness to pay relatively high rates to ensure against small losses (Rabin and Thaler, 2001). Individual differences in reflection, or the capacity to second-guess intuitions, tracks with a willingness to make more optimal (i.e., rational in the classical economic sense) risk decisions (Frederick, 2005).

From the standpoint of democratic theory, the concern is less about the sorts of economic decisions that people make than it is about their political decisions. In our application of the dual-process model of the mind, partisan identities influence people's intuitions. Most people's gut reaction is to root for their political team, to see the politicians associated with their party as the good guys, and to see the members of the opposing party as a threatening and menacing force. Rationality does not imply freedom from having these impulses. Rather, it is about the ability to override these initial reactions when the circumstances warrant it. When politicians on our team take political positions that are at variance with our values, reflection applies the break on the temptation to take the same position. Reflection leads us to vote against incumbents from our party who have displayed incompetence or have violated the public trust. Reflection bolsters democratic accountability not through dispassionate reasoning but through *managing passions that threaten to lead us astray*. In our theoretical account, individual differences in reflection account for why people are different when it comes to reasoning about politics and explains important differences in how partisanship shapes attitudes and behavior. Individual differences in reflection predict the type of people who behave like party loyalists as well as the type of people who put their values and accuracy before party loyalty.

Our account, which we call the Intuitionist Model of Political Reasoning, differs from classical models of rationality in that we do not expect everyone to behave in ways that are consistent with either a formal definition of rationality or a commonsense notion of reasonableness. Some individuals go with their gut reaction, evidence to the contrary be damned. In this respect, our account is consistent with models of motivated reasoning. Nonetheless, we differ from these models in one crucial respect. Theories of motivated reasoning, particularly when applied to politics, are skeptical that reflection can reliably overcome people's biases. According to currently received theories of motivated reasoning in the domain of politics, at best reflection does little good, and at worst people use thinking to bolster their preexisting attitudes and rationalize their decisions (e.g., Kahan, 2012; Lodge and Taber, 2013). Our account holds out hope that some individuals can reliably overcome their biases through thought, recognizing that individuals have different capacities for reflection.

We think that adopting this new approach to thinking about rationality is useful because the "are partisans rational?" debate that serves as an important fault line between optimists and pessimists presumes a model of the human mind that is at variance with accumulating evidence about how the mind actually works. The (often implicit) presumption regarding rationality defines the rational mind as one that evaluates evidence by thinking in a cool and logical way through the dispassionate application of decision rules (e.g., Bartels, 2002; Bullock, 2009; Gerber and Green, 1998; Grynaviski, 2006; Redlawsk, 2002). Partisan identities interfere with the rational mind by creating an emotionally laden "perceptual screen" that obscures the thought process (Campbell et al., 1960, 133). Yet half a century of research in psychology and neuroscience shows that there is not a neat division between thought and emotion. In fact, emotional processing occurs before conscious thought, and as a result, thinking is necessarily influenced by emotions (Abelson, 1963; Lodge and Taber, 2013). Moreover, while emotional states can bias how people reason about the world (Redlawsk, 2002), they can also aid people in reaching accurate conclusions about the state of the world (Bechara, 2004) and can even minimize the influence of partisanship (Brader, 2006; Marcus, Neuman, and MacKuen, 2000). So, if people's partisan identities cause them to see the world through a particular screen, it is not simply a function of their emotional state.

We also believe that our approach enriches the study of democratic accountability by providing an insight into why elected officials are held accountable for their behavior some of the time and not other times. Democratic accountability is a system-level concept. We observe it insofar as voters, on average, hold politicians accountable for their actions. In some contexts, voters appear capable of doing so (e.g., Canes-Wrone, Brady, and Cogan, 2002), whereas in other contexts, voters clearly come up short by punishing or rewarding politicians for irrelevant events (e.g., Achen and Bartels, 2016; Healy, Malhotra, and Mo, 2010). If we presume that voters reach decisions in the same way, these disparate findings appear inconsistent and paradoxical. By allowing individuals to vary in the degree to which they are reflective, and thus willing to punish their team and reward the opposing team when times warrant it, an explanation emerges for why the efficacy of democratic accountability would vary across elections and contexts. Not only do places vary with respect to the relative balance of reflective to less reflective individuals, but also particular circumstances may temporarily cause individuals who are typically less reflective to be more reflective as well as individuals who are typically more reflective to be less so.

1.4 PLAN OF THE BOOK

In the next chapter, we elaborate on the dual-process model of the mind, individual differences in reflection, and what all of it means for the influence of partisan identities on political attitudes and behavior. We also place our work in the context of recent research that seeks to incorporate behavioral insights into models of information processing (Lau and Redlawsk, 2006; Lodge and Taber, 2013) as well as incorporate individual differences into models of partisan identity (Groenendyk, 2013; Huddy, Mason, and Aarøe, 2015; Lavine, Johnston, and Steenbergen, 2012). We conclude this chapter by explicitly comparing our Intuitionist Model of Political Reasoning to prominent models of information processing in political science.

In Chapter 3, we propose an empirical strategy for measuring individual differences in reflection. We draw on the psychological literature on cognitive style, which considers how people's motivations influence the ways in which they attend to information. Our strategy goes beyond previous attempts to measure individual differences in reflection, which tend to focus on people's propensity to devote significant cognitive effort to thinking through their decisions. We also entertain individual differences in the propensity to attach strong emotions to attitudes, which gives rise to strong intuitions. We predict that people are more likely to be reflective when they are motivated to think *and* have weaker intuitions, and therefore we suggest that both of these propensities play a central role in an individual's capacity for reflection. We devote much of this chapter to empirically validating our measurement approach by demonstrating that these measures correlate with markers of reflection and are not simply proxies for other politically relevant individual differences, such as political knowledge, education, and ideology.

With our measurement strategy placed on sure footing, we turn our attention in Chapters 4, 5, and 6 to investigating how individual differences in reflection shape political decision making and, ultimately, democratic accountability. Chapter 4 takes on the first prong of the textbook model of democratic accountability, which assumes that people form coherent and consistent political preferences attached to a shared ideological worldview. Drawing on experimental data, we show that people predisposed to be more reflective tend to adopt policy positions that are ideologically consistent, even when their political party takes the opposite position. Using observational data, we explore the implications of these findings – namely, that the predisposition to be reflective makes people more open to changing their partisan identity.

In Chapter 5, we consider the second prong of the textbook model, which assumes that partisans are capable of putting aside their partisan blinders and updating their evaluations of politicians in light of how they perform in office. Drawing on experimental and observational data, we find that people who are predisposed to be reflective are more likely to punish politicians of their own party and reward politicians of the opposing party when the facts warrant it. As a result, reflective individuals are also less likely to vote a straight party ticket in national elections.

Taken together, Chapters 4 and 5 demonstrate that some individuals are capable of living up to the demands of the textbook model of democratic accountability, while others are less so. Individuals who are predisposed to be less reflective are more likely to behave in ways that vex the pessimists. They tend to be knee-jerk partisans who toe the party line. Because partisan identities are a type of social group identity, we surmise that polarization among political elites helps fuel partisan cheerleading by making people more hostile toward opposing partisans. We address the implications of partisan polarization in Chapter 6 and find that less reflective individuals tend to have stronger negative emotional reactions toward members of the opposing party (as well as stronger positive reactions toward members of their own) than more reflective individuals. Experimental evidence points to the behavior of party elites as an important culprit. When prominent Democrats and Republicans sharply criticize one another, they create feelings of anger, which helps explain why some partisans develop antipathy for the other side.

Finally, we reflect on these findings in Chapter 7, summarizing their implications for democratic politics. Our first order of business is to offer a preliminary analysis of outcomes in congressional elections that shows that members of Congress are more likely to be held accountable for their legislative behavior as the proportion of reflective voters in their district increases. These findings suggest that reflection influences people's voting behavior and, ultimately, election outcomes – as opposed to simply how they answer questions on surveys or behave in experimental settings. We then devote the remainder of the chapter to discussing the limitations of our theoretical model and empirical findings, ponder future avenues of research – including a brief discussion about what steps could be taken to either induce individuals to be more reflective about politics or minimize the need to be reflective – and conclude with general thoughts about the future direction of the field.

2

A Theory of Individual Differences in Reflection and the Intuitionist Model of Political Reasoning

Before citizens can hold elected officials accountable for their decisions, they must make sense of those decisions. Are they consistent with citizens' values? Did they generate outcomes citizens liked or disliked? In order to understand how citizens answer these questions and arrive at opinions about politics, we need a model of how people process political information. The rational choice and social psychological models introduced in the previous chapter offered scholars a useful place to start. The rational choice framework provides a normative benchmark, while the social psychological framework provides an explanation for the gap between democracy in its ideal form and democracy in practice. But like all starting points, theoretical parsimony can become an obstacle to achieving a more complete explanation for how the world works.

The purpose of this chapter is to present an updated model of how people process political information that is more descriptively accurate than extant models. Fortunately for us, the behavioral revolution in the decision sciences, which lies at the intersection of economics and psychology, challenges the simplistic assumptions about human decision making that have been central to many rational choice and social psychological models of political behavior. Other scholars have drawn on behavioral insights to study how citizens form attitudes about politics and hold their elected representatives accountable (e.g., Dickson, 2006; Woon, 2012), and we extend their work by incorporating individual differences in psychological motivations into our updated model of political reasoning. Doing so is important because people do not process information in the same way. Some individuals critically evaluate information and behave in ways that approach idealized models of rationality while others do not.

Building on this approach, we offer a theoretically grounded framework for capturing individual differences in reflection and apply this general framework to accomplish the specific aim of this book: understanding how people's partisan identities shape their political attitudes.

2.1 OPENING THE BLACK BOX

When people express an opinion – be it about politics, sports, food, fashion, or anything else – we observe the outcome of some internal process that occurs within the brain. That process involves making sense of the information received externally and deciding how it should influence one's attitudes, choices, and behavior (Lau and Redlawsk, 2006). For instance, let's say someone is trying to decide which candidate she should vote for in the upcoming presidential election. If she knows nothing about the candidates running for office, she needs to form an opinion about each one and decide which one she likes better than the others. The information that informs her choice could come from an active search or from incidental contact with political messages delivered through advertising or news coverage of the campaign. If she already has an opinion about the candidates running for office, she must decide whether additional information changes her opinion. The psychological task of sorting out information is potentially complex. Does the information come from a credible source? Is it positive, negative, or neutral? If the piece of information contains factual claims, how strong is the evidence behind those claims? These sorts of epistemological questions motivate an entire branch of philosophy!

So how does the human brain go about answering these questions? Before the emergence of neuroscience, studies of individual decision making treated the brain as a "black box" (Camerer, Loewenstein, and Prelec, 2005). Influenced by Greek philosophers' demarcation between thought and emotion, social science models of decision making until a few decades ago presumed that conscious, calculating thought – or *cognition* – was the primary mechanism by which people arrived at decisions, while emotion – or *affect* – interfered with our ability to reason and clouded our judgment (Marcus, Neuman, and MacKuen, 2000). Both the classical model of rational choice decision making and early social psychological models presumed that conscious cognition is the appropriate arbiter for our beliefs. To the extent that emotions play a role, they are a nettlesome byproduct of cognition that can only serve to undermine our ability to arrive at accurate judgments.

As neuroscientists began to peek inside the black box, they discovered that the human mind does not work this way. First, conscious thought is not the primary mechanism by which we arrive at decisions. In fact, conscious thought is often not involved at all. It turns out that people feel before they think (Zajonc, 1980).[1] In a now-famous neuroscience study (Bechara et al., 1997), researchers asked research subjects to play a simple game where they were given an endowment of money and asked to select cards from four decks. The cards bestowed either awards or penalties to be added to or subtracted from the initial endowment. Two of the decks had larger awards and larger penalties, while the other two had smaller awards but smaller penalties. The best strategy for maximizing one's overall gains was to take cards only from the small-reward/small-penalty decks. However, the subjects had no way of knowing this fact at the beginning of the study. They could only form impressions about the decks of cards by drawing from them. The game ended after 100 draws. The study's investigators connected subjects to a machine that measured electrodermal activity – a measure of perspiration and an indicator of emotional response. At fixed intervals in the game, the researchers asked participants what they thought and felt about the game. What they found is that electrodermal responses preceded people's ability to articulate what they thought about the deck of cards and why. People got a "feeling" for which decks were good and which were bad *outside of conscious awareness*, which is not a rare occurrence. Most mental processes – including those that formulate goals – happen "off line," blissfully outside of conscious awareness (Bargh and Chartrand, 1999; Camerer, Loewenstein, and Prelec, 2005).

Second, cognition and affect are not in opposition. Returning back to the Bechara et al. (1997) study, the researchers conducted the same study among a group of patients with damage to their ventromedial prefrontal cortex, which regulates behavioral responses to emotions. Because of their brain injuries, these patients were unable to connect affective reactions to their cognitive processing. Their brain damage did not impair their ability to think – they were just as capable as people with normal functioning brains to do math or read a map – they were just unable to connect feeling and thinking. In other words, these individuals had the ideal mind envisioned by Greek philosophers and adherents to classical economic theory. So, without affect to get in the way of cognition, did they perform better at the game? No. In fact, they did quite a bit worse than the neurotypical participants, whose feelings guided them to draw from the good decks well before they understood why. The brain-impaired patients, in contrast, never figured out which deck of cards was better. The lesson here is that feeling and thinking are intertwined mental processes. We feel before we think, and feeling sometimes helps us think (Bechara, 2004).

Third, conscious cognition is not always in the driver's seat. It is intuitive to think of the conscious part of the human mind as a homunculus that makes decisions about what we believe, prefer, and do. This conception of the human mind is intuitive, in part, because this is how we experience the world. By definition, we do not observe off line mental processes at work. Although we may, from time to time, get a glimpse of off line processes – those times that we drive home from work deep in thought and arrive with no memory of taking the necessary turns and stops along our familiar route, for instance – it is impossible to be fully cognizant of everything that goes on beneath the surface.

To appreciate how the brain works, it helps to consider how it evolved. Like any other organ or biological entity, the human brain was built on the architecture of our ancestors' brains. Conscious awareness was late to the game and was tacked on to a brain that was built to perform most tasks without it – from breathing, to sensing the presence of predators, to forming behavioral responses, such as eating, mating, fighting, and fleeing from danger. As evolutionary psychologists Cosmides and Tooby (2004, 91) explain, the mind is "a crowded zoo of evolved, domain specific programs."[2] Controlled conscious thought is just one component of the mind and not the most important. In fact, emotions play a more pivotal role, since they referee conflicts among automatic processes. Emotions also play an important role in directing conscious thought by recruiting controlled cognitive functions to make decisions. Sometimes cognition is recruited to take over and direct our behavior, but sometimes it is simply asked to rationalize behavioral responses formulated off line. Fifty years of "split-brain" studies of patients whose left and right brain hemispheres cannot communicate demonstrate that the job of the executive function located in the left hemisphere, which is where conscious cognition takes place, is often less about making decisions than it is about providing post-hoc narratives for our behavior (Gazzaniga, 2011).[3]

An influential model of the human mind, emerging from current-day research in psychology and neuroscience, characterizes the brain as processing information via two channels that operate simultaneously as well as in collaboration. This dual-process model of the brain categorizes mental functions as either automatic (System 1 processes) or controlled and conscious (System 2 processes) (Stanovich and West, 2000). Of course, this categorization is a simplification, since mental functions can work in complex ways, but it is a useful simplification that has become central to the behavioral models in the decision sciences (see Evans and Stanovich, 2013; Stanovich, 2009).[4]

System 1 processes work beneath the surface, out of our conscious awareness. Some System 1 mental processes are "innately prepared" cognitive modules that were hardwired by evolution into the architecture of the human brain (Haidt and Joseph, 2004). These innate modules include (among many others) a fear of spiders and snakes (New and German, 2015; Ohman and Mineka, 2003), an aversion to losses (McDermott, Fowler, and Smirnov, 2008), and an ability to process the emotional content of people's facial expressions (Dimberg, Thunberg, and Elmehed, 2000). Other System 1 modules are acquired through learning and repetition: simple arithmetic $(2 + 2)$, the capital of one's home state, and a concert pianist's ability to sight-read music.

The quintessential characteristic of System 1 processing is that it is effortless, fast, and always working. System 1 processes information first, and emotions are central to how it works (Lufityanto, Donkin, and Pearson, 2016). As Lodge and Taber (2013, 174) explain, affective information enters the processing stream before "the retrieval of semantic considerations, cognitive associations, and emotional appraisals ... influencing the retrieval and interpretations of these and other forms of subsequent information." Emotions are a way for System 1 to label things (e.g., ideas, objects, people) as good, bad, or neither. In addition to tagging associations as positive or negative, emotions also provide a way for System 1 to communicate with System 2. For instance, anxiety is a way to get System 2's attention ("Hey, I think that might be a spider") and, in doing so, command conscious attention and focus to evaluate the severity of the perceived threat (Gray, 1987).

System 2, in contrast, requires effort and is, therefore, much slower than System 1 is at processing information. System 2 processes operate above the surface and embody conscious cognition. These are the mental modules that the brain uses when we engage in deliberate thinking – solving a difficult math problem, figuring out the best route to get somewhere in an unfamiliar place, or deciding whether to take a job offer. Because System 2 processes are more mentally taxing and time intensive than System 1 processes (and are often in response to System 1 requests for attention), the main job of System 2 processes is to attend to the spontaneous intuitions generated by System 1 processes. These intuitions or gut feelings provide System 2 with suggestions about which decisions "feel right."

Before continuing, we should note that there are critics of dual-process theories of information processing. Some critics contend that most of what we do arises from automatic processes and that the notion that action arises from conscious thought is overblown if not downright illusory (Bargh and Chartrand, 1999; Wegner, 2003). Others argue that a single-process model offers a more parsimonious framework in which all decisions, whether they derive from automatic or conscious processes, follow similar "if-then" rules (e.g., Kruglanski and Gigerenzer, 2011; Osman, 2004). Still others advance the opposite claim that one needs more than two systems to capture the complex workings of the mind (e.g., Schooler et al., 2015). In short, we draw from an area of scientific research that is under active investigation. Without a doubt, there is much to be learned about how the mind works, and future insights may well lead us to modify our own model. It is the nature of science that extant knowledge is provisional, and while our knowledge about the world – including how the mind works – grows, it will never be complete. Consequently, we must make decisions about where to start. We are largely persuaded by Evans and Stanovich (2013) that the critiques of the specific dual-process model on which we build our theory (elaborated below) miss the mark. The preponderance of evidence amassed from psychology and neuroscience support the contention that the mind uses two types of processing – one that does not require conscious attention and one that does. Even if the lines between System 1 and System 2 processing are blurred at the edges, it does not mean that the distinction is not a useful one. In particular, we agree with Evans and Stanovich (2013, 234–235) that dual-process models provide an explanation for why people vary in their ability and willingness to behave in ways that are consistent with normative models of rationality. Indeed, the evidence we offer in Chapters 3, 4, and 5 bolsters Evans and Stanovich's account.

2.2 VARYING DEGREES OF RATIONALITY

In this project, we adopt a narrow definition of what it means to be "rational." As we elaborate in this section, we do not view rationality as a character trait. People are not rational or irrational. We can only describe the specific decisions that people make in this way. Moreover, we do not evaluate the rationality of a choice in light of a prescriptive notion about what is in people's best interests. For instance, we are agnostic about whether it is irrational for poor people to support economically conservative policies or for rich people to support economically liberal ones. Instead, we consider a choice to be rational to the extent that it is "optimally related to [one's] beliefs and goals" that are connected to a coherently organized set of preferences and rooted in reality (Chong, 2013, 96). Therefore, it could be entirely rational for a poor person to support economically conservative policies if he or she holds conservative political predispositions about the role of the government in society. We will say more in Chapters 4 and 5 about how we empirically evaluate the rationality of people's choices in the domain of democratic accountability.

2.2.1 Two Pathways to Rationality

From the standpoint of the dual-process model of the mind summarized in the last section, there are two pathways to making rational choices. The first is that people's intuitions can lead them in the optimal direction. It just so happens that in the course of confronting and solving recurring adaptive problems faced by early humans – e.g., avoiding predators, finding mates, maintaining social reputations – natural selection endowed the human mind with intuitions that point us in the right direction when we face problems that resemble the ones our ancestors faced. These intuitions offer an efficient and effective way to cope with uncertainty and minimize costly mistakes, creating an "adaptive rationality" in which people are able to arrive at rational choices without needing to rely on System 2 processes (Haselton et al., 2009; see also Kelman, 2011; Gigerenzer, 2007). [5]

Unfortunately, there are times when our intuitions, adaptively rooted or otherwise, lead us astray. After all, nothing is foolproof and modern environments sometimes pose problems that are not neatly aligned with the types of problems our ancestors faced. We possess an evolutionary, deep-seated fear of snakes, which were a continual threat to early humans, but not for cars or electrical outlets, even though these recent technological innovations represent a greater lethal threat to most modern humans than snakes do (Confer et al., 2010). What happens when our gut reactions point in a suboptimal direction? Ideally, System 2 processes step in and override our intuition to arrive at an optimal decision. As such, System 2 evaluation of System 1-generated intuitions provides the second pathway for making rational choices (Rand, 2016).

Like the first pathway to rationality, there is no guarantee that the second pathway will work. The problem, to use the words of Daniel Kahneman (2011), who received a Nobel Prize in Economics for his pathbreaking work that laid the foundation for the behavioral revolution, is that System 2 tends to be a "lazy controller" for most people. It is easier to accept the effortlessly formulated answer suggested by System 1 – even a suboptimal one – than it is to suppress it and engage in reflection. That is not to say that everyone always gives in to System 1. People are capable of reflection. It is also not to say that everyone is equally "lazy." In fact, some individuals are much more likely to push back against System 1 suggestions than others (Frederick, 2005). Individual differences abound in System 2 processes (Stanovich, 2009). We use this fact as a launching point.

Keith Stanovich (2009, 2011) offers a useful way to think about individual differences within the dual-process framework. As depicted in Figure 2.1, he subdivides System 2 processes into two classes. *Algorithmic* processes reflect raw cognitive abilities, such as the ability to solve differential equations or grasp the subtle details of a logic puzzle. *Reflective* processes are concerned with higher-order goals and motivations. Individual differences in algorithmic processing are a function of differences in general intelligence. IQ tests attempt to measure this quality by placing people on a continuum that captures differences in computational abilities. Individual differences in reflective processes are a function of differences in one's proclivity to critically evaluate System 1 recommendations and one's willingness to override System 1 recommendations when they conflict with higher-order goals (e.g., a goal

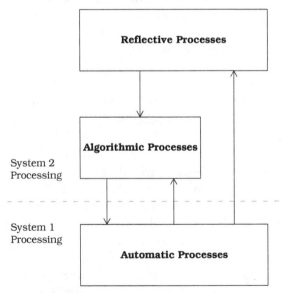

FIGURE 2.1. Dual-Process Model of Information Processing

Note: Figure adapted from Stanovich (2011, 33, Figure 2.1).

to be accurate). In support of the notion that algorithmic and reflective processes serve separate functions – even though they all operate at the conscious System 2 level – Stanovich and his team find that raw intelligence, as measured by IQ, does not predict the degree to which people engage in actively monitoring System 1 suggestions.[6]

From Stanovich's perspective, the reflective part of our minds, as opposed to the algorithmic part, is responsible for helping people arrive at rational choices when their intuitions point them in a different direction. He writes,

Thus, there is an important sense in which rationality is a more encompassing construct than intelligence – it concerns both aspects of System 2. The reason is that rationality is an organismic-level concept. It concerns the actions of an entity in its environment that serve its goals. To be rational, an organism must have well calibrated beliefs (reflective level) and must act appropriately on those beliefs to achieve its goals (reflective level). The organism must, of course, have the algorithmic-level machinery that enables it to carry out the actions and to process the environment in a way that enables the correct beliefs to be fixed and the correct actions to be taken (Stanovich, 2009, 59).

This account of rationality offers a constructive modification to economic models that emphasize the algorithmic processes for reaching optimal decisions. Whether people are capable of engaging in or even just approximating the calculations necessary to arrive at an optimal choice is beside the point if people are unmotivated to do it. Stanovich's approach helpfully moves us beyond skepticism about the particular assumptions of rational choice models that motivate critiques of the approach (e.g., Green and Shapiro, 1994). Rationality is not about being able to effortlessly generate the complex computations that populate formalized rational choice models, or even about imperfectly approximating complex calculations in ways offered by models of "bounded rationality" (Simon, 1959). Rather, it is about the willingness to second-guess one's self in an attempt to get to an accurate answer. Formalized rational choice models almost certainly mischaracterize the process by which individuals actually arrive at decisions, but that does not mean, to paraphrase the renowned statistician George Box, that they cannot be useful.[7] It is possible that people are capable of thinking through things in a way that approximates formal decision rules. The point here is that it is less about capability, which rests in the algorithmic mind, than it is about willingness to think through things when we already like a suboptimal, but intuitive, answer. That willingness rests in the reflective mind.

2.2.2 Capturing Individual Differences in Reflection

If IQ accounts for individual differences in algorithmic processes, what accounts for individual differences in reflective processes? While the answer to this question remains under active investigation, previous scholarship boils the answer down to differences in psychological motivations (e.g., Chaiken, Liberman, and Eagly, 1989; Cohen, Stotland, and Wolfe, 1955; Kruglanski, 1989; Petty and Cacioppo, 1986; Stanovich, 2009). The notion that psychological motivations structure human behavior has a long and rich history in psychology. Formalizing the concept over 70 years ago, Maslow (1943) posited that human motivations arise from needs that must be satisfied for the overall health and, ultimately, survival of an individual. Physiological needs offer the clearest example. Without food and water, one will perish. Hunger and thirst are motivational states that arise from these needs and trigger goal-directed action to satisfy them (e.g., eat and drink). Yet as Maslow eloquently explains, humans also possess psychological needs that are essential for a healthy life. These include needs for affection, belongingness, self-esteem, and self-actualization. Psychological needs are less acute than physiological needs. Perhaps it is possible to die of a "broken heart," but one will surely die of starvation first. Nonetheless, psychological needs also trigger goal-directed action aimed at satisfying physiological needs.

Although less clearly stated, Maslow treated needs and the motivations that arise from them as universal tendencies that can vary in intensity from individual to individual. For instance, we all need to feel safe, but a neurotic person may have more difficulty fulfilling this need than others (379–380). Accordingly, we see needs as fundamental predispositions that operate in the way we described in Chapter 1. They create stable tendencies within individuals. The particular pulls of these tendencies vary across individuals and interact with situations to shape observed behavior.

Working from the needs-and-motivations framework, Cohen, Stotland, and Wolfe (1955, 291) distilled what Maslow considered "higher" psychological needs into "... a need to understand and make reasonable the experiential world." In the parlance of the dual-process framework, this need triggers goal-directed action in the algorithmic mind. It is a *need for cognition*, in the terminology proposed by Cohen et al. and adopted by John Cacioppo and John Petty, who developed the concept further (see Cacioppo and Petty, 1982; Petty and Cacioppo, 1986). As the name implies, the need for cognition captures the quintessentially human drive to use thought to make sense of the world. It is a need that the science fiction writer Kurt Vonnegut (1963, 182) summed up well in his novel *Cat's Cradle*: "Tiger got to hunt, bird got to fly; Man got to sit and wonder 'why, why, why?' Tiger got to sleep, bird got to land; Man got to tell himself he understand."

Yet as we discussed in the previous section, thinking is taxing, so while all humans may have a drive to use System 2 processing to make sense of the world, we are not unlimited in our capacity to do so. The key insight Cohen and his colleagues offer is that the degree to which people engage in effortful thinking is partially a function of their psychological need to do so. Simply put, some people find thinking to be fun, while others see it as a chore.

Individual differences in need for cognition predict how likely people are to engage in effortful thinking. Individuals who are high in need for cognition are more likely to scrutinize persuasive messages and evaluate arguments based on the quality of the evidence presented, while individuals low in need for cognition tend to ignore argument quality if a heuristic, such as a trusted source cue, is available (Petty and Cacioppo, 1981, 1986). Individuals who are high in need for cognition may not always engage in effortful processing – just as individuals who are low in need for cognition may sometimes devote their mental energy to thinking through something thoroughly – but individual differences in need for cognition tend to predict how deeply individuals process information on average (Cacioppo et al., 1986).

Individuals who are high in need for cognition also tend to "base their judgments and beliefs on empirical information and rational considerations" (Cacioppo et al., 1986, 216). Nonetheless, scholars have also observed instances in which this is not the case. In particular, when individuals possess strong prior attitudes, higher levels of need for cognition can actually facilitate counter arguing and disconfirmation bias (Petty and Brinol, 2002; Petty and Wegener, 1998). In other words, the need for cognition may also help people use System 2 processes to generate rationales that reinforce their System 1 suggestions, which is inconsistent with Stanovich's notion of rationality. Reflection is more than thinking deeply. It also involves a willingness to scrutinize one's deeply held opinions and beliefs.

Consequently, we believe that need for cognition provides an incomplete marker of reflection. It tells us something about the motivation to use System 2 processes to engage in algorithmic processing, but it does not fully tell us about the willingness to override System 1 intuitions. In order to get a more complete picture, we argue that one must also consider what is going on below the surface in System 1. One of the main jobs performed by the automatic mind is creating and maintaining a network of associations that constitute our attitudes and beliefs (Greenwald et al., 2002; Lodge and Taber, 2013). Figure 2.2 offers a simplified representation of an associative network. The circles represent basic memory objects (people, places, statements, etc.), the positive and negative signs represent the valence of the affective tag linked to the memory objects, and the size of the positive and negative signs connotes the strength of the affective charge. The links among memory objects represent beliefs that an individual holds, and the affective tags summarize the attitudes that the individual holds.

The hypothetical person represented by this figure – let's call her Linda – believes that the Democratic Party fights for workers and that her mother identifies with the party. She likes fighting for workers and especially likes her mother, which accounts for the large positive affective tag attached to the Democratic Party and memory objects associated with the Democratic Party. In contrast, Linda believes that the Republican Party sides with business interests and opposes taxes. She dislikes business interests that threaten workers' rights but likes opposing taxes, and as a result, her attitude toward the Republican Party is somewhat more

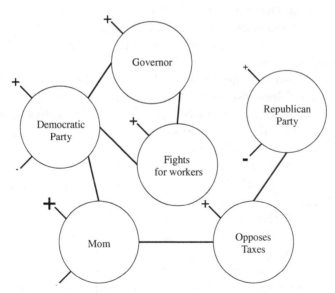

FIGURE 2.2. Hypothetical Example of an Associative Network

ambivalent, consisting of a more equal distribution of positive and negative affective tags.

When a person is prompted to think about something, System 1 quickly searches the associative network to retrieve relevant attitudes. For instance, imagine that Linda read a news story about allegations that the Democratic governor of her state engaged in shady dealings with the mob. System 1 would quickly retrieve the associations connected with her governor and remind her that she likes him. This chain of *spreading activation* – which all occurs in milliseconds outside of conscious awareness – is how System 1 goes about forming intuitions that are then offered as suggestions to System 2. In this example, Linda's System 1 intuition would be to discount the story and continue to like her governor.

Our argument is that the strength of people's intuitions influences their willingness to override those intuitions. The strength of people's intuitions is proportional to the affective tags connected to the attitudes that System 1 retrieves when constructing intuitions. The stronger the affective tag, the more one must be motivated to entertain considerations with which he or she very much disagrees. Extant research suggests that the need for cognition supplies this motivation, but at some point, we argue, it is not enough. Once preexisting attitudes become strong enough, the need for cognition can turn the powers of reflection into the powers of rationalization. Our proposition is that one's *general* capacity to exhibit rationality is a function of not only System 2 engagement, but also System 1's forcefulness. There is no doubt that the forcefulness of System 1's suggestions varies across attitude objects within an individual. Everyone feels strongly about some things and less so about others. Nonetheless, System 1 forcefulness also varies across individuals, such that some people tend to connect stronger affective tags to their attitudes than others do, on average. And individual differences in System 1 forcefulness also serve as a potent marker of rationality.

Individual differences in System 1 forcefulness, like individual differences in the depth of System 2 processing, reflect differences in psychological motivations. In contrast to differences in System 2 processing, which reflect a desire to think, we contend that differences in System 1 forcefulness reflect, at least in part, the motivation to seek out and experience emotions. This motivation or *need for affect*, as Maio and Esses (2001) refer to it, encompasses a desire to either experience emotions or attempt to minimize them. The need for affect is not about emotion regulation – that is, the desire to maintain positive mood states (cf. Gross, 1998). Rather, it is about a motivation to "... seek a broad range of emotional experiences" (Maio and Esses, 2001, 586). While the need for affect is a general motivation that influences people's behavior across situations, it has important implications for attitude formation and, therefore, the nature of people's associative networks maintained by System 1 processes. When evaluating information, individuals who are high in need for affect are more likely to attach strong emotions to their judgments, which in turn causes them to form stronger attitudes (Britt et al., 2009). Moreover, as need for affect increases, individuals are more likely to attend to the emotional content of messages when forming attitudes (Haddock et al., 2008; Huskinson and Haddock, 2004; Mayer and Tormala, 2010). Individual differences in the need for affect are not so much individual differences in how System 1 processes information as they are individual differences in how affectively charged individuals' attitudes are *on average*. Consequently, as people's need for affect increases, so should the forcefulness of their System 1-generated intuitions. We cannot emphasize enough that need for affect is a domain general indicator of System 1 forcefulness. Whether people possess strong intuitions in a specific domain (e.g., politics) is not simply a function of need for affect. In order to make domain-specific predictions about System 1 forcefulness, we must know more about the individual. As we explain in the next section and empirically validate in Chapter 3, people's partisan attachments play a crucial role in shaping their intuitions in the domain of politics, and need for affect predicts how powerful these intuitions are.

We place need for affect and need for cognition motivations in the context of Stanovich's dual-process model in Figure 2.3. Individual differences in need for cognition influence people's willingness to crank up effortful mental processes housed in the algorithmic mind that make up "thinking." Need for affect, in turn, influences the forcefulness of System 1 intuitions. Taken together, we contend that individual differences in the willingness to override System 1 suggestions in an attempt to reach accurate conclusions and avoid the pitfalls of motivated reasoning (e.g., one-sided thinking) – that is, "rationality" in Stanovich's sense of the term – are the joint product of the depth of System 2 processing and the intensity of System 1 intuitions. While there may be alternative approaches to capturing individual differences in these two domains, we focus on the need for cognition and need for affect, given the depth of their theoretical development within the field of psychology.

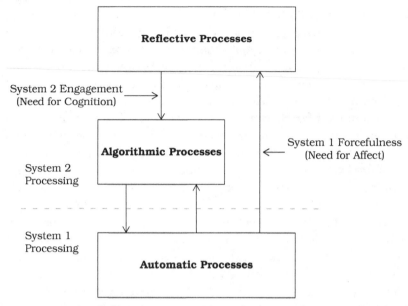

FIGURE 2.3. Psychological Motivations and the Dual-Process Model of Information Processing

Figure 2.4 summarizes how we expect System 1 forcefulness and System 2 engagement – and, specifically, our operationalizations of these theoretical constructs – to jointly influence people's willingness to engage in reflection, on average. We say "on average" because people's willingness to be reflective is not a deterministic function of need for affect and need for cognition. Individual differences in need for affect and need for cognition tell us something about people's *predisposition* to engage in reflection, yet whether an individual actually does so in a particular instance depends on situational factors. For instance, when people are asked to accomplish a secondary task (e.g., remembering a long string of numbers) while completing a decision task, the additional load on their conscious executive functions makes it more difficult for many individuals to override their intuitive responses (e.g., De Neys, 2006). Consequently, we view the predictions in Figure 2.4 as expectations that average across situations.

All things being equal, we expect individuals to be more reflective, and thus more willing to override their intuitions, as their need for affect decreases and their need for cognition increases. The type of individual who is low in need for affect and high in need for cognition has weaker affective tags and a strong inclination to more deeply evaluate his or her

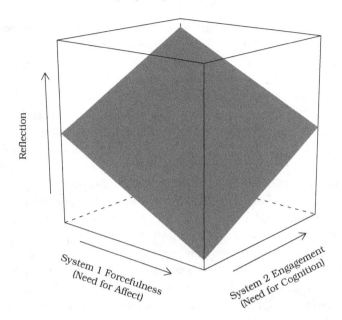

FIGURE 2.4. The Expected Influence of System 1 Forcefulness and System 2 Engagement on Reflection

Note: Reflection, System 1 Forcefulness, and System 2 Engagement are theoretical constructs derived from the dual-process theory of information processing. "Need for affect" and "need for cognition" are placed in parentheses to indicate that they are empirical operationalizations of System 1 Forcefulness and System 2 Engagement, respectively. The degree to which these operationalizations map onto their theoretical constructs likely varies across situations. Consequently, the predictions summarized by the plane in the figure should be treated as expectations that average across situations.

initial, System 1-motivated responses. Conversely, we expect individuals to be less reflective, and thus less willing to override their intuitions, as their need for affect increases and their need for cognition decreases. The type of individual who is high in need for affect and low in need for cognition possesses strong affective tags and little inclination to second-guess his or her gut reactions.

We have less precise expectations regarding individuals who are either low or high on both need for affect and need for cognition. Individuals who are low on both dimensions should tend to have weaker intuitions but also lack the motivation to push back against them. Consequently, their behavior should fall, on average, somewhere between individuals who are high in need for affect/low in need for cognition and individuals who are low in need for affect/high in need for cognition. Individuals who are high on both dimensions have strong intuitions but also possess a strong motivation to think. How they apply their cognitive energy depends on the situation. On the one hand, they may use thought to construct elaborate rationalizations, making them the embodiment of motivated reasoning. On the other hand, because these individuals do enjoy thinking, there is a limit to how much they can rationalize something. As Kunda (1990, 482) explains, even motivated reasoners "attempt to be rational and to construct a justification of their desired conclusion." We believe that this contrasts with individuals who are high in need for affect and low in need for cognition, because these folks are not very motivated to form a justification. They just go with their gut. Consequently, individuals who are high on both dimensions should also fall, on average, somewhere between individuals who are high in need for affect/low in need for cognition and individuals who are low in need for affect/high in need for cognition, albeit for reasons that are different from individuals who are low on both dimensions.

For any given decision, it would be difficult for us to make precise predictions about what individuals who are low on both need for affect and need for cognition or high on both dimensions will do without an additional set of auxiliary hypotheses. Perhaps if an issue is particularly important to them, they would engage in less reflection, or if they are placed in a context where they are explicitly asked to provide a detailed rationale for their decision, they would be more reflective. Because we wish to first establish that the dual-process theoretical model helps us understand the influence of partisan attachments on political decisions, we begin by evaluating the model's clearest predictions. As such, in the pages that follow, we focus on the behavior of individuals who are high in need for affect and low in need for cognition (i.e., those predisposed to be less reflective) and individuals who are low in need for affect and high in need for cognition (i.e., those predisposed to be more reflective). We leave the other combinations of need for affect and need for cognition to future research – a point we will return to in the conclusion.

Note that our framework for individual differences in reflection is about people's stable predispositions with respect to particular *psychological motivations* and not about the relative importance of cognitive and affective functions within the brain. As we explained at the outset of this chapter, affective processes play a crucial, if under-appreciated, role in information processing. Affect is intertwined with cognition. To be clear, we are not arguing that people low in need for affect and high in need for cognition behave like robots who only think and do not feel. The minds of people who are low in need for affect and high in need for cognition work like other people's minds. Their attitudes are endowed with affective tags. They feel before they think, and in many contexts feeling aids rather than hinders their ability to form accurate and useful attitudes. Our contention is more specifically about people's willingness to override System 1 intuitions in those instances when the available evidence points to their intuitions being biased or wrong. Need for affect and need for cognition influence people's proclivity to engage in critical reflection, a System 2 process, to interrogate System 1 intuitions.

2.3 THE INFLUENCE OF PARTISAN ATTACHMENTS AND THE INTUITIONIST MODEL OF POLITICAL REASONING

At the foundation of our thesis is a simple proposition: individual differences in reflection shape how people process information about politics in the same way they affect how people process information about anything else. We find ourselves mostly in agreement with Lau and Redlawsk (2006, 21), who contend that "[v]oter decision making *cannot* be much different from most other decisions people make in their daily lives" (emphasis in original). We say "mostly" because we believe that it is certainly true that humans use the same physical and psychological mechanisms to process all information, including political stimuli. However, political stimuli have at least two salient differences from the types of information that people confront when making quotidian decisions, like how to navigate a crowded street or what to eat for lunch. For one, political opinions, if adopted as policy by the government, are collectively binding. The distinction here is that in politics, people are not simply trying to decide what they want to eat for lunch; they are being asked to decide what everyone should eat for lunch. Second, because politics is about making collective decisions, it activates group conflict. To take the lunch analogy to the extreme, ordering a turkey sandwich for yourself makes you someone who likes turkey sandwiches; asking everyone to do the same makes you part of the turkey sandwich faction – a faction no doubt bitterly opposed by the pastrami on rye faction. As a result, political information often contains references to socially relevant groups (gender, race, ethnicity, etc.).

In fact, people often use group references as a way to sort out their opinions on political issues – like the things liked by the groups you like and dislike the things liked by the groups you dislike (Brady and Sniderman, 1985). As we discussed in Chapter 1, political parties provide a crucial organizational structure within an electoral democracy and, therefore, a potent reference group (Key, 1964; Schattschneider, 1942). In modern American politics, general elections for federal and state offices are by and large contests between a candidate who calls him- or herself a Democrat and a candidate who calls him- or herself a Republican. Likewise, most citizens develop a preference for one major party over the other. According to the American National Election Survey conducted during the 2012 presidential election, approximately 56 percent of Americans say that they think of themselves as a democrat or a republican, and an additional third of the electorate indicates that they lean in the direction of one of the two major parties when pushed, meaning that nearly 90 percent of the American electorate identifies with either the Democratic or Republican Party.

We believe that the centrality of group attachments, and partisan attachments in particular, in the political domain is of crucial importance for understanding how people arrive at rational political choices. Electoral competition pits parties against one another, potentially activating the psychology of intergroup competition and an us-versus-them mentality among partisan adherents. Indeed, people's partisan attachments are powerful enough to influence their decisions that lie outside of the political domain. People are more likely to give scholarships to students who share their partisan identity as well as share more money with individuals from their party than with individuals from the opposing party in stylized trust games (Carlin and Love, 2016; Iyengar and Westwood, 2015). People's partisan attachments affect decisions about what to buy, whom to marry, and how religious to be (Alford et al., 2011; Gerber and Huber, 2009; Margolis, Forthcoming). As a result, intuitions about political choices may reflect people's bias toward their partisan ingroup and against their partisan outgroup(s). Ingroup favoritism helped early humans resolve social dilemmas that surround extending trust to strangers, and accordingly, it serves as a powerful innately prepared intuition (Brewer, 2007). That said, innately prepared intuitions that evolved over 12,000 years ago are not guaranteed to function as intended in modern, large-scale political environments (Petersen, 2015), and ingroup bias often leads to perverse decision making in modern-day heterogenous environments (Kelman, 2011).

Consequently, partisan attachments may frustrate the adaptive rationality pathway. As long as people's partisan intuitions are in line with their political values and presuppositions, people's partisan intuitions should function as a useful heuristic. However, in those instances where people's partisan intuitions are at variance with their values and predispositions, people will need to use reflection as a pathway to make a rational choice. The dual-process model of information processing discussed in the last section helps cut through the debate between rational choice and social psychological approaches by placing their divergent predictions about the effects of party identification in a unified framework. As we discussed in Chapter 1, rational choice approaches characterize partisan identification as a useful heuristic, while social psychological approaches categorize partisan identities as a kind of social identity. In our framework, party identification can function as both a social identity and a heuristic. As a social identity, one's party identification influences the affective tag connected to incoming information. In general, people like good news about their party and bad news about the opposing party as well as dislike bad news about their party and good news about the opposing party. These affective reactions to incoming group-relevant information happen spontaneously and outside of our conscious awareness in the domain of System 1 (cf. Cikara, Botvinick, and Fiske, 2011).

When processing political information, System 1 processes show a clear bias toward one's party and against the opposing party (Westen et al., 2006), which leads people to form intuitions that reflect partisan biases. System 1 nudges people to support the policies and candidates of their party and oppose the policies and candidates of the other, even if one should pause and think. In this way, System 1 treats partisan information as a heuristic. Whether it is a useful heuristic depends on the context. Is an inparty candidate advocating a position that clashes with one's ideological principles? Is an outparty candidate advocating a position that is consistent with one's guiding principles? Does an inparty politician deserve to be punished for violating the public trust? Answering these questions is the job of System 2. Individuals who are unmotivated to be reflective will generally not engage these questions. They will toe the party line, and that will be the end of it. Individuals who are motivated to be reflective will ask these questions, and if the answers lead them to diverge from their System 1 partisan intuition, they will take a different course of action.

Figure 2.5 summarizes our application of the dual-process theory of information processing, discussed in the last section, to the domain of politics, which we call the Intuitionist Model of Political Reasoning. Our model is intuitionist in the sense that intuitions come first and directly influence cognition.[8] Once people receive political information

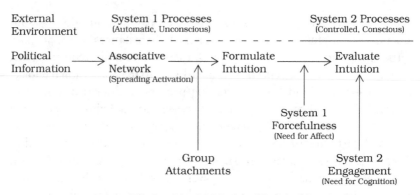

FIGURE 2.5. The Intuitionist Model of Political Reasoning

from their external environment – be it from a news story, a campaign advertisement, a politician's speech, or a neighbor – System 1 processes take the first crack. The information automatically triggers the mind to search the associative network through the process of spreading activation to summon relevant beliefs and attitudes. With the help of these considerations, System 1 formulates an intuition about what should be done with this new information. People's group attachments shape the intuitions people form. Of importance to our current project, people's partisan attachments influence the content of their intuitions in ways that reinforce their partisan beliefs and attitudes. The stronger people's partisan identities, the more likely their gut reaction will be to advocate toeing the party line.

With the intuitive reaction in place, System 2 takes over and evaluates whether one should go with his or her gut response or engage in critical reflection. This is where individual differences in reflection enter into the picture. Stable differences in motivational dispositions influence the depth and character of System 2 processing. System 1 forcefulness (operationalized by need for affect) causes people's attitudes, including partisan attitudes, to have stronger affective tags, generating stronger gut reactions. The motivation to engage System 2 (operationalized by need for cognition) influences the degree to which people enjoy going through the trouble of effortful thinking to scrutinize their gut reactions. Taken together, differences in both motivational dispositions give rise to varying degrees of motivated partisan reasoning.

All things being equal, we expect that higher levels of need for cognition coupled with lower levels of need for affect will cause people's partisan identities to behave more in line with rational choice accounts; and we expect that lower levels of need for cognition coupled with higher levels of need for affect will cause people's partisan identities to behave more in line with social psychological accounts. We extract many predictions from these two propositions with respect to the effects of partisanship on political attitude formation and behavior. As we discussed in the previous section, we focus on instances where need for affect and need for cognition are divergent from one another because these instances generate the clearest predictions in the dual-process framework and, therefore, offer the most sensible place to begin. We return to this point in the concluding chapter and consider other combinations of need for affect and need for cognition.

We also hasten to emphasize the importance of the phrase "all things being equal" that prefaces our expectations about the effects of need for affect and need for cognition. We do not expect that people's partisan identities *always* win out when need for affect is high and need for cognition is low. As we explained at the end of the previous section, situational context matters. The psychological motivations on which we focus create stable tendencies, or defaults, in how reflective people tend to be. On average, individuals low in need for affect and high in need for cognition are more likely to be reflective, while individuals who are high in need for affect and low in need for cognition are less likely to be reflective. Nonetheless, particular situations may push individuals temporarily away from their defaults. It would be premature for us to construct a theory of how situational variables interact with people's predisposition to be reflective, as our first order of business is to demonstrate that individual differences in reflection are relevant for political attitude formation. That being said, in the interest of probing the boundary conditions of our model's core hypothesis, we consider the role that a crucial situational variable, issue salience, plays in motivating people to be temporarily reflective. We chose to consider issue salience (as opposed to other situational variables) because it is central to canonical models of public opinion formation (e.g., Carmines and Stimson, 1989; Iyengar and Kinder, 1987; Zaller, 1992). Furthermore, research directly relevant to the question at the heart of our project suggests that as issue salience increases, people are more likely to have a preexisting opinion on an issue, and if they encounter information counter to that opinion – even from a trusted partisan source – people are more likely to devote cognitive resources to reconcile the information with their preexisting attitude (Arceneaux, 2008; Ciuk and Yost, 2016). Consequently, we investigate whether this motivation extends to less reflective individuals in Chapter 4.

In the coming pages we elaborate and empirically assess the effects of individual differences in reflection on how people form political attitudes and evaluate political leaders. These form the basic ingredients of the textbook model of democratic accountability discussed in the previous chapter. Our approach helps square the differences between the competing accounts offered by optimists and pessimists by showing that each group of scholars is right in part and wrong in part. By accounting for individual differences in reflection, and sacrificing only a bit of parsimony, we are able to provide a unifying framework for the dominant competing explanations of partisanship in American politics.

2.4 OUR CONTRIBUTION

The Intuitionist Model of Political Reasoning builds on and refines prominent models of political attitude formation. It incorporates a more realistic account of how the human mind works than does Zaller's (1992) Receive-Accept-Sample (RAS) model. In the RAS framework, when people are asked to form a political attitude, they consciously search their memory for "considerations" relevant to the attitude, sample from among those that are most accessible, and average across them to fashion an attitude. The mixture of considerations that tend to be at the top of people's heads is influenced by their attentiveness to politics. Individuals who regularly follow politics are better than less politically attentive individuals at rejecting considerations that are inconsistent with their political predispositions. As a result, politically attentive individuals tend to have more consistent political attitudes and possess what Converse (1964), who provides the theoretical edifice of the RAS model, would consider a "sophisticated" belief system in which individuals know what issue positions go together and which ones do not. In one respect, the Intuitionist Model of Political Reasoning is compatible with the RAS framework. In both, people survey their associative network to arrive at a summary attitude. The key difference is that in our model, this step takes place quickly outside of conscious awareness, and the resulting attitude is an intuition that provides a starting point in the attitude formation process.

Because our approach is built on a more descriptively accurate model of the mind than Zaller's cognitively taxing memory-based account, it offers a better way to theorize about individual differences in information processing than the RAS framework's emphasis on political awareness. That is not to say we do not see the value in political awareness as a theoretical concept. It does an excellent job explaining why some individuals have more knowledge about politics as well as more internally consistent belief systems. Following politics is a prerequisite for knowing about politics. Nonetheless, the motivation to be attentive to politics is conceptually separate from the motivation to be reflective (or not). Being reflective about politics may lead people to be more politically aware, but being politically aware about politics does not necessarily make one more reflective. As a matter of logic, there is no reason that one cannot simultaneously follow politics religiously and, thus, know a lot of facts about political personalities and the details of policy debates (i.e., the standard way in which scholars measure political awareness), while at the same time interpreting political and social outcomes in a way that affirms their particular worldview (see also Gaines et al., 2007; Gvirsman, 2015; Jerit and Barabas, 2012). It is also unclear what the RAS model predicts with respect to whether political awareness causes people to rely more on party cues or the policy information contained in political messages. On the one hand, politically aware individuals are more likely to have partisan attachments, but on the other hand, they should also be more likely to possess coherent ideological belief systems. As evidence for the inchoateness of this aspect of the RAS model, extant research offers a conflicting set of findings regarding the influence of political awareness on partisan-motivated reasoning. Some studies find that politically aware individuals are more likely to rely on partisan cues than less aware individuals (e.g., Groenendyk, 2013; Lau and Redlawsk, 2001; Rudolph and Popp, 2007), while other studies find the opposite (e.g., Arceneaux and Kolodny, 2009a; Kam, 2005). In contrast, the Intuitionist Model of Political Reasoning offers a more incisive prediction for individual differences in partisan-motivated reasoning. As people make sense of "what goes with what" (Converse, 1964, 212), less reflective individuals are more likely to rely on party cues, while more reflective individuals are more likely to rely on policy information and their ideological worldview.

Our model also refines the multimodel information-processing approach offered by Lau and Redlawsk (2006). With a focus on how individuals arrive at voting decisions, Lau and Redlawsk present a typology of processing strategies that generates four abstract models of decision making. Model 1 ("Dispassionate Decision Making") describes the textbook rational choice model of vote choice as articulated by Downs (1957). Voters actively search for a full array of information that allows them to evaluate each alternative and select the one that maximizes their self-interest. Model 2 ("Confirmatory Decision Making") is the archetype of the early social psychological model of voting established by *The American Voter* (Campbell et al., 1960) and describes voters as seeking out information that is consistent with political attitudes developed early in life, such as party identification. Model 3 ("Fast and Frugal Decision Making") describes voters as valuing efficiency by seeking out information about candidates that pertains to the issues they care most about and, in doing so, minimizing the costs associated with finding information and making comparisons across multiple dimensions. Model 4 ("Intuitive Decision Making") characterizes voters as satisficers who seek out the minimum amount of information necessary to make a decision, leading people to lean heavily on stereotypes and other heuristics that afford an easy decision. Our model refines this approach in two important respects. First, it makes clear that information-processing strategies fall on a continuum ranging from the rational ideal to an intuitively driven approach, as opposed to fitting neatly into discrete classifications. Second, we do not presume that decision making must reflect an active search for information and conscious cognitive processing. Even Model 4 in Lau and Redlawsk's typology describes "intuitive" decisions in cognitive terms. In contrast, our model's definition of intuition jibes with the way in which this term is currently used in cognitive psychology and neuroscience, which emphasizes the automatic nature of how people arrive at a starting point for all decisions. Whether people choose to engage in active reflection depends on their psychological motivations.

Finally, we believe that our model builds on and extends Lodge and Taber's (2013) John Q. Public (JQP) model of information processing. The JQP model provides a theoretical account that is far more in line with current-day theories of decision making in cognitive psychology and neuroscience than either Zaller's RAS model or the typologies developed by Lau and Redlawsk. Furthermore, we are deeply indebted to Lodge and Taber's decades of research on the ways in which automatic processes shape political evaluations. They teach us that the affectively laden intuitions that arise from unconscious processing cause many people to engage in rationalization when it comes to justifying a political attitude or choice rather than a rational assessment that fashions an optimal attitude or choice. The Intuitionist Model of Political Reasoning also recognizes the importance of automatic processes and the potential for intuitions to lead people to engage in motivated reasoning. Yet it also extends Lodge and Taber's JQP model by explicitly incorporating individual differences in reflection into the model of conscious processes. Lodge and Taber (48) contend that the primacy of affectively laden intuition in the decision making process "undermines the deliberative foundations of Enlightenment rationality" because "… conscious deliberation is the wake behind the boat, while automatically stimulated affective and cognitive processes control the rudder" (for a similar argument, see Kahan, 2012). We believe this line of argument is too strong. Many people rationalize their political attitudes for sure, but people are not prisoners to their gut reactions. Dozens of studies show that deliberation and reflection can help people arrive at nonintuitive, rationally optimal decisions (Rand, 2016). Some people are motivated to reach accurate conclusions (Kunda, 1990) and, thus, willing to second-guess their affectively charged intuitions. Our theoretical model explains why, and as a result, we come away with a less pessimistic view of political decision making.

In addition to scholarship on information processing, we join a recent push by scholars to investigate individual differences in partisan reasoning, and we see our contribution as building upon as well as advancing this emerging line of research. In his investigation of partisan identification, Eric Groenendyk (2013) argues that partisans face two competing motivations. On the one hand, they want to be loyal to their party, but on the other hand, they also feel the need to justify why they identify with a particular party. Contrary to Green, Palmquist, and Schickler (2002), Groenendyk contends that keeping partisan identities isolated from negative evaluations of party leaders is an unsustainable strategy. At some point, something must give. If people encounter enough negative information about their party, they will find it impossible to justify their partisan identity and will begin to shift the way they categorize themselves. Individuals differ in how much negative information is enough, and in this respect, high levels of interest in and knowledge about politics strengthens individuals' ability to find ways to justify their partisan identities and insulate themselves from negative information. In the context of our framework, Groenendyk draws our attention to how people's motivation to defend their identities interacts with individual differences in System 2 processing, particularly the ability to deploy cognitive resources defensively. We believe that our approach helps place Groenendyk's findings in a more comprehensive theoretical framework. By drilling down to more fundamental needs and motivations that influence the interaction between System 1 and System 2 processes, we provide insights about why a range of individuals, including those with the same level of political knowledge, would be more or less likely to engage in partisan reasoning.

In a related vein of research, Howard Lavine and colleagues (2012) leverage the fact that, while people by and large view their party in positive terms, they differ in how uniformly they do so. Some individuals hold a mix of likes and dislikes about their party, making them more *ambivalent* about their partisan identity than individuals who hold mostly positive feelings about their party. Lavine et al. find that ambivalent partisans are much more likely to devote cognitive resources to reach accurate decisions and are less likely to simply toe the party line. They link individuals' partisan ambivalence to evidence of poor performance when their party is in power, internal value conflicts, and heterogenous social networks. As with Groenendyk's research, we interpret Lavine et al. as underscoring an important outcome – partisan ambivalence – of individual differences in System 2 processing (see also Rudolph and Popp, 2007). We see their findings as compatible with our theoretical approach, since we also place a great deal of importance on dispositional differences in reflective processes, which reside in System 2. We also place their model in a more comprehensive framework by going beyond proximal causes of individual differences in partisan ambivalence, such as the willingness to hold incompatible values, choose friends with different views, and interpret poor economic performance as evidence of poor party stewardship. Our approach points to the more fundamental psychological motivations that would cause individuals to differ in these ways.

Finally, while our theoretical framework highlights the importance of emotional processing within System 1, it is important for us to separate ourselves from the stream of research devoted to understanding the effects of specific emotional states (e.g., anxiety, disgust, anger, etc.). Most relevant to our project, feelings of anxiety promote deeper information search, cognitive processing, and a willingness to depart from partisan loyalties (Brader, 2006; Marcus, Neuman, and MacKuen, 2000; Valentino et al., 2008), while feelings of enthusiasm and anger can promote partisan reasoning (Marcus, Neuman, and MacKuen, 2000; Valentino et al., 2011). We have little doubt that emotional states can have profound effects on how people reason about politics.[9] Our tack here is to focus on people's motivational predispositions rather than particular emotional states. This decision is a matter of emphasis as opposed to an assertion that predispositions hold greater explanatory power than situational characteristics. The truth of the matter is that people's predispositions interact with situational context (Bowers, 1973; Dworkin and Kihlstrom, 1978).

Although it is beyond the scope of our current project, one could incorporate emotional state effects into our theoretical framework. For instance, one could treat people's incidental emotional states as a situational variable that temporarily pushes people away from their predisposed level of reflection. An unreflective person may be pushed to devote temporarily more cognitive resources to think through an issue when placed in a state of anxiety; and a typically reflective person may temporarily turn his or her mind off, so to speak, in those moments when he or she is angry. To be clear, our theoretical model, like all social science models, is a probabilistic one. We do not predict that need for affect and need for cognition cause people to *always* behave in a particular way, nor do we deny that other situational and individual-level factors are important. However, we must start somewhere, and we have chosen to start by building our theory on the basis of stable individual differences out of the belief that we must demonstrate that they exist and matter politically before we move on to a more complicated interactionist model.

3

Measuring Individual Differences in Reflection

The purpose of this chapter is to elaborate on and justify our empirical approach to measuring individual differences in reflection. To do so, we look to the ways in which psychologists measure how people differ in their *cognitive style*, or the way in which people mentally attend to information. We recruit two measures of cognitive style, briefly discussed in the previous chapter, that capture one's need for affect and need for cognition. These measures of cognitive style capture differences in how much people are motivated to seek out and feel emotions and how much they are motivated to think. As we explain, we believe that together these differences in psychological motivations shape people's willingness to engage in reflection.

Because these measures are somewhat novel to the study of politics and we propose using them in somewhat novel ways, we begin this chapter by placing the need for affect and the need for cognition in the context of the fields in which they were developed and explain why we believe they can also be leveraged to serve our goals. We then spend the remainder of the chapter empirically evaluating the validity of these measures as a way to capture people's propensity to engage in reflection by demonstrating that they are correlated with theoretically related constructs and uncorrelated with distinct constructs. In doing so, we also introduce the data, drawn from several studies, that will serve as the basis for the empirical tests undertaken in the remaining chapters.

3.1 NEED FOR COGNITION

The empirical study of individual differences in cognitive style begins with the need for cognition. Originally proposed by psychologists Arthur

46

Cohen, Ezra Stotland, and Donald Wolfe (1955, 291), the need for cognition was defined as "a need to structure relevant situations in meaningful, integrated ways." They argued that this need varies across individuals in intensity, causing those with a stronger need for cognition to devote more energy to making sense of the world, especially when confronted with ambiguous situations where one must figure out how facts and events are connected. A little over twenty-five years later, John Petty and John Cacioppo (1981, 1986) placed the concept at the center of their Elaboration Likelihood Model (ELM) of persuasion and refined its measurement. Initially it consisted of more than forty items, but they shortened the need for cognition battery to a more manageable number (Cacioppo, Petty, and Kao, 1984). The items from the short-form battery, which we employ in our empirical research, are shown in Table 3.1. The ELM constitutes the first dual-process model of information processing and set in motion the stream of research leading to Stanovich and West's (2000) integrative System 1/System 2 framework discussed in Chapter 2. The ELM framework specifies two "routes" by which people process persuasive appeals. The central route involves thought and deliberation (i.e., elaboration), while the peripheral route relies on simple heuristics (e.g., the credibility of the source) to reach a decision quickly. Need for cognition is a stable and heritable trait (Cacioppo et al., 1996; Ksiazkiewicz, Ludeke, and Krueger, forthcoming) that captures people's motivation to take the central route. To put it in more concrete terms, the type of people who are high in need for cognition enjoy solving puzzles as well as thinking about and discussing all of the plot holes in the movie they just saw. In contrast, those low in need for cognition go out of their way to avoid onerous mental tasks; they would rather play checkers than chess, and, no, they do not want to discuss all of those plot holes because it ruins the fun of watching movies.

The ELM, and the measure of need for cognition in particular, has been immensely influential in the study of persuasion as well as numerous other aspects of decision making (Furnham and Thorne, 2013). Nonetheless, need for cognition has been used less in political science research (Sohlberg, 2015), and among the handful of studies that do employ the measure, the results are somewhat mixed. Need for cognition appears to be correlated with self-reported political interest and knowledge about politics (Ahlering, 1987; Cacioppo et al., 1986; Condra, 1992). There is less agreement over how and to what extent it influences the way in which people process political information. On the

TABLE 3.1. *The Need for Cognition Battery*

Below is a list of statements. You will find that some of these statements describe you, and some do not, to various degrees. For each of the statements below, please indicate how well each statement describes you on the following scale: extremely uncharacteristic of you (not at all like you), somewhat uncharacteristic of you, uncertain, somewhat characteristic of you, extremely characteristic of you (very much like you).

I would prefer complex to simple problems.
I like to have the responsibility of handling a situation that requires a lot of thinking.
Thinking is not my idea of fun.
I would rather do something that requires little thought than something that is sure to challenge my thinking abilities.
I try to anticipate and avoid situations where there is a likely chance I will have to think in depth about something.
I find satisfaction in deliberating hard and for long hours.
I only think as hard as I have to.
I prefer to think about small, daily projects to long-term ones.
I like tasks that require little thought once I've learned them.
The idea of relying on thought to make my way to the top appeals to me.
I really enjoy a task that involves coming up with new solutions to problems.
Learning new ways to think doesn't excite me very much.
I prefer a task that is intellectual, difficult, and important to one that is somewhat important but does not require much thought.
I feel relief rather than satisfaction after completing a task that required a lot of mental effort.
It's enough for me that something gets the job done; I don't care how or why it works.
I usually end up deliberating about issues even when they do not affect me personally.

---

one hand, need for cognition correlates with greater ambivalence toward the two major political parties in the United States (Rudolph and Popp, 2007), consistent with the notion that effortful processing causes people to entertain and sometimes accept beliefs that are inconsistent with a neat view of the world in which their team is always right and the other is always wrong. People high in need for cognition are also less likely to rely on heuristics to arrive at political opinions, such as adopting the majority opinion (Lee, 2014; Mutz, 1998) or siding with their political party (Arceneaux and Vander Wielen, 2013; Bullock, 2011). On the other hand, some scholars fail to find evidence that need for cognition affects other aspects of political reasoning, such as the ability to place presidential candidates on a simple left/right ideological scale (Holbrook, 2006) or evaluate information about novel political issues (Kam, 2005).[1]

Our interest in need for cognition lies in its ability to indicate people's propensity to behave rationally. As we elaborate in Chapter 2, we draw on Stanovich and West's (2000) refinement of the dual-process framework, which defines rationality as a product of reflection. In their framework, need for cognition is more than the willingness to devote cognitive energy to thinking; it is a willingness to devote cognitive resources to thinking put in the service of questioning and, if necessary, overriding System 1 intuitions. However, the empirical evidence does not neatly align with need for cognition as a *complete* measure of reflection. Need for cognition can also aid motivated reasoning. Individuals high in need for cognition are more likely to resist arguments advanced by news outlets with which they disagree ideologically (Arceneaux, Johnson, and Cryderman, 2013) and reject scientific studies that are contrary to their preexisting notions (Kahan, 2012). Moreover, need for cognition does not reliably predict that people will override System 1 intuitions (LeBoeuf and Shafir, 2003; Sohlberg, 2015).

One possible explanation for this less-than-coherent mix of results is that a high need for cognition is not synonymous with a motivation to be accurate. Need for cognition is simply a measure of how much people enjoy thinking. People can simultaneously enjoy thinking and defending their preexisting attitudes. Indeed, coupling deep thought with a desired outcome makes for excellent lawyers and theologians. Joking aside, when people are motivated to maintain an existing opinion, psychological research demonstrates that the need for cognition correlates with the effort allocated to generating justifications to ignore or discount countervailing information (Petty and Brinol, 2002; Petty and Wegener, 1998). Politics is exactly the sort of domain where people are likely to possess a powerful motivation to defend their worldview and maintain their partisan identities. When these motivations are strong, people's System 1 intuitions will be particularly forceful and difficult to override. In order to measure the propensity to engage in reflection, we must measure people's motivations to hang on to their preexisting attitudes in addition to their capacity for thought.

3.2 NEED FOR AFFECT

We contend that another individual difference in cognitive style offers insight into the forcefulness of people's System 1 intuitions, and thus how committed they are to preexisting attitudes: the need for affect. A relatively new concept, Gregory Maio and Victoria Esses (2001) developed the need for affect battery as the affective complement to the need for cognition battery. The need for cognition gauges how much people enjoy thinking, and the need for affect captures how much people enjoy experiencing emotions. The twenty-six-item battery, shown in Table 3.2, includes questions about how much people like experiencing strong emotions as well as the degree to which they want to avoid them. As we explained in the previous chapter, need for affect does not tap the degree to which people *feel* emotions. All humans feel emotions. Some people are motivated to put a damper on them, while others like to revel in them. It is this stable disposition that need for affect taps (see Maoi and Esses, 2001, 594). To offer some concrete examples, people high in need for affect would choose to watch a tear jerker over a documentary; when they feel down, they wallow in their sadness, and when they feel up, they let everyone know it. In contrast, people low in need for affect would prefer to watch a documentary over a tear jerker, and they like to keep a lid on their emotional reactions.

Note that we describe need for affect as a complement to need for cognition. We do so deliberately. The two motivations are not in opposition to each other. A high need for affect does not necessarily imply a low need for cognition. In fact, the two measures evince a modest *positive* correlation (see Maio and Esses, 2001, 595). As need for affect increases, need for cognition tends to as well, with a great deal of variance – many people are high on both scales, low on both, on opposite sides, or simply fall in the middle on both. Consequently, need for affect is not simply the inverse of one's propensity to enjoy effortful thinking. It is something different.

We are interested in need for affect because it gives insight into the magnitude of the affective tags that people tend to attach to their attitudes and beliefs. Because need for affect motivates people to seek out and experience emotions, individuals who possess a high need for affect should be more likely to attend to their affective states when forming attitudes, and the evidence supports this contention. As need for affect increases, people are more likely to bring their attitudes in line with their feelings about objects (e.g., whether something makes them feel sad or angry) (Huskinson and Haddock, 2004). Individuals who are high in need for affect are also more likely to be persuaded by appeals to emotion ("this drink makes you feel good") than they are by appeals to practical

TABLE 3.2. *The Need for Affect Battery*

For the statements below, please indicate how much you agree with each one on the following scale: strongly disagree, disagree, neither agree nor disagree, agree, strongly agree.

If I reflect on my past, I see that I tend to be afraid of feeling emotions.
I have trouble telling the people close to me that I love them.
I feel that I need to experience strong emotions regularly.
Emotions help people get along in life.
I am a very emotional person.
I think that it is important to explore my feelings.
I approach situations in which I expect to experience strong emotions.
I find strong emotions overwhelming and therefore try to avoid them.
I would prefer not to experience either the lows or highs of emotion.
I do not know how to handle my emotions, so I avoid them.
Emotions are dangerous – they tend to get me into situations that I would rather avoid.
Acting on one's emotions is always a mistake.
We should indulge our emotions.
Displays of emotions are embarrassing.
Strong emotions are generally beneficial.
People can function most effectively when they are not experiencing strong emotions.
Humans couldn't survive if we didn't experience emotions.
It is important for me to be in touch with my feelings.
It is important for me to know how others are feeling.
I like to dwell on my emotions.
I wish I could feel less emotion.
Avoiding emotional events helps me sleep better at night.
I am sometimes afraid of how I might act if I become too emotional.
I feel like I need a good cry every now and then.
I would love to be the type of person who is totally logical and experiences little emotion.
I like decorating my bedroom with a lot of pictures and posters of things emotionally significant to me.

---

information ("this drink is made of natural ingredients") (Haddock et al., 2008; see also Mayer and Tormala, 2010).

Because high levels of need for affect cause people to attend more to their affective state, they should also motivate people to attach strong affective tags to their attitudes (see Ryan, Wells, and Acree, 2016). Stronger affective tags should, in turn, lead to stronger attitudes (Krosnick and Petty, 1995). There is evidence for this contention: higher levels of need for affect predict stronger and more certain attitudes (Britt et al., 2009). As we discussed in the previous chapter, System 1 processes have the first crack at processing political information. In the course of processing information, if System 1 activates existing attitude structures that are connected to large affective tags, it should spontaneously generate intuitions that are more forceful and thus more difficult to override. In this way, need for affect is a domain-general indicator of System 1 forcefulness. We see this as a strength, because it means that the measure of need for affect is not confounded with politics. Since we are ultimately interested in measuring something more domain-specific – the forcefulness of people's partisan intuitions – we must gather information about whether people identify as a democrat or republican. In concert with partisanship, need for affect serves as a predictor for the affective weight attached to preexisting attitude structures connected to people's partisan identities. As need for affect increases, people who identify as democrat or republican should find it more difficult to override partisan-motivated intuitions.

Of course, there are other measures of cognitive style that scholars have used to measure attitude strength. Individuals vary in the degree to which they are motivated to form attitudes, especially strong attitudes. The need to evaluate scale created by Jarvis and Petty (1996) measures this individual difference by asking questions such as, "I form opinions on everything" and "It is very important for me to hold strong opinions." Higher values on the need to evaluate scale correspond to people offering more opinions about political candidates as well as stronger correlations between voting preferences and both partisan identities and issue opinions (Bizer et al., 2004). Individuals high in the need to evaluate show higher levels of ideological constraint (Weber and Federico, 2007) and more stable political attitudes (Chong and Druckman, 2010). Consequently, the need to evaluate also appears to contribute to ideologically motivated reasoning, wherein individuals seek to maintain ideologically coherent attitudes even in the face of countervailing information (Nir, 2011).

Since there are likely multiple pathways through which psychological motivations influence System 1 forcefulness, the need to evaluate undoubtedly plays a similar role as the need for affect. However, the available evidence shows that need for affect and need to evaluate are only weakly correlated (Maio and Esses, 2001), and both measures have independent effects on attitude strength when accounted for simultaneously (Britt et al., 2009). Consequently, need for affect and need to evaluate influence System 1 processing in different ways. Because our theoretical framework focuses on the affective component of System 1 processes (affective processing is, after all, central to what System 1 does), we believe that need for affect is more conceptually relevant to our framework.

The need for cognitive closure is another measure of cognitive style often used as a marker for motivated reasoning. The measure, developed by Webster and Kruglanski (1994), taps the degree to which people are motivated to reduce uncertainty by forming attitudes quickly. While the need for cognitive closure undoubtedly shapes how individuals process political information (see Jost et al., 2003), we do not think it is a good indicator of System 1 forcefulness. From a theoretical perspective, the need for closure should motivate people simply to go with their System 1 intuition not because it is difficult to override, but because they are not motivated to be reflective. In this way, need for cognitive closure seems to us to be the obverse of need for cognition, and the available evidence supports our supposition (see also Ksiazkiewicz, Ludeke, and Krueger, forthcoming). Need for cognitive closure is negatively correlated with both need for cognition and need for affect. Accordingly, the measure does not achieve our theoretical goal to tap System 1 forcefulness.

More important, these other measures of cognitive style do not appear to be mere proxies for need for affect and need for cognition, nor do they strike us as being as appropriate for capturing the relevant processes of our theoretical model. While it may be a worthy goal to combine these various measures of cognitive style into a coherent framework, it is beyond the scope of our project. Our goal at hand is to operationalize individual differences in reflection, rather than produce a unified model of psychological motivations. In the remaining pages of this chapter, we evaluate whether or not need for affect and need for cognition offer us useful measures of individual differences in reflection.

3.3 DO NEED FOR AFFECT AND NEED FOR COGNITION MEASURE INDIVIDUAL DIFFERENCES IN REFLECTION?

The self-report batteries for need for affect and need for cognition shown in Tables 3.1 and 3.2 have been assessed and validated by psychologists. Nonetheless, we seek to use them for a specific purpose – as an indicator of reflection – that goes beyond the original intent of these measures. We also seek to apply them to a domain – politics – for which they were not explicitly developed. Neither of these facts is inherently problematic. On their face, these measures are related to the key elements of the dual-processing model of the mind, and other scholars actually have recognized this with respect to need for cognition (e.g., Frederick, 2005; Stanovich and West, 2000). We also see it as a benefit that these measures do not make explicit references to politics or political attitudes. First, we are interested in capturing individual differences in the general propensity to be reflective, rather than people's propensity to be reflective about politics in particular. Second, if the batteries included overt references to politics, we would worry that the resulting measures are commingled with individual differences in political predispositions (e.g., ideology) and thus capture something other than information-processing predispositions.

Even though we believe that there is a theoretical and practical case for using need for affect and need for cognition to measure individual differences in reflection, the fact that we are using these measures in a somewhat novel way means that we should take the extra step to validate them for our purposes. We are particularly interested in assessing their *construct validity*, which is the extent to which these measures capture the elements of information processing that we think they do. We evaluate the construct validity of these measures by evaluating two important characteristics that comprise construct validity. The first is *discriminant validity*. That is, these measures should *not* overlap too much with measures from which they should be distinct. For instance, other personality measures should not account for need for affect or need for cognition. The second, *convergent validity*, gets at the obverse: these measures should be related to theoretically relevant measures. Need for affect should be related to System 1 forcefulness, and need for cognition should be related to effortful thinking.

3.3.1 The Data

Between 2012 and 2016, we conducted five studies to investigate how individual differences in reflection shape political reasoning.[2] These studies, which are briefly summarized in Table 3.3, include over 4,300 participants in total, drawn from both nationally representative samples and convenience samples. We designed each with specific hypotheses in mind, and we make use of both observational and experimental methods. We will say more about these studies in the coming chapters, and a full accounting of each study's methodology is located in Section 1 of the Appendix. For now, the fact that each of these studies includes measures of need for affect and need for cognition allows us to assess the construct validity of these measures.

TABLE 3.3. *Summary of Empirical Studies*

Study Name	Year	Study Type	Sample Type	N	Scale Reliability
2012 Campaign	2011–2012	Observational	Census-matched Internet sample	1000	$\alpha_{NFA} = 0.640$ $\alpha_{NFC} = 0.613$
Governor Evaluation	Spring 2013	Experiment	Internet convenience	661	$\alpha_{NFA} = 0.883$ $\alpha_{NFC} = 0.911$
Emotion Processing	Fall 2014	Observational	College students	105	$\alpha_{NFA} = 0.889$ $\alpha_{NFC} = 0.852$
Party Cues	Spring 2015	Observational and experiment	Internet quota sample	1258	$\alpha_{NFA} = 0.852$ $\alpha_{NFC} = 0.898$
Issue Polarization	Summer 2015	Observational	Internet quota sample Internet	1302	$\alpha_{NFA} = 0.836$ $\alpha_{NFC} = 0.858$

Note: Need for affect and need for cognition were measured with shortened four-item batteries in the 2012 Campaign Study, while they were measured with the full batteries displayed in Tables 3.1 and 3.2 for the other studies. See the Section 1 of the Appendix for more details.

For each study, we have participants' answers to the questions shown in Tables 3.1 and 3.2 (or a subset of those questions in the case of the 2012 Campaign Study). Ultimately, we want to use the answers to generate two scores for each person, one that summarizes their level of need for affect and one that summarizes their need for cognition. In order to accomplish this goal, our first task is to convert people's responses to the individual items into numbers using a 1 to 5 scale and coding them so that higher values correspond to higher levels of need for affect and need for cognition. For example, participants who said that "thinking is not my idea of fun" is extremely characteristic of them would be coded as a "1," and those who said that it was extremely uncharacteristic of them would be coded as a "5" (somewhat characteristic would be a "2," uncertain would be a "3," and so on).

Our next task is to assess whether it is appropriate to combine these responses into a single measure for each need for affect and need for cognition. The standard way to do this is to see how well the answers correlate with one another. If they are indeed tapping the same underlying construct, then people's answers to one question should give us some sense of how they will answer another. For instance, the theory behind need for affect predicts that people who strongly agree with the statement "It is important for me to be in touch with my feelings" should also agree with the statement "I think that it is important to explore my feelings." We can summarize the correlations of the responses within the need for affect and need for cognition batteries using a statistic called Cronbach's α. This quantity tells us how much consistency there is within the answers to these items, which statisticians call *scale reliability*. The higher the number, the more reliable the scale. The Cronbach's α for each scale in each study is reported in the last column of Table 3.3. Across our studies, the indicators of need for affect and need for cognition all show high levels of scale reliability.

Now that we have numerical values for the participants' responses to the individual items and we know that they form a reliable scale, our final task is to generate a number that summarizes people's level of need for affect and a number for their level of need for cognition. The simplest approach would be to take the average of the numerically coded responses for the respective need for affect and need for cognition batteries. An argument for this approach is that it is straightforward and intuitive. It does not take an advanced degree to add and divide. However, the fatal drawback to this approach is that it gives each item equal weight even though we know that some items may be better than others at discriminating people's level of need for affect and need for cognition. A standard way to deal with this problem is to use a statistical technique called factor analysis to figure out how much weight each item should be accorded before essentially taking the average of all responses. The argument in favor of this approach is that it is common, and statistical programs can do the necessary calculations quickly and with ease. Nonetheless, the downside to this approach is that it assumes that we can measure people's true levels of need for affect and need for cognition without any error. We would need to assume that respondents did not accidentally enter the wrong response on some items, for instance, or that people did not become fatigued as they answered the questionnaire and failed to give us an accurate response. Assumptions like these are certainly false. All measurement – be it something as mundane as people's height or as complex as people's information-processing dispositions – is bound to have some amount of error.

Failure to account for measurement error could introduce bias into statistical analyses that use these measures (Treier and Jackman, 2008). Consequently, we use a statistical technique called Bayesian ordinal factor analysis (Martin, Quinn, and Park, 2013) to estimate people's levels of need for affect and need for cognition from their responses to the batteries shown in Tables 3.1 and 3.2. This technique not only generates a single score for each individual on each scale, but it also quantifies the amount of measurement error that exists for each score. In doing so, we are able to gauge how accurate (or inaccurate) our placement is of each individual on the need for affect and need for cognition scales, and as a result, we can incorporate this uncertainty into the statistical models we use to estimate the measures' effects on people's political attitudes and behavior. We provide a more technical explanation in Section 2 of the Appendix for interested readers, but stated briefly here, Bayesian methods provide a straightforward and statistically rigorous means of generating uncertainty estimates. Markov chain Monte Carlo algorithms, such as that used in the analysis, explore the parameter space by means of a "random tour," in which locations in the parameter space are visited (i.e., recorded) at a rate proportional to their posterior probability. Upon completion of the tour, the output of its visits offers a summary of the distribution over the parameter space. The amount of uncertainty surrounding the estimation of the latent variable is simply measured as the dispersion of the iterated recordings of the tour (i.e., the posterior density). As noted elsewhere, other scaling techniques often estimate uncertainty in a less principled fashion (e.g., relying on ad hoc assumptions) or fail to account for it entirely (see, for discussion, Clinton and Jackman, 2009; Clinton, Jackman, and Rivers, 2004).

Therefore, the Bayesian approach we use to estimate need for affect and need for cognition scores offers both point estimates and reliable information regarding the uncertainty surrounding the measurement of these latent variables. Why is it important to account for this measurement error? It is generally problematic to assume that observed data (i.e., item responses) are deterministically generated when including measures of latent attributes as explanatory variables in analytical models. Social scientists frequently ignore the errors-in-variables problem by simply assuming that explanatory variables are measured with perfect precision. This is particularly common in the literatures relating to the subject of this manuscript. However, failure to account for measurement error in explanatory variables can lead to parameter estimates that are biased and inconsistent, which can result in erroneous conclusions. Recent work suggests that Bayesian methods can be used to address this problem and finds that accounting for measurement error in explanatory variables can dramatically affect the results of analytical models when compared to conventional methods (see, e.g., Trier and Jackman, 2008). The approach we use in this study accounts for uncertainty in both the estimation of the latent need for affect and need for cognition scores and in modeling their effects.

Figure 3.1 shows the distributions of posterior means for the need for affect and need for cognition scales from the Party Cues Study. We chose this study as an exemplar because it offers a large and nationally diverse sample that asked respondents the full need for affect and need for cognition batteries. Nonetheless, the results do not differ markedly from any of the other studies. As these distribution graphs show, both need for affect and need for cognition follow a single-peaked distribution where most respondents cluster around the center of the scales and fewer people fall in the tails of the distributions. This is a common aspect of most individual differences in psychological dispositions: most people cluster in a "normal" range, and a smaller group of people evince extremely low or high levels of a particular trait.

Because we are ultimately interested in how the intersection of need for affect and need for cognition influences political reasoning, we show the joint distribution of these two traits in Figure 3.2. The top panel is a joint density plot, and it shows that most people fall somewhere in the middle range of both scales, which should not be surprising based on the univariate density plots shown above. Yet it also demonstrates that

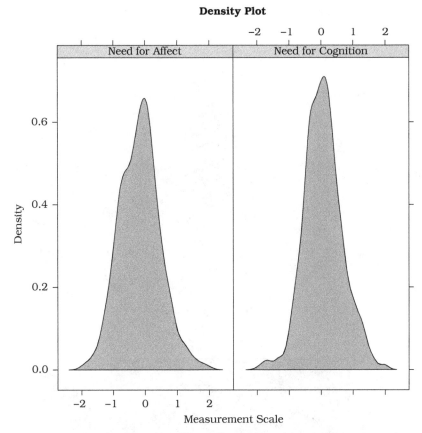

FIGURE 3.1. Distributions of Need for Affect and Need for Cognition, Party Cues Study

there is a good bit of variance, with a considerable number of individuals falling higher on one scale and lower on the other. The contour plot in the bottom panel offers another way to visualize the variance in the two distributions. It shows a weak positive relationship between need for affect and need for cognition (consistent with previous research) but also drives home the wide range of variance. It is this variance that gives us the necessary leverage we need to study the effects of individual differences in the predisposition to be reflective.

For illustrative purposes, Figure 3.3 presents the proportions of the subjects in the various studies who we could categorize as being high on one scale and low on the other – the types of individuals who are of central interest to this project. In this exercise, we define individuals

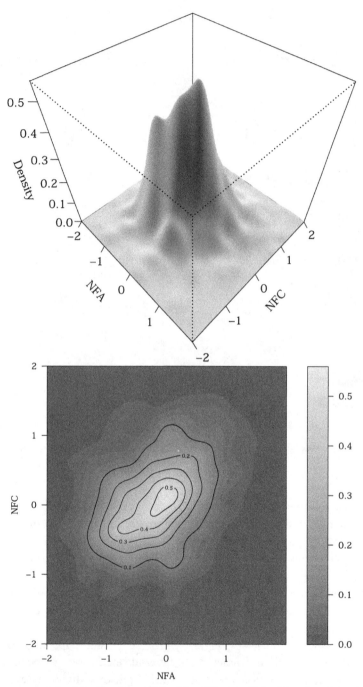

FIGURE 3.2. Joint Distributions of Need for Affect and Need for Cognition, Party Cues Study

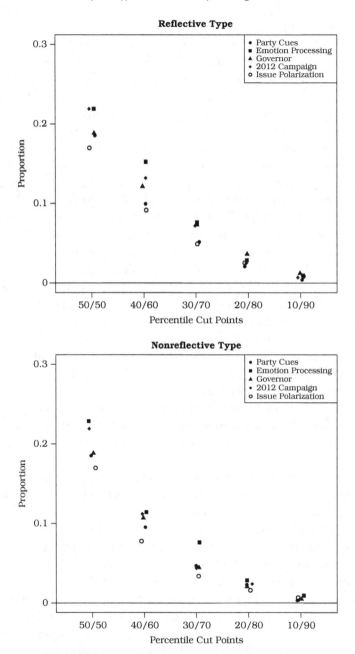

FIGURE 3.3. Percentage of Reflective and Nonreflective Types of Individuals across Various Cut Points

who are low in need for affect and high in need for cognition as "reflective," and those who are high in need for affect and low in need for cognition as "nonreflective." Since a discrete categorization approach involves making the somewhat arbitrary decision of where to draw the cut points for the "high" and "low" classifications, Figure 3.3 shows the proportions of each type using various cut point criteria. For instance, the results corresponding to the 50/50 percentile cut points for categorizing respondents as reflective report the proportions of subjects in our studies who were simultaneously below the median on the need for affect scale and above the median on the need for cognition scale (note that the scatterplots are jittered for presentation's sake). Similarly, the results for the 40/60 percentile cut points for categorizing respondents as nonreflective show the proportion of individuals who were simultaneously above the sixtieth percentile on the need for affect scale and below the fortieth percentile on the need for cognition scale. Clearly, the proportions of respondents categorized as reflective and nonreflective fall considerably as the cut point decision rule becomes more stringent (i.e., simultaneously increasing on one scale and decreasing on the other). When using a modest cut point criterion like the medians, nearly 40 percent of subjects fall, on average, into one of the types of interest. But even for a relatively strict criterion, such as using the thirtieth and seventieth percentiles for cut points, we find that an average of approximately 11 percent of subjects fall into these categories, which is still a magnitude of substantive importance in democratic politics. After all, election outcomes can be decided by a one- or two-percentage point swing in votes.

We wish to emphasize that the foregoing analysis was carried out to illustrate the joint distributions of need for affect and need for cognition. Placing respondents into reflective and nonreflective categories offers a convenient shorthand for thinking about our theoretical predictions. However, our theoretical model presumes that people's propensity to be reflective falls on a continuum, and as a result, people can be more or less reflective as opposed to either reflective or not reflective. Furthermore, from the standpoint of statistical modeling, there are well-established reasons for maintaining the continuous properties of our need for affect and need for cognition measures, because doing so makes use of all available information (i.e., variability), improves statistical power, and increases validity (Cohen, 1983; Royston, Altman, and Sauerbrei, 2006; Rucker, McShane, and Preacher, 2015).[3] For these reasons, we maintain the continuous measures in the empirical analyses in the rest of the book (with one exception in Chapter 5 where data limitations forced us to categorize individuals). Consequently, when we discuss results with respect to individuals being more or less reflective, we are drawing inferences by adjusting the values of need for affect and need for cognition in simulations that use regression coefficient estimates connected to the continuous measures of these variables.

3.3.2 Discriminant Validity

We evaluate the discriminant validity of need for affect and need for cognition in two ways. First, we assess whether these measures are merely proxies for individual differences that previous research has identified as key explanatory variables of political attitudes and behavior. While we would not be surprised to find that need for affect and need for cognition correlate with many of these variables – after all, there should be some overlap in psychological motivations and personality characteristics, for instance – we should also uncover evidence that they are sufficiently distinct. If we can account for need for affect and need for cognition using education or political knowledge, for example, then we might as well stick with these more familiar and well-understood variables. Second, we empirically examine the claim that we made at the end of Chapter 2 that need for affect and need for cognition measure differences in motivations rather than emotional processing. In doing so, we offer assurances that these measures tell us about how people process information as opposed to how they experience the world.

We accomplish the first approach by calculating the bivariate correlations among need for affect and need for cognition and a host of demographic, political, and personality differences in all of the studies listed in Table 3.3. The results are summarized in Figures 3.4, 3.5 and 3.6. The markers represent Pearson's r correlation coefficients, and the horizontal lines are the 95 percent confidence intervals around the correlations. A positive correlation coefficient indicates that as the variable named along the y-axis of the figure increases, need for affect or need for cognition also increases; and a negative coefficient indicates the opposite. The magnitude of the coefficient indicates the strength of the correlation, where 0 indicates no correlation and 1 indicates a perfect correlation. The confidence intervals tell us how certain we should be about the correlation coefficients, which were estimated from a sample of people. Because we were only able to interview a small slice of the American population, we cannot be completely sure that the correlations we observe in these data perfectly match the correlations that actually exists. The wider the confidence intervals, the more uncertain we are about our sample estimate, and when the confidence interval crosses the zero (vertical) line, then we cannot be statistically certain that any relationship exists between the variables.

The top panel of Figure 3.4 shows the correlations with need for affect and personality differences, and the bottom panel shows the correlations with need for cognition and personality differences. The first thing to observe is the correlation between need for affect and need for cognition. Consistent with previous research and across all five studies, we find a modest positive correlation between the two variables. These findings remind us that these two psychological motivations are not in opposition to each other. The remainder of these graphs shows the correlations with personality differences, which we measured along five important traits: agreeableness, conscientiousness, extroversion, neuroticism, and openness to new experiences (question wording for these measures is located in Section 3 of the Appendix). These traits, dubbed the "Big Five" by personality psychologists, capture stable core differences in how individuals orient themselves toward the social world (Goldberg, 1990; McCrae and Costa, 1987). For instance, agreeable people try to be more friendly with strangers; individuals high in conscientiousness tend to be orderly and punctual; extroverted individuals tend to be outgoing and at ease in social situations; neurotic individuals tend to be more emotionally volatile than less neurotic individuals; and people who are more open to experiences enjoy learning and traveling.

Recent work shows that these dispositional traits explain notable variation in political attitudes (Gerber et al., 2010) and political behavior (Mondak et al., 2010). It is important to note that while these five traits capture core differences in personality traits, they do not account for all of the ways in which people are different. People also differ in terms of their psychological motivations, of which need for affect and need for cognition are prime examples. Although personality traits may give rise to particular motivations, those motivations are not merely byproducts of personality traits either (McAdams and Pals, 2006, 208–209). The results shown in Figure 3.4 are consistent with the notion that need for affect and need for cognition are not simply different labels for the five core personality traits. Conscientiousness, extroversion, and neuroticism are weakly correlated (if at all) with need for affect and need for cognition. Agreeableness correlates modestly with these two motivations. Openness correlates modestly with need for affect and more

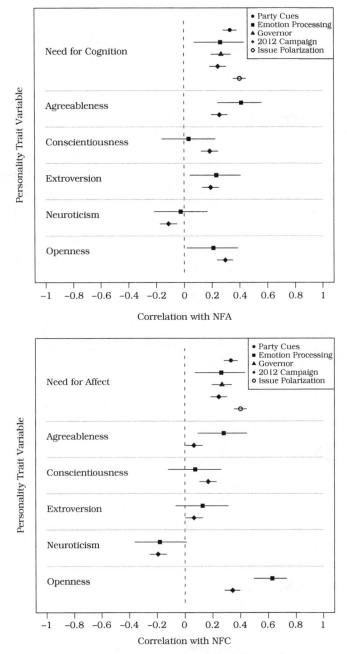

FIGURE 3.4. Bivariate Correlations among Need for Affect and Need for Cognition and Personality Differences

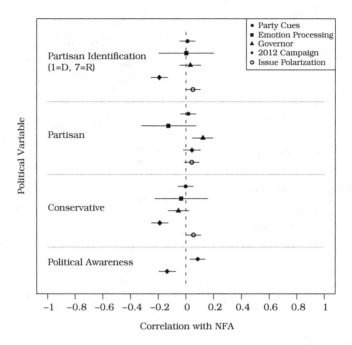

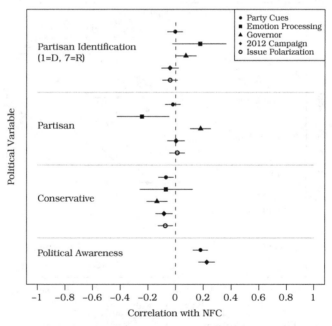

FIGURE 3.5. Bivariate Correlations among Need for Affect and Need for Cognition and Political Characteristics

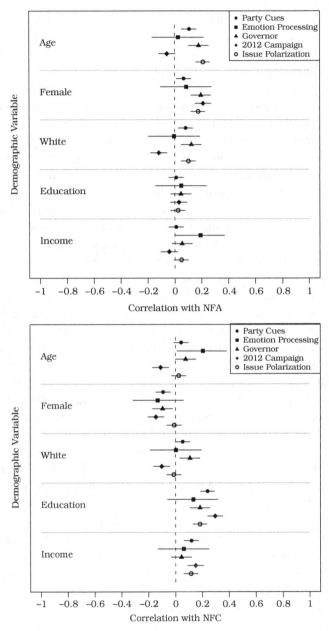

FIGURE 3.6. Bivariate Correlations among Need for Affect and Need for Cognition and Demographic Characteristics

strongly with need for cognition. The robust positive correlation between openness and need for cognition makes sense, because an interest in ideas and learning (openness) should overlap with a motivation to think (see Ksiazkiewicz, Ludeke, and Krueger, forthcoming). Nonetheless, two things are noteworthy. First, the correlation between openness and need for cognition is more modest in the 2012 Campaign Study, which drew on a nationally representative sample. Second, even if openness does explain some (but apparently far from all) of the motivation to engage in effortful thinking, it also predicts people's need to feel strong emotions. Consequently, openness to experience, like need for cognition, is unlikely to be a comprehensive measure of reflection.

The panels of Figure 3.5 display how need for affect and need for cognition correlate with four key individual differences that are proximal to politics. Party identification, as we have already touched upon, predicts a wide range of political attitudes and is central to understanding political behavior in the United States (Campbell et al., 1960; Green, Palmquist, and Schickler, 2002). We use the standard seven-point classification system that asks people to rank themselves on a scale that ranges from strong democrats to strong republicans, with those who do not lean in the direction of either major party as independents. We then fold this measure to create a 4-point partisanship scale that goes from independents to independents who lean toward one of the major parties, to weak party identifiers, and ending with strong party identifiers. Partisan intensity, aside from the direction of party identification, predicts partisan reasoning (Gaines et al., 2007). Next, we consider self-reported ideology, which ranges from liberal to conservative, with moderates falling in the middle. Individual differences in ideology predict a host of political and nonpolitical attitudes (Hibbing, Smith, and Alford, 2013), and conservatism has been linked to close-mindedness (e.g., Rokeach, 1960; for a review, see Jost et al., 2003). Lastly, we take into account political awareness, which was measured by asking people a series of political facts (e.g., "Who is the speaker of the House of Representatives?"). People who know more about politics tend to have more consistent political attitudes that are more impervious to persuasive messages (Zaller, 1992), and political awareness has been advanced as a better measure of information processing than need for cognition in the domain of politics (Kam, 2005).

As Figure 3.5 makes plain, the political variables measured here do not correlate reliably with either need for affect or need for cognition. Party identification and partisan intensity are virtually uncorrelated with these motivational variables. It appears that democrats and republicans as well as strong partisans are just as likely to be high in need for affect and need for cognition. This is an important finding that calls for more discussion, which we provide later in this chapter. There is little correlation between need for affect and conservatism and only a very small negative correlation between conservatism and need for cognition. While these results are in line with work that links close-mindedness to conservatism, they are hardly arresting. Conservatism is not a proxy for low levels of need for cognition. With respect to political awareness, its relationship with need for affect is ambiguous, as it is positive in one study and negative in the other – both studies draw on nationally representative samples. Whichever is the case, the correlation is marginal at best ($-0.2 < r < +0.2$). In contrast, need for cognition is consistently positively correlated with political awareness, but even here the relationship is quite small.

The panels of Figure 3.6 show the relationships between need for affect and need for cognition and a host of important demographic variables. Age, gender, race, education, and income are reliable guides to political attitudes and behavior and have been central to theories of political attitudes at least since the initial studies of voting in the United States (Berelson, Lazarsfeld, and McPhee, 1954; Campbell et al., 1960). Quite simply, there is no evidence that demographics account for substantial variation in either need for affect or need for cognition. The correlations that do exist are modest at best. For instance, as education increases, people are only slightly more likely to evince a greater need for cognition.

We believe that the results presented in Figures 3.4, 3.5, and 3.6 demonstrate convincingly that need for affect and need for cognition are not merely proxies for other individual differences that are more familiar to the study of politics. That said, we do uncover evidence of some overlap, which suggests that we should account for these variables in our empirical analyses to ensure that some other variable is not driving the effects we wish to ascribe to psychological motivations.[4] Moreover, while we believe this is a useful demonstration of discriminant validity – need for affect and need for cognition are distinct from other psychological, political, and demographic characteristics – we can do more to assess discriminant validity on purely theoretical grounds.

As we explained in Chapter 2, individual differences in need for affect and need for cognition reflect differences in how people are motivated to process information. They do not reflect individual differences in the physiological architecture that dictates how people process emotions. All human beings experience emotions, and they guide behavior in similar ways across individuals, at least for those who fall within the normal range of brain function (Cosmides and Tooby, 2004; Stanovich, 2009).[5] To underline a point we have already made: despite the intuitive appeal, people high in need for affect are not "feelers" just as people high in need for cognition are not "thinkers." Moreover, need for affect and need for cognition should not reflect a proclivity to experience particular types of emotions, such as anxiety or sadness. Trait differences in mood states arise from different psychological processes, such as neurological differences in how neurotransmitters are processed (Caspi et al., 2003) as well as early childhood trauma (Huddy, Feldman, and Weber, 2007). Consequently, need for affect and need for cognition should not predict how people experience emotions or the degree to which people experience particular emotions. The only thing these measures should predict, particularly need for affect, is the degree to which people attend to the emotions that they experience and the strength of the emotional tags attached to their attitudes.

Evaluating this claim constitutes our second approach to assessing the discriminant validity of need for affect and need for cognition. As the name implies, we measured emotional processing with the aid of the Emotion Processing Study. We used a procedure that replicated the Oxley et al. (2008) study of emotional arousal and political ideology. Subjects – all undergraduates at Temple University – were asked to view emotionally arousing photographs while we recorded how much their hands perspired, which psychophysiologists call electrodermal activity (EDA). EDA is an indicator of arousal and is often used to measure the intensity of people's emotional experiences (Dawson, Schell, and Filion, 2001). The emotionally arousing photographs were drawn from the International Affective Picture System (IAPS) database, housed by the Center for the Study of Emotion and Attention (CSEA), which includes hundreds of images that have been rated for emotional content (valence and arousal) and validated through numerous studies (Lang, 1995). Study participants viewed a blank screen for twenty seconds followed by a randomly rotated image that was then viewed for twenty seconds. This procedure was repeated for twelve images: three that evoke anxiety from threats (a ferocious dog, a snake, the Twin Towers on fire after the 9/11 attacks), three tapping sadness (a cemetery, a crying child, and a disabled child), two that evoke happiness (cute puppies and an island paradise), two that elicit excitement (sky diving and a ski jump), and two mundane objects (a basket and a spoon). Participants' EDA was measured (in microsiemens) every millisecond throughout the entire viewing session.

Following the protocol used by Oxley et al. (2008), we measured individual differences in emotional arousal by first taking the natural log of EDA (in order to minimize the effects of extreme outliers), calculating the average logged EDA scores during each of the blank screens and screens with images, and then taking the difference between averaged scores when the image was present from the blank screen that proceeded the image, which acts as a baseline. These logged differences in EDA constitute how participants' emotional arousal changed in response to the emotion-inducing images. Scores above zero indicate that the person's emotional arousal increased above the baseline, negative values indicate a suppressed emotional response (relative to the baseline), and zero indicates no change in emotional response.

The scatterplots shown in Figures 3.7 and 3.8 graphically depict the correlation between psychological motivations (i.e., need for affect and need for cognition) and participants' emotional responses to the five groups of images (mundane, excitement, happiness, sadness, and threat). In every case, it looks like someone shot a canvass with a shotgun – these are textbook examples of "no correlation." The lines drawn through the data points make a similar case. They are all close to being flat, which tells us that as need for affect and need for cognition increase, emotional responses neither increase nor decrease on average. If we squint, we can see very slight negative relationships between need for affect and happy images as well as need for cognition and threatening images. However, in both cases the results are substantively unimportant, and we cannot rule out sampling variability as an explanation ($p > 0.05$). In the case of need for affect and happiness, the correlation is the exact opposite of what one would predict if need for affect were in fact a proxy for emotional arousal. We also continue to find the same lack of correlations if we break the results down by each image, rather than lumping them into the groups that we do. Moreover, we observe a similar story if we examine how need for affect and need for cognition are distributed across various levels of emotional responses. It turns out that the distributions of need for affect and need for cognition are highly similar (i.e., not statistically discernible) across high, medium, and low ranges of emotional responses. Both the image-by-image results and distributional analysis are located in Section 4 of the Appendix.

In sum, individual differences in need for affect and need for cognition do not reliably correlate with participants' individual differences in

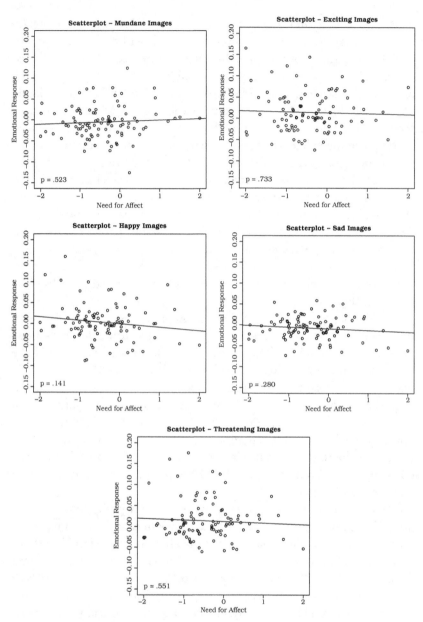

FIGURE 3.7. Bivariate Correlations between Need for Affect and Emotion Response, Emotion Processing Study

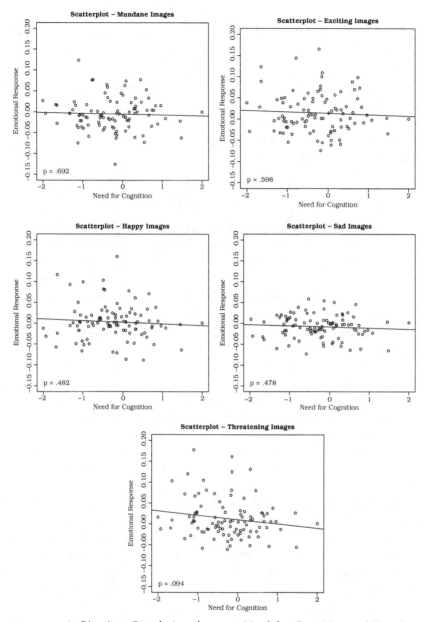

FIGURE 3.8. Bivariate Correlations between Need for Cognition and Emotion Response, Emotion Processing Study

emotional arousal. Consequently, they do not appear to manifest from physiological differences in people's reactions to emotional stimuli. These results are consistent with our claim (as well as the claims advanced by the underlying psychological research) that need for affect and need for cognition are neither a product of individual differences in emotional processing nor a reflection of one's proclivity to experience particular types of emotions. Instead, they map onto particular psychological motivations that cause people to process information in particular ways. We turn to evaluating this claim in the next section.

3.3.3 Convergent Validity

Having demonstrated what need for affect and need for cognition are not, we now turn to the task of evaluating whether they are what we think they are. We begin with the claim that need for affect increases the strength of the affective tags in people's associative networks. Because we are interested in the effects of partisan identification in this project, we look specifically at whether need for affect increases people's affective attachment to the party with which they identify. People who say they "strongly" identify with a party and who are high in need for affect should have stronger positive affective tags connected to their party and stronger negative tags attached to the opposing party. The relationship between need for affect and partisan affective tags should diminish as people become less identified to a party. Independents who are high in need for affect should be less likely to hold strong attitudes about either party, because they are unlikely to consistently attach either positive or negative affective charges to one party.

Recall that in the bivariate correlations reported in the last section, we found both need for affect and need for cognition to be uncorrelated with whether individuals strongly identified with one of the major parties. Does that mean that the evidence undermines the claim that need for affect contributes to stronger affective attachments to people's partisan identities? In a word, no. Although the standard seven-point measure of partisan identification is often treated as a measure of people's affective attachments to the parties, the question itself asks people how they "think" of themselves and makes no mention of emotional attachments (Burden and Klofstad, 2005). People can identify as a strong democrat or republican because they have a strong affective attachment to their party, or because they find through a dispassionate assessment that they agree with their party's issue positions (Petersen, Giessing, and Nielsen, 2015). Consequently, it is necessary to measure people's affective attachments using a different approach.

We could simply ask people to tell us how they feel about the parties, but we do not believe this to be a fair test. Need for affect taps how much people enjoy feeling emotions and how useful they think emotions are. So, people high in need for affect may simply be more likely to report feeling strong emotions about their party than people who are low in need for affect. Rather than asking people to tell us how they feel about the parties, we directly measure the strength of people's affective attachments to the parties within their associative networks using an Implicit Attitude Test (IAT). Implicit attitudes comprise the content of associative networks. They are the positive and negative affective charges attached to people's evaluations of ideas, things, and people, as illustrated with a hypothetical example in Figure 2.2.

The IAT, developed by psychologists Anthony Greenwald, Debbie McGee, and Jordan Schwartz (1998), measures people's implicit attitudes with a clever and unobtrusive method. Study participants are seated in front of a computer monitor and asked to classify objects as quickly as possible that appear at the middle of the screen into one of two groups that are labeled on either the left or right side of the screen. One set of objects are positive or negative words, which people categorize as "Good" or "Bad" by typing the key that corresponds with the side of the screen associated with those labels (e.g., the E key for the left-side label and the I key for the right-side label). The other set of objects relate to the implicit attitudes under investigation. For instance, if researchers wanted to measure people's implicit attitudes about the racial groups white and African American, participants would be asked to categorize photos of white individuals and African American individuals by typing the key associated with those labels (e.g., E if "African American" is on the left and I if "White" is on the right). Participants go through a series of practice runs where they practice typing the key as quickly as possible for one set of objects at a time (e.g., either the good/bad words or "African American"/"White"). Next, the test phase begins. The two sets of objects are combined, and participants are asked to categorize both the good/bad words and the objects that relate to the implicit attitude under investigation. Doing so couples "Good" and "Bad" with the two categories under investigation (e.g., "African American" and "White"). Participants' performance during the test portion of the IAT protocol provides an insight into the affective tags connected to the two categories under investigation. Keeping with the racial IAT example, individuals who tend to associate positive attributes with whites and negative attributes with African Americans will be slower at categorizing photos of whites when the labels "White" and "Bad" are on the same side of the screen and "African American" and "Good" are on the same side.

To measure people's implicit partisan affect, we asked participants in the Emotion Processing Study to complete the Partisan IAT as developed by Iyengar and Westwood (2015) (for a related approach, see Theodoridis, forthcoming). The positive words that people were asked to categorize as "Good" were wonderful, best, superb, and excellent; the negative words people were asked to categorize as "Bad" were terrible, awful, worst, and horrible. For the partisan stimuli, participants saw various logos that represent the Democratic and Republican parties (and to make it as clear as possible, the name of the party was incorporated into the logo) and asked to categorize them as "Democratic Party" or "Republican Party." For the practice run, participants were first asked to categorize good/bad words twenty times and then Democratic Party/Republican Party logos twenty times. We randomly rotated whether words or party logos came first as well as on which side of the screen the labels appeared. We then combined the tasks for the test portion, keeping the labels on the same side of the screen as participants had just encountered in the practice run, and asked participants to make forty categorizations randomly drawn from the good/bad stimuli and the Democrat/Republican stimuli. After completing these categorizations, we reversed the association between good/bad words and party labels by reversing the side of the screen on which either the good/bad label appeared or where the Democratic Party/Republican Party label appeared. For instance, a participant who had "Good" and "Republican Party" on the left side of the screen would be asked to re-do the categorization procedure with either "Good" and "Democratic Party" on the left side of the screen or "Bad" and "Republican Party" on the right side of the screen. With the switch in labels made, participants went through forty practice runs again in which they categorized either words or party labels, before coupling words and party logos (again categorized forty times). Figure 3.9 shows two examples of screens that participants would have encountered during the test portion.

The amount of time it took people to correctly categorize objects in the task where words and party logos were combined forms the basis of our measure of people's implicit partisan affect. Following the procedure outlined in Greenwald, Nosek, and Banaji (2003), we calculated the

FIGURE 3.9. Examples of Screens from Implicit Partisan Affect Test

standardized difference (called a *d* score) in the average amount of time it took people to make categorizations when the "Democratic Party" label was on the same side of the screen as "Good" from the average amount of time it took people to make categorizations when the "Republican Party" label was on the same side of the screen as "Good." Positive values on this measure indicate that people have more negative associations with the Democratic Party and more positive associations with the Republican Party. Negative values indicate the opposite: positive associations with the Democratic Party and negative associations with the Republican Party. A score of zero indicates indifferences (or ambivalence) between the two parties.

Because we ultimately want to know if need for affect increases positive attachment to the party with which an individual identifies, we use the absolute value of the *d* score, so that higher values mean stronger affective attachment to one party over the other.[6] We model the effects of need for affect and need for cognition on implicit partisan affective attachment by using a Bayesian linear regression model in which we account for our measures of need for affect, need for cognition, and the interaction of need for affect and need for cognition, as well as their interactions with explicitly stated partisan strength (i.e., independent, lean partisan, weak partisan, strong partisan). As we do throughout the following analytical models when possible, we also include controls for political, personality, and demographic characteristics. See Section 2 of the Appendix for a more technical discussion of our general statistical modeling approach.

Figure 3.10 shows the results restricted to pure independents and strong partisans, for whom we have the clearest predictions.[7] The evidence corroborates our theoretical model. As need for affect increases, strong partisans exhibit a stronger affective attachment to their party, while we see little change among independents. We see virtually no relationship between need for cognition and implicit partisan affective attachment for self-described strong partisans. In addition, strong partisans who are high in need for cognition have, on average, less affectively charged partisan attitudes than strong partisans who are high in need for affect. Meanwhile, need for cognition weakens partisan affective attachments for independents, which may reflect the unhindered willingness of individuals high in need for cognition to consider positive and negative attributes of both parties. If we include weak partisans and leaning partisans in the graphical presentation, which can be found in Section 5 of the Appendix, the results also confirm our expectations. The positive relationship between need for affect and implicit partisan affect remains positive but becomes less steep for weak partisans and leaning partisans.

Having demonstrated that need for affect is associated with a key indicator of System 1 forcefulness in the domain of politics – affective partisan attachments – we now evaluate the claim that both need for affect and need for cognition predict people's *general* tendency to engage in reflection. To accomplish this goal, we draw on two approaches to measuring reflection in domains that fall outside of politics. The first is the *cognitive reflection task*, developed by psychologist Shane Frederick (2005) to measure individual differences in people's willingness to override their intuitive answers to simple logic problems (see also Kahan, 2012). The second involves replicating a simple optimization problem used by Kahneman and Tversky (reported in Kahneman, 2011)

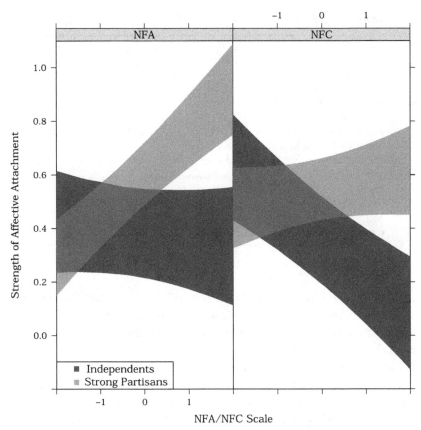

FIGURE 3.10. Associations between Need for Affect, Need for Cognition, and Implicit Partisan Affective Attachment for Strong Partisans and Independents, Emotion Processing Study

to gauge people's ability to overcome their intuitive responses when making decisions over a series of risky choices.

We begin with the cognitive reflection task. It consists of three logic puzzles, which are shown in the left-hand column of Table 3.4. These are not difficult problems that require one to have a high IQ in order to arrive at the correct answer. However, the immediate intuitive responses to these questions, shown in the second column, are wrong. In order to answer the questions correctly (correct answers shown in the third column), one must take a moment to reflect on the intuitive response, recognize that it is wrong, and come to the correct answer. Like many psychological measures, the cognitive reflection task has been administered to many samples of college students. Entry into college requires some degree of

TABLE 3.4. *The Cognitive Reflection Task*

Question	Intuitive Response	Correct Response
1. A bat and a ball cost $1.10 in total. The bat costs $1.00 more than the ball. How much does the ball cost?	10 cents	5 cents
2. If it takes 5 machines 5 minutes to make 5 widgets, how long would it take 100 machines to make 100 widgets?	100 minutes	5 minutes
3. In a lake, there is a patch of lily pads. Every day, the patch doubles in size. If it takes 48 days for the patch to cover the entire lake, how long would it take for the patch to cover half of the lake?	24 days	47 days

intelligence, at least of the "book smarts" variety of intelligence. Of course, colleges vary in their selectivity, and when the task has been administered to students at less prestigious universities, more than half get all of the answers wrong and about a fifth get two to three answers correct. Before condemning the nation's higher education system, consider that when this test is administered to students at highly selective Ivy League universities, less than half of the sample is able to get two to thee items correct and nearly a quarter get all three wrong (see Frederick, 2005, 29). It appears that when it comes to being reflective, book smarts help, but are not enough by themselves.

We placed the cognitive reflection task among a series of questions on the survey instrument given to participants in the Party Cues Study. The participants in this study were drawn from a nationally descriptive sample, and the overall performance on the task was similar to that of students at less prestigious universities. Around 22 percent of the sample performed well, getting two to three responses correct, while a whopping 57 percent got none of the answers correct. Moreover, incorrect answers clustered around the intuitive responses to the questions. Figure 3.11 shows how need for affect and need for cognition correlate with performance on the cognitive reflection task. The models that generated these predictions account for the interaction between need for affect and need for cognition as well as the influence of demographics and political variables. The width of the line communicates the statistical uncertainty about the estimated relationships.

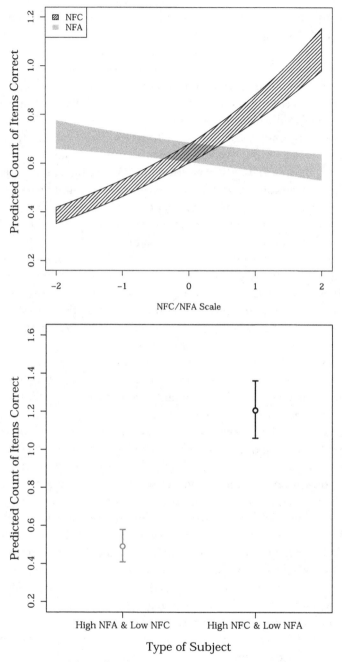

FIGURE 3.11. Need for Affect and Need for Cognition Predict Performance on the Cognitive Reflection Task, Party Cues Study

The top panel of Figure 3.11 shows a strong positive relationship between need for cognition and performance on the cognitive reflection task. As participants' need for cognition increases, their performance improved markedly, moving from essentially getting no answers correct to getting at least one correct, on average. We also see a weak negative relationship between need for affect and cognitive reflection. Individuals with a high need for affect perform marginally worse on the cognitive reflection task than those with low levels of need for affect, but the difference is not substantively meaningful. More importantly, individuals who are high in need for affect perform much worse than individuals who are high in need for cognition, and we can rule out sampling variability as an alternative explanation for this difference. The bottom panel of Figure 3.11 summarizes the interaction between need for affect and need for cognition. Consistent with our expectations developed in the previous chapter, individuals who have low levels of need for affect and high levels of need for cognition perform much better on the cognitive reflection task than individuals who have high levels of need for affect and low levels of need for cognition.[8] These results suggest that one's levels of need for affect and need for cognition are important determinants of one's inclination to reflect on the task at hand.

How people handle risky choices offers another way to assess reflection. The classic theory of economic rationality offers a straightforward answer: do the math. Risks are about uncertainties (e.g., will this stock make me money or lose me money?), and uncertainties can be expressed in probabilities (e.g., there is a 25 percent chance it will make me money). Life is all about making choices under uncertainty. Every day, we encounter situations that can be thought of as gambles. Should I gamble that there will be no major accidents on the route to work and get an extra ten minutes of sleep? Should I pay more money for a new appliance that is less likely to break down or take a gamble on a less expensive, slightly used one? If I go with the new appliance, should I pay for the extended warranty? And so on. The classical rational choice model says that all we need to do is grab some paper and a pencil to figure out the optimal choice when deciding what to do over a series of gambles.

Unfortunately for classical economic theory, decades of work in behavioral economics – which draws on the descriptive theory of the mind discussed in Chapter 2 – throws cold water on the notion that people consistently try to optimize their choices when faced with risk. Instead, people have a tendency to take sure gains when they can and avoid sure losses as much as possible, even when doing so is not the optimal choice.

Kahneman (2011, 334–335) offers a useful framework to assess people's adherence to the classical rational choice model, taken from a study he conducted with his long-time collaborator and co-luminary in behavioral economics, Amos Tversky. Pretend that someone was presented with two gambles and asked to consider both of them before making a decision.

Gamble 1. Choose between:

A. A sure gain of $240

B. A 25 percent chance to gain $1,000 and a 75 percent chance to gain nothing

Gamble 2. Choose between:

C. A sure loss of $750

D. A 75 percent chance to lose $1,000 and a 25 percent chance to lose nothing

What should this person do? From the standpoint of classical economic rationality, the answer is easy. Consider the probabilities of Gamble 1 and 2 jointly and pick the pair of options that yields the highest expected payoff. Yet most people treat each of these gambles as a separate problem and take the sure $240 in the first gamble (option A) and then the loss-averting option in the second gamble (option D). Admittedly, both of these responses are intuitive ones and fit with the intuitionist model of the mind that tells us to take sure gains and avoid losses. However, if one simply does the math, it becomes crystal clear that options A and D fare worse than, say, options B and C. The choice pair B and C offers a 25 percent chance of gaining $250 and a 75 percent chance of losing $750. These are not great odds, but they beat the far more commonly selected choice pair A and D. Folks who go the intuitive route (A and D) are taking the joint gamble of winning $240 with a 25 percent chance and losing $760 with a 75 percent chance.

We placed this problem on the survey for the Party Cues Study to see whether individual differences in reflection, as measured by need for affect and need for cognition, predict which choice pair people select. Consistent with previous studies, most respondents chose the loss-averse pair that represents risk aversion toward taking gains and risk acceptance toward avoiding losses (A and D), while barely 4 percent chose the dominant pair (i.e., producing a higher expected utility) that involves risk-acceptance with gains and risk-aversion with losses (B and C).[9] The results, summarized in Figure 3.12, show that need for affect and need for cognition serve as powerful predictors for whether people optimize or choose the more intuitive, loss-averse alternative. As need for affect

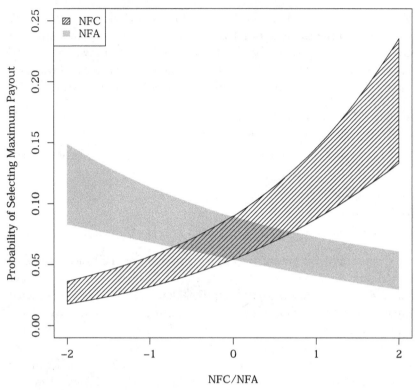

FIGURE 3.12. Associations between Need for Affect, Need for Cognition, and Risk Optimization, Party Cues Study

increases, people are less likely to choose options B and C. At the high end of the need for affect scale, the empirical model predicts a 4 percent chance of choosing the optimal pair, which is in line with the sample average. In contrast, individuals with higher levels of need for cognition are much more likely to choose options B and C, with the empirical model predicting about an 18 percent chance of making this choice, which is 4.5 times higher than the prediction for those with high need for affect. Note that we include the participants' performance on the cognitive reflection task as one of the control variables (along with demographics, political predispositions, and political knowledge), so that we capture the effects of need for affect and need for cognition on individuals' propensity to be reflective beyond a measure of reflection that is commonly used in the literature. We believe that this analysis offers compelling evidence that by including measures of System 1 forcefulness (i.e., need for affect) and motivation to use System 2 processes for engaging in thought (i.e., need for cognition), we are able to do a better job of empirically capturing individuals' propensity to engage in critical reflection than by simply using the cognitive reflection task.

3.4 ARE DEMOCRATS MORE REFLECTIVE THAN REPUBLICANS?

In the remainder of the book, we plan to use these empirical measures of need for affect and need for cognition to explain variation in partisan reasoning. Before we do, we address a question that we often receive about whether democrats and republicans differ in meaningful ways with respect to the predisposition to be reflective. In his *New York Times* bestseller, *The Republican Brain*, science journalist Chris Mooney (2012) points to a number of psychological studies that find that conservatives tend to be less open to new experiences, more likely to seek cognitive closure, and more likely to take dogmatic stands to build an argument. By way of connection, he concludes that republicans are less rational and reflective than democrats. In making his case, Mooney points to issues where republicans reject scientific evidence that is inconsistent with the conservative take on things.

There are good reasons to doubt Mooney's thesis. First, all political ideologies, including conservatism, reflect psychological motivations to some extent. The need for certainty correlates with political conservatism in the United States, but this correlation is not perfect nor is it universally observed across other polities (Malka et al., 2014), and recent research shows that liberals can be just as dogmatic when it comes to their political attitudes as conservatives (Conway et al., 2016). Second, the Republican Party (and Democratic Party, too) is a coalition of ideological groups. Not all conservatives agree on all issues. The conservative coalition in the Republican Party separates along economic and social issues. Economic conservatives tend to prefer less state regulation in both economic and personal domains, while social conservatives welcome state regulation aimed at reinforcing traditional cultural norms and moral behaviors. With respect to psychological motivations, economic conservatives do not appear to fit with the rigidity hypothesis in the United States, while social conservatives do (Feldman and Johnston, 2014). Consequently, it would be inaccurate to paint all republicans as the same kind of conservative. Third, democrats can be just as likely to reject scientific evidence when it suits their political worldview (Kahan, 2012), and both

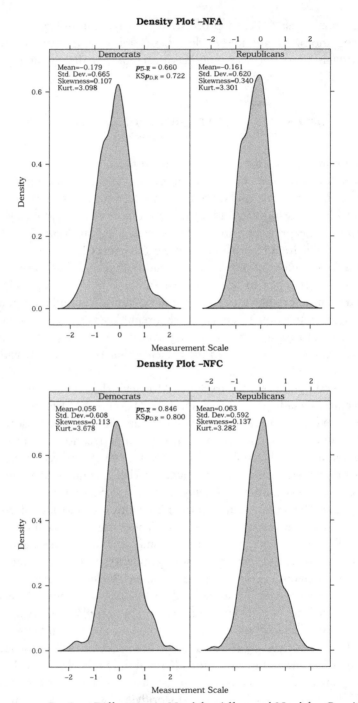

FIGURE 3.13. Partisan Differences in Need for Affect and Need for Cognition, Party Cues Study

democrats and republicans are willing to view straightforward facts (e.g., unemployment) through less of a partisan lens when given incentives to be accurate (Bullock et al., 2015; Prior, Sood, and Khanna, 2015).

We can easily assess Mooney's argument empirically. Figure 3.13 shows the distributions for need for affect and need for cognition by party identification in the Party Cues Study, which again drew on a nationally descriptive sample. As this figure makes clear, democrats and republicans have virtually identical distributions on these measures, and formal statistical tests confirm it (the p-values for the difference of means and Kolmogorov-Smirnov tests are shown in the figures). If anything, democrats evince slightly (but not meaningfully) lower levels of need for cognition relative to republicans, contrary to what we would expect from from Mooney's thesis.

3.5 SUMMARY

In this chapter, we went into greater depth on the theory behind need for affect and need for cognition, providing our rationale for why we believe they are useful indicators of individual differences in reflection. We then offered empirical support for what these measures do and do not capture. They do not duplicate other measures of individual differences more familiar in the study of politics. They do not simply capture differences in how people process emotions. Instead, they reflect differences in psychological motivations that predict how affectively charged people's partisan identities are as well as their willingness to scrutinize their intuitive responses in domains beyond politics. Finally, the willingness to engage in critical reflection is not owned by the adherents of one party in the United States. Democrats and republicans are equally reflective (or not).

With these measures in place, we devote the remainder of the book to empirically demonstrating how individual differences in reflection explain why some people behave like partisan cheerleaders while others are more inclined to behave according to classical models of rationality. We show that need for affect and need for cognition increase our understanding of the micro-foundations that underlie macro-theories of democratic accountability, including attitude formation, political evaluations, and the nature of party polarization.

4

Toeing the Line: Partisan Identities and Policy Attitudes

For the remainder of the book, our goal is to assess the effects of reflection on political reasoning and its implications for democratic accountability. Before embarking on this endeavor, it is important that we reiterate the textbook model of democratic accountability we introduced in Chapter 1. At its base lies a simple notion. The public holds elected officials accountable by reelecting incumbent office holders who perform in ways that conform with the public's preferences and by voting for candidates challenging incumbents when their actions do not conform with the public's preferences. Put simply, democratic accountability is about throwing the rascals out when they do a poor job. If the public is incapable of throwing the rascals out, there is nothing stopping incumbent officeholders from following their own personal preferences and interests at the expense of the public's (Ferejohn, 1986).

To briefly summarize the problem presented in Chapter 1, people's partisan identities may make it difficult for them to identify who the rascals are. The textbook model of democratic accountability is built on a few micro-foundations that concern the behavior of individuals in the polity. First, the model assumes that people possess coherent preferences that are logically connected to an ideological system, or political worldview, that encapsulates guiding principles for what government should do (Lenz, 2012). Second, the model assumes that people are capable of evaluating incumbent politicians on the basis of their preferences and in light of the facts about elected officials' performance in office (Ferejohn, 1986). In this chapter we focus on the first assumption, and we visit the second assumption in Chapter 5.

What does it mean for people to possess coherent preferences? In this context, we do not use the term "preferences" in its colloquial sense as a tendency to want something. Rather, we use it as a technical term that lies at the center of rational choice models. A preference is a clear rank ordering of what people want and do not want, and that rank order must be logically consistent. In order for people to have preferences over flavors of ice cream, to take a silly example, they must be able to rank flavors from most liked to least liked, and that preference ordering must follow the dictates of logic, such as the law of transitivity (Chong, 2013). For example, if someone prefers chocolate to vanilla and vanilla to strawberry, then he or she must also prefer chocolate to strawberry.

In politics, policy preferences reflect a logically consistent rank ordering of policy options. One way to impose order on policy preferences is to tie them to an overarching ideology. While one could find other ways to structure policy preferences, rational choice models typically invoke the left/right dimension of economic policy that has distinguished political philosophies since the Enlightenment (Stokes, 1963). On the far left of the dimension is a preference for government regulation of every aspect of the economy as a way to manage risks and uncertainties created by free markets; on the far right is a preference for the government to take a minimal role in regulating the economy that involves merely enforcing contracts and property rights. Given the ubiquity of the left/right ideological dimension in studies of democratic accountability and responsiveness, we also rely on it as an organizing principle and benchmark.

Partisan identities do not complicate this simple model of policy preferences provided that policy preferences behave as an exogenous force in people's political decisions, including the formation of people's partisan identities. The textbook model of democratic accountability requires that people ally with left-leaning and right-leaning parties, because they are either left- or right-leaning themselves. Yet if partisan identities also influence people's policy preferences, citizens give incumbent politicians an opening to exploit them. If partisan identities are exogenous to policy preferences, it means that people simply adopt the positions taken by their party's elites (or reject positions taken by the opposing party) rather than forming preferences that are consistent with a worldview and then evaluating incumbents in light of those preferences. Allowing incumbent politicians to dictate policy preferences lets them escape being held accountable for taking positions that are contrary to people's political worldview (see Broockman and Butler, 2015). It is this complication that we contemplate in this chapter.

4.1 PARTIES, PREFERENCES, AND ATTITUDES

After twelve years of Republican presidents, former Democratic governor of Arkansas Bill Clinton entered the White House in 1993 with an ambitious domestic agenda and a Congress dominated by his party. During his campaign, he promised a comprehensive reform of the health care system, which is something no president had attempted for a generation. President Clinton asked his wife, Hillary Clinton, to lead a task force charged with developing a proposal. After months of work, the task force produced a complex plan that resulted in a bill of more than 1,300 pages. Formally called the Health Security Act, the proposal devised a universal health care system by creating a standardized insurance package that the government would provide through regulated health insurance companies and that would be funded largely by a tax on employers.

Derisively dubbed "Hillarycare" by conservative groups, business lobbies, and the insurance industry, opponents attacked the plan as an unworkable government takeover of the health care system that would reduce the quality of medical care in the United States. In response, Republicans offered a counterproposal, largely developed by conservative think tanks, that left the health insurance system intact and simply required individuals – as opposed to employers – to purchase health insurance. Republicans defended the "individual mandate" as congruent with the principle of personal responsibility, while Democrats rejected it as a regressive plan that would punish the working poor. Opinion polling at the time showed the same partisan split in the electorate. An October 1993 poll conducted by NBC News and the *Wall Street Journal* found that 55 percent of republicans were not all that concerned about the individual mandate, while 56 percent of democrats were very concerned about it (NBC News, 1993). The Clinton health care plan died in Congress, and the Democratic hope to reform health insurance was shelved for another fifteen years, but the individual mandate remained very much a part of the Republican approach to health care reform in the years that followed. Over a decade later, Republican candidates in the 2008 election championed it, while the Democratic nominee, Barack Obama, opposed it.

As president, Mr. Obama came under pressure from his Democratic allies in Congress to include the individual mandate in his own health care reform plan as a way to secure Republican support. Eager to remove an obstacle to a bipartisan victory on an issue he had staked his campaign on, Obama grudgingly agreed. The gambit did not pan out for Obama, though. Rather than attracting bipartisan support for the Affordable Care Act, now derisively called "Obamacare" by its conservative detractors, congressional Republicans assailed the plan they once championed by decrying it as a "job-killing tax" (see Cooper, 2012). Partisans in the electorate followed suit. An NBC News/*Wall Street Journal* opinion poll conducted in June 2011 found that 61 percent of democrats would be more likely to vote for a candidate who supported the individual mandate, while only 17 percent of republicans would do so (NBC News, 2011).

This example gets at the heart of the debate between optimists and pessimists over preference formation. Optimists presume that people either *have* political preferences or can behave *as if* they do. A pessimistic interpretation of this example is that people do not have preferences about policy in the classical sense defined above. Republicans who presumably saw it as a good proposal in 1993 and 2008 had no reason to drastically change their rank order of possible health care policies in 2010. This story also challenges the notion that people simply use partisan heuristics to behave as if they have meaningful preferences. It is understandable that many individuals look to partisan sources for help in making sense of complex policy options in the same way they look to mechanics for advice about how to fix their cars. The operative assumption here is that partisan heuristics communicate preferences that are consistent with some shared belief system about how the world should work. Yet in this example, nothing happened between 2008 and 2010 that changed the individual mandate from being an element of personal responsibility to a job-killing tax from the standpoint of economic ideology. The only thing that changed was that President Obama was against it and then he was for it. The position flipping at the elite level was entirely strategic.

Before we write this example off as a cute anecdote, there is a wealth of evidence that people's opinions about policy can be swayed by irrelevant shifts in language (see Chong and Druckman, 2007). Kahneman and Tversky were first to show that subtle shifts in the way one frames a policy option can lead to drastic shifts in opinions. In an oft-cited and replicated experiment (Tversky and Kahneman, 1981), they asked people to choose among two policies to confront an "unusual Asian disease" that was expected to kill 600 people. Half of the study participants were told that with Policy A, 200 people would be "saved" and with Policy B, there was a 33 percent chance that all 600 people would be saved and a 67 percent chance that no one would be saved. The other half of the study participants were told essentially the same thing, but the options were framed in terms of the number of people who would be expected to die. So, with Policy A, 400 people would die and with Policy B, one could take the gamble in which no one dies 33 percent of the time or 600 people die the remaining 67 percent of the time. Policies A and B in both of the scenarios are equivalent from the standpoint of the laws of probability. A 33 percent chance of saving 600 people can also be stated as saving 200 people on average (33 percent × 600), and a 67 percent chance of 600 people dying is equivalent to 400 people dying on average (67 percent × 600). Nonetheless, people tended to prefer one policy over the other. If the policies were framed as saving lives, people overwhelming preferred the sure thing (Policy A) over the gamble by a three to one margin. However, if the policies were framed as letting people die, the opposite was the case. By a three to one margin, people chose to take a gamble with Policy B. Even if we chalk up the overwhelming preference for one option over an equivalent one to innumeracy, one cannot attribute such a drastic reversal in opinions to a coherent rank order of preferences. There is no world in which it is logical to prefer saving 200 out of 600 lives over letting 400 out of 600 die.

In everyday politics, we confront the added wrinkle that people do not simply evaluate policy options presented in the detached way Kahneman and Tversky asked their subjects to do. Instead, they encounter arguments for and against particular policy proposals from partisan sources. In general, people tend to be more receptive to persuasive arguments from sources that they trust and resistant to those from sources that they do not trust (Hovland and Weiss, 1951). People tend to trust that their party makes good arguments and that the opposing party makes bad ones (Zaller, 1992). Insofar as parties take policy positions that line up with their supporters' interests and worldview, relying on party cues to pick sides in political debates saves time and cognitive energy (Lupia and McCubbins, 1998). However, in order to incentivize elite responsiveness, it is essential that the public be willing to punish politicians from their party when they betray those interests. Consequently, strict reliance on party cue heuristics does not offer a reliable way for citizens to achieve democratic accountability. At the end of the day, party adherents must keep policymakers from their party honest, and that means people must evaluate the content of persuasive messages, rather than reflexively toeing the partisan line.

What happens when people encounter persuasive messages from their party that are inconsistent with their political worldview? The more than a dozen studies that have pitted party cues against policy positions paint a somewhat complicated picture. Over a third find unambiguous evidence that people tend to put party cues above policy information (Berinsky, 2009; Cohen, 2003; Druckman, 2001; Nicholson, 2012; Rahn, 1993), while over a fifth find the opposite – policy information trumping party cues (Bullock, 2011; Boudreau and MacKenzie, 2014; Nicholson, 2011). The remaining studies show that the relative influence of party cues versus policy information depends on some other contextual variable. People tend to privilege party cues on less familiar issues, while attending to policy information on highly salient issues (Arceneaux, 2008; Bechtel et al., 2015; Ciuk and Yost, 2016) as well as when they know more about politics (Kam, 2005; but see Groenendyk, 2013). Party cues also matter more when politicians take ambiguous stands on issues relative to instances when they do not (Tomz and Van Houweling, 2009). Finally, the presence of party division on a topic (Democrats taking one side and Republicans taking another) diminishes the influence of policy information (Druckman, Peterson, and Slothuus, 2013; Riggle et al., 1992).

We take two lessons from this stew of findings. First, across the vast majority of studies, there is consistent evidence that people are willing to toe the party line even when it goes against their political worldview at least some of the time. This reinforces Kahneman and Tversky's contention that people do not reliably behave as if they have coherent rank-ordered preferences. Instead, people have attitudes. They like some things and dislike other things, but they do not necessarily rank their likes and dislikes in a systematic way. To stick with the Asian disease experiment that started all the fuss, people can like sure things when they think their choice is going to lead to a gain (saving lives) and like taking gambles when they their choice is about avoiding a loss (letting people die). Attitudes, unlike preferences, are not bound by the strict rules of logic. As the old joke goes, people can simultaneously dislike a meal because it tasted terribly and the portions were too small.

Second, the context in which people make decisions influences the pull of party cues. People tend to rely on party cues when the policy options at stake are abstract and they have little knowledge about the alternatives. Sometimes abstruseness is inherent in the issue itself (Carmines and Stimson, 1980). Is mark-to-market accounting a useful way to value derivatives or a threat to the financial system? Unless individuals have steeped themselves in the principles of accounting, a partisan source can serve as a lifeline on where to even begin thinking about this issue. Conversely, should an abortion clinic be allowed to sell aborted fetal tissue for a profit? Should the American military be allowed to torture suspected terrorist suspects? One need not look to a partisan source to construct an initial opinion on these subjects. For other kinds of issues, the degree to which people are able to make intuitive sense of policy options depends on how they are presented (Cobb and Kuklinski, 1997). For instance, if complex policy options are framed in terms of group beneficiaries (e.g., veterans, seniors, taxpayers, etc.), then people can use their attitudes toward those groups to formulate an opinion rather than rely on partisan cues (Boudreau and MacKenzie, 2014; Nicholson, 2011).

An optimist may view these results as vindication for the notion that everyday people are more than knee-jerk partisans. Policy information can push through the partisan screen at least some of the time. A pessimist would likely say that the mere fact that people have *policy attitudes* as opposed to *policy preferences* shatters the foundation on which the optimists have built their conception of democratic accountability. Even if people are capable of looking past partisan cues, they often do not, and they are less likely to do so on the kinds of complex policy questions that make up the day-to-day work of what government does. These are both valid viewpoints, and by taking one over the other, we risk creating a caricature of how democratic accountability works in practice. A realistic account seeks to understand the contingent influence of party cues. When are they most influential and for whom? We turn to these questions next.

4.2 THE ROLE OF REFLECTION IN ATTITUDE FORMATION

The Intuitionist Model of Political Reasoning offers a more constructive way to think about rationality and anticipates a range of outcomes with respect to the influence of partisan cues. The model places attitudes, rather than preferences, at its center. Assuming that people order their attitudes into preferences is a useful abstraction for mathematical models of decision making. Insofar as those models approximate decision contexts in which people either have a clear ordering of policy options or behave as if they do, we see little harm in making this assumption. Yet there are many instances in which people do not possess well-formed preferences, and we risk being led astray by the abstraction that they do (Egan, 2014). By relaxing the assumption that people have well-ordered preferences, our model builds on a realistic account of how people form attitudes and make decisions in light of them.

The general prediction from our model is that reflection helps people place their policy attitudes before partisan cues. Individuals low in need for affect and high in need for cognition will be more likely to reject messages incongruent with their political worldview, even when offered by a trusted partisan source, and they will be more likely to accept messages congruent with their political worldview, even when offered by an opposing partisan source. In contrast, individuals who lack the motivation to be reflective will be more likely to follow the partisan cue. Individuals high in need for affect and low in need for cognition will be more likely to accept a message offered by a trusted partisan source, even when it is incongruent with their political worldview, and they will be more likely to reject a message offered by an opposing partisan source, even when it is congruent with their political worldview.

That said, the literature we reviewed in the previous section leads us to believe that the political context places boundary conditions on when the general prediction of our model should hold. In particular, when people are confronted with salient issues – issues on which people tend to have strong preexisting attitudes and the political parties have taken clear stands – it motivates individuals to be more reflective and rely more on policy aspects of political messages (Ciuk and Yost, 2016). In these instances, partisan cues should be less of a force, especially if the message comes from a co-partisan taking a stand that is at variance with the established party line on an issue. To give an example, most Americans have crystalized attitudes about abortion policy, and when they confront messages about it, they can figure out what their position should be without help from a partisan cue. Accordingly, democrats can easily discount messages from the rare pro-life Democratic politician (Arceneaux, 2008).

Obversely, in those instances where people have little knowledge or experience with an issue, party cues should play a more dominant role. For instance, when President Obama took a position against mark-to-market accounting practices and Republican presidential candidate Mitt Romney took the opposite side, democrats and republicans who were unversed in complex accounting rules had some clue about what their opinion should be on the issue by simply following a trusted source. At the same time, when people do not have much knowledge about a specific issue, reflection is crucial for helping people ensure that the party line is also consistent with their political worldview. To continue with the mark-to-market example, liberals prefer state regulation of economic risks, while conservatives prefer to let the organic forces of the market play out with minimal government oversight. Consequently, with a little reflection, liberals should be able to come to the conclusion that letting big banks set the value of their own assets and liabilities is not consistent with their political worldview, while conservatives should come to the opposite conclusion.

Our model's general prediction taken together with the issue salience boundary condition leads to the observational implication that individuals, when presented with a co-partisan source who has taken a position that is at odds with their ideology (or an opposing party source who has taken a position consistent with their ideology), will be more likely to place party before policy when they are unmotivated to be reflective and confront an issue on which they have few, if any, crystalized attitudes. Although the incongruence between party positions and ideology may be the exception rather than the rule, there are certainly instances where politicians strategically take ideologically inconsistent positions. We began with the example of President Obama embracing a policy born in conservative think tanks, but we can offer a number of other high-profile examples from recent history. Republican President Nixon supported price controls to tackle inflation and a rapprochement with communist China. Ronald Reagan, the conservative touchstone of today's Republican Party, supported changes to the tax code that created net tax increases several times during his presidency. Democratic President Clinton supported liberalizing trade regimes over the objections of organized labor, and embraced conservative-leaning policies on welfare and criminal justice. For his part, Republican President George W. Bush instituted a substantial centralization of education standards and expanded health coverage for seniors. These were consequential policies, illustrating that party is not always a reliable heuristic if one wishes to form ideologically consistent policy attitudes.

4.3 PARTY CUE EXPERIMENTS

We isolate the influence of party cues on policy attitudes with the aid of the experimental method. This approach has a long history in the study of source cues, stretching back to path-blazing research on persuasion initiated by Yale psychologist Carl Hovland (Hovland and Weiss, 1951) and continuing up to today – and for good reason. Experiments give the researcher full control over which messages study participants receive. This practice creates different groups of participants. For example, some participants might receive an argument for a particular policy attributed to a representative from their party, while other participants receive the same argument attributed to a representative from the opposing party. Borrowing from the parlance of medical experiments, the different groups of participants are said to receive different "treatments." In order to ensure that different treatment groups are comparable, the experimental method involves assigning participants to treatment groups at random. Because of this, each study participant has an equal chance of receiving a particular treatment, making it unlikely that one treatment group has more partisans, fewer reflective individuals, and so on. One can see the simple logic underlying random assignment by imagining what would happen if a researcher randomly assigned study participants to different treatment groups but then forgot to actually administer the treatments. Because the individuals in each of the groups are similar to one another, we would expect to see no differences in their responses, on average, to questions that were supposed to be influenced by the treatments. By implication, this means that if the researcher were to re-run the study and this time remember to administer the treatments, observed differences in responses to the questions that follow the treatments can be attributed to the treatments.[1]

In short, randomized experiments allow researchers to make judgments about cause and effect. The alternative approach would be to let people sort themselves into different groups organically, observe their attitudes, and try to make inferences from differences in their attitudes. While this observational approach has benefits, a major downside inherent in the approach is that we can never be sure what causes people in organically constructed groups to differ from one another. Consider the influence of party cues. In an observational study, we might survey individuals and ask them questions about various policy positions, recording whether they know where the parties stand on these issues. We could then ask their opinion on those issues and see if their policy attitudes correspond to their beliefs about where the parties stand on the issues. It would be tempting to attribute a correspondence between party positions and policy attitudes to the influence of party stances. Yet it could be just as easily the case that people project their own policy attitudes onto their party (Page and Jones, 1979). A randomized experiment pushes past this limitation by separating the party cues that people encounter from their partisan identities. The researcher ensures that democrats and republicans are just as likely to encounter the same political messages embedded with the same party cues.

We investigated the influence of party cues in the aptly named Party Cues Study, summarized in Table 3.3. To reiterate the important elements of the study, we collected a nationally representative sample with the help of an Internet survey firm. The 1,258 participants in our sample were demographically similar to the nation at large in terms of income, education, and gender, although the sample had a slightly higher concentration of whites than the general population (86 percent identified as white). The partisan composition of the sample also mirrored the general American population: just over 47 percent identifying as or leaning toward democrat, 39 percent identifying as or leaning toward republican, and just shy of 14 percent identifying as independents with no partisan leanings. Because we are interested in the behavior of party identifiers, we restrict our experiment to the 1,088 participants who identified as or leaned toward the Democratic or Republican parties.

We conducted two experiments that built directly on the more than a dozen partisan cue experiments discussed in the last section. Participants read a political messages in which we manipulated various aspects. We administered a 3 (source cue) × 2 (policy position) design, creating six possible treatment groups. The political message advocated either a policy position that was consistent with the participants' political worldview (i.e., in the liberal direction for Democrats and the conservative direction for Republicans) or a position that was inconsistent (i.e., in the conservative direction for Democrats and the liberal direction for Republicans). In addition, the message was attributed to an inparty cue (the Democratic caucus for democrats and the Republican caucus for republicans), an outparty cue (the Republican caucus for democrats and the Democratic caucus for republicans), or a nonpartisan cue (a nondescript policy institute). This design allows us to estimate the effects of policy information when different party cues are present. In order to evaluate the influence of issue salience, we conducted two experiments using this design. Roughly half of the participants were assigned to read a political message about a high salience issue, while the other half were assigned to read about a low salience issue. As we describe in greater detail below, both issues are central to ideological disagreements between the Democratic and Republican parties but differ with respect to how salient the issue is in the current polarized environment. We consulted the extant literature to select the issues, settling on health care policy for the high salience issue (Bullock, 2011) and the functional level of responsibility (federal or state) for environmental regulation for the low salience issue (Arceneaux, 2008).

4.3.1 Party Cues on a Low Salience Issue: Federalism

The debate surrounding the appropriate reach of the federal government and the scope of state's rights has animated conflict between the two major political parties in the United States since the ratification of the US Constitution in 1789 (Aldrich, 1995). Nonetheless, the issue remains a technical one largely about policy means, as opposed to policy ends. All things being equal, individuals tend to have stronger opinions about policy ends than means (Carmines and Stimson, 1980), and as a result, partisan identities are more powerful than are considerations about functional responsibilities within the federal system (Brown, 2010). For this reason, we believe that the debate about federalism offers a quintessential example of a low salience issue. Only committed ideologues or individuals personally affected by some policy should have strong opinions about whether the federal government or the state government should be responsible for something. One could make strong arguments on both sides – either for keeping government close to the people or emphasizing national interests and duties. We suspect that which argument wins the day will be heavily influenced by *who* makes the argument.

In previous work, we show that people tend to follow their party, rather than their ideology, when it comes to dividing the responsibility for developing and administering environmental protection policy within the federal system (Arceneaux, 2008). Building on this work, we presented 537 participants in the Party Cues Study with the following experiment:

One of the issues on the legislative agenda in the United States is environmental policy. Please read the recommendation recently advanced by [*a public policy institute/members of the Democratic caucus in Congress/members of the Republican caucus in Congress*] and then share your opinion.

[Randomly Assign to Conservative or Liberal Argument]

Conservative Argument. State and local governments should have more responsibility for developing and implementing environmental policy. Every state and city operates within a different environmental context, and so they – and not the federal government – should play the most prominent role in determining the laws that fit their specific needs. Quite simply, state and local governments are closer to the people and can do a better job deciding what is best for the environment.

Liberal Argument. The federal government should have more responsibility developing and implementing environmental policy. The health of the environment affects everyone in the country, not just people in a particular state. So, the federal government should take the lead in ensuring its protection. It's in our national interest to have clean air and clean water.

Everyone read the opening statement requesting that they read a recommendation on environmental policy that was attributed to members of their party's congressional caucus, the opposing party's caucus, or an independent think tank (the emphasis was added in the text to highlight random assignment; the text was not italicized on the survey instrument). Next participants were randomly assigned to read either the conservative or the liberal argument. The conservative argument made the case that state and local government should control environmental policy, while the liberal argument took the position that the federal government should do it. Because the Democratic Party supports federal action to regulate and protect the environment, while the Republican Party generally resists federal action, we coded the argument as *proattitudinal* (i.e., consistent with one's political worldview) if democrats received the liberal argument and republicans received the conservative argument. Conversely, we coded the argument as *counterattitudinal* (i.e., inconsistent with one's political worldview) if democrats received the conservative argument and republicans received the liberal argument.

After reading the environmental policy recommendation, participants were asked, "Which level of government do you think should be more involved when it comes to environmental policy?" They could place their answers on a multipoint scale that went from 1 (the federal government) to 7 (state and local governments). We recoded these answers so that higher numbers represented increasing consistency between the positions articulated by subjects and their party's ideological worldview. So, democrats received higher scores the closer their response was to the federal government and lower scores the closer their response was to state and local governments, while the opposite was the case for republicans. If people place party cues before policy information, then people's responses to this question should reflect movement toward the position espoused by their party in the experiment and away from the position taken by the opposing party in the experiment. In contrast, if people place policy information before party cues, their responses should be ideologically consistent and unaffected by the partisan cue.

We can gauge the relative influence of party cues and policy information by separating the sample according to whether participants were assigned to the inparty treatment or the outparty treatment and then subtracting the mean response among participants in the counterattitudinal treatment from the mean response in the proattitudinal treatment.[2] Taking the difference in treatment group means is a standard way to measure the effect of a treatment. Breaking out the policy information effect by the party cue treatment allows us to say whether people respond to policy information differently when they receive inparty versus outparty cues. Positive numbers indicate that the respondents, on average, were more likely to go in the direction of their expected political worldview. That is, democrats were more likely to say the federal government should have more control and republicans were more likely to say that the state and local governments should have more control. Negative numbers indicate the opposite: people were more likely to move away from their expected ideological response.

Because we are interested in testing whether levels of reflection shape participants' responses to party cues and policy information, we use a statistical model to estimate whether the size and direction of the treatment effect changes across levels of need for affect and need for cognition. We included measures for political knowledge and demographics in the statistical model to ensure that need for affect and need for cognition are not simply proxies for political awareness or something else. Interested readers can find more information about this statistical model in Section 2 the Appendix, and the full model results are reported in Section 6 of the Appendix. We report the findings in Figure 4.1. The gray shaded line shows the effect of the policy information (proattitudinal versus counterattitudinal) for participants who received the inparty cue, and the line with diagonal hatch marks shows the effect of policy information for participants who received the outparty cue. The thickness of the line communicates the degree of statistical uncertainty by showing the range of possible treatment effects. We calculated the range so that overlap of the inparty and outparty intervals communicates information regarding statistical differences in the effect of the party cue treatment. If the lines are clearly distinct (i.e., they do not overlap), it indicates that the treatment effects in the inparty cue condition are statistically different from those in the outparty cue condition. If the lines do overlap, then it indicates that we cannot say with certainty whether the party cue treatment had an effect.

The pattern of results in Figure 4.1 are consistent with the general prediction we drew from the Intuitionist Model of Political Reasoning. With need for cognition set at its mean, as need for affect increases, participants are significantly more inclined to put the party cue before policy information. Individuals high in need for affect are much more likely to accept the proattitudinal recommendation when it is attributed to their party and much less likely to accept it when it is attributed to the opposing party. Moreover, these effects are quite large. At higher levels of need for affect, respondents moved in the direction of the party cue by two (inparty cue) to four (outparty cue) points on a seven-point scale, and we can easily rule out sampling variation as explaining the effects of the party cue. In contrast, with need for affect set at its mean, as need

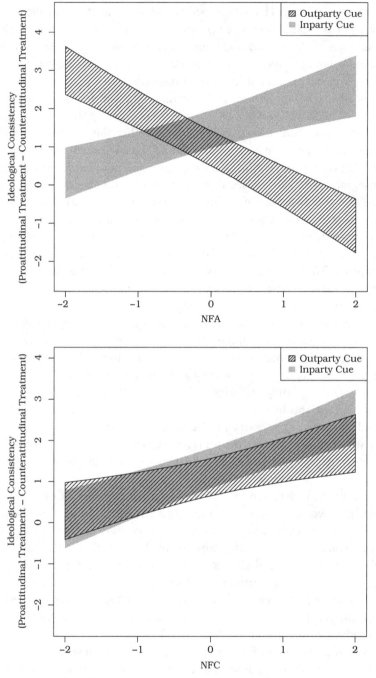

FIGURE 4.1. The Effects of Party Cues versus Policy Information on a Low Salience Issue, Party Cues Study

for cognition increases, people go in the direction of the proattitudinal message irrespective of whether it was attributed to their party or the opposing party.

In the language of the dual-process model, when people rely on affective attachments and are disinclined to be reflective, then party cues dominate people's intuitions and they are more likely to go in the direction of those party cues. Conversely, when individuals are more inclined to engage in critical evaluation, they resist party cues when those cues conflict with their political worldview. When it comes to less salient political issues, party cues *can* help less reflective individuals make decisions that are in line with their ideological predispositions, consistent with the rationale for heuristics laid out by (Lupia, 1994), but only when parties take positions that are aligned with their supporters' ideological predispositions.

4.3.2 Party Cues on a High Salience Issue: Health Care

We now turn our attention to an instance where people's political worldview should dominate partisan cues in their responses to political messages: high salience issues. On these issues, democrats and republicans should already possess strong opinions about the appropriate course of action and thus are more likely to engage System 2 processing in a way that checks their System 1 partisan intuitions. While there are a number of high salience issues from which to choose, we looked to John Bullock's (2011) research on the relative influence of partisan cues and policy information about health care policy. Bullock finds that the participants in his experiments were more likely to place policy information before partisan cues, and we hypothesized that the salience of health care policy in current-day American politics could be part of the explanation. As illustrated by the continuing and highly partisan debate over the Affordable Care Act, passed under President Obama's watch with only Democratic votes in Congress, as well as the shrill partisan debate over President Clinton's failed health care plan in the 1990s, it seems abundantly clear that proposals aimed at expanding health care coverage to those who cannot afford it strikes at the core of what separates liberal and conservative political philosophies in the United States. From the liberal standpoint, the government has a moral duty to make health care affordable and accessible to everyone, and from a conservative standpoint, government-subsidized health care constitutes an intolerable intrusion in people's personal lives as well as the free market.

Modeling our experiment on the ones conducted by Bullock (2011), we used funding for Medicaid, which provides coverage to low-income individuals, as the specific issue. Recall that in the aftermath of passing the Affordable Care Act, the question of whether the federal government should provide additional funds for Medicaid (and whether states should accept those funds) was subject to intense partisan debate. Republicans in Congress bitterly opposed the expansion of the Medicaid program, and many Republican governors refused to accept funding at the time the experiment was administered. Consequently, it is exactly the sort of issue on which people should have clearly formed, crystalized opinions. We presented the following experiment, which follows the form of the low salience issue experiment, to 551 participants in the Party Cues Study:

One of the issues on the legislative agenda in the United States is health care coverage for low-income individuals. Please read the recommendation recently advanced by [*a public policy institute/members of the Democratic caucus in Congress/ members of the Republican caucus in Congress*] and then share your opinion.

[Randomly Assign to Conservative or Liberal Argument]

Conservative Argument. In this year's budget we should reduce Medicaid health coverage for tens of thousands of low-income citizens. The cuts are needed for a balanced budget that increases school funding without seeking higher taxes or cutting other social welfare services. Combining these cuts with new measures that cut waste and reduce fraud will ensure that our country is doing the most it can to promote fiscal responsibility.

Liberal Argument. In this year's budget we should expand Medicaid health coverage for tens of thousands of low-income citizens. The expansion is needed to protect the disabled, elderly and parents who currently lack coverage. Combining these expansions with new measures that cut waste and reduce fraud will ensure that our country is doing the most to protect the poorest among us.

After reading the health care policy recommendation, participants were asked, "Which option below is closest to your opinion when it comes to health coverage for low-income individuals?" They were then prompted to place their response on a multipoint scale that ranged from 1 (expand coverage) to 7 (reduce coverage to balance budget). Following the procedure described in the previous section, we recoded responses so that higher values are consistent with people's expected political worldview. For democrats, higher values indicate support for expanding coverage, whereas for republicans, higher values indicate support for reducing coverage. We also followed the same procedure for coding treatment assignment (inparty cue, outparty cue, nonpartisan cue, proattitudinal argument, counterattitudinal argument) and use the same statistical model to estimate the effects of party cues versus policy information.

The results are shown in Figure 4.2. Party cues have little effect, irrespective of people's level of cognitive reflection. It does not matter whether participants received an inparty or an outparty cue; we observe the same pattern of results in both panels.[3] As need for affect increases, people's attitudes move more in the direction of the proattitudinal message, and we do not observe any effect of the policy information at high levels of need for cognition. This pattern of results is consistent with our expectations. First, political worldview overwhelms party cues as evidenced by the lack of statistical difference between the party cues. Second, System 1 forcefulness, as captured by need for affect, increases the chance of moving further in the direction of the proattitudinal argument and rejecting the counterattitudinal argument. Third, high levels of System 2 engagement, as measured by need for cognition, led subjects to respond with analogous levels of ideological consistency regardless of what treatments they received (across the inparty and outparty cues). These results illustrate the boundaries of our model's general prediction. Some people may be predisposed to be less reflective, but that does not mean they never engage in critical reflection.

4.4 EXPLAINING VARIATION IN PARTISAN STABILITY

If reflection causes people to depend more on their values when forming attitudes about political issues, it stands to reason that it should do the same with respect to their partisan identities. As originally conceived by Campbell et al. (1960), partisan identities were considered highly stable and formed early in life, like other social identities. They were treated as a fundamental building block of political attitudes – an "unmoved mover" that influenced and structured people's other political attitudes (Johnston, 2006, 329). The exogeneity and stickiness of partisan identities are central tenets of social psychological theories of party attachments (Green, Palmquist, and Schickler, 2002). In contrast, rational choice theories of partisan attachments treat people's partisan identities as simply the product of one's evaluations of the political parties. People identify with one party over another to the extent that it is doing better than another at managing the economy or taking policy positions that align with one's ideology. That decision is subject to change as people adjust their evaluations of the parties in light of the actions that the

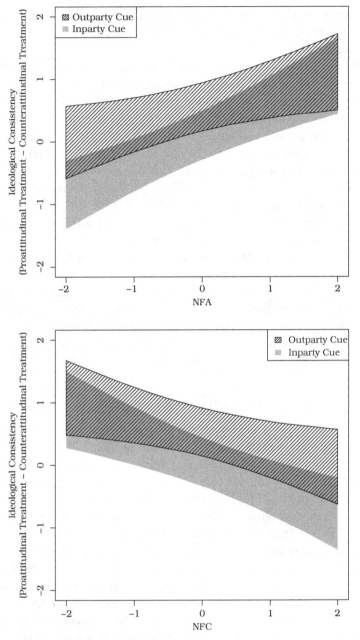

FIGURE 4.2. The Effects of Party Cues versus Policy Information on a High Salience Issue, Party Cues Study

parties actually take. If the economy collapses when one's party controls the government or if one's party leaders take positions on issues with which they disagree, they will adjust their evaluations of the party as well as their attachment to the party accordingly (e.g., Fiorina, 1981; Franklin and Jackson, 1983; Weinschenk, 2010). In the rational choice framework, people's partisan identities are stable to the extent that the parties' relative positions with respect to competence and issue positions are unchanged or the change is so marginal that it fails to move the needle, as opposed to stability arising from people's partisan identities behaving as an unmoved mover (Achen, 1992).

Recent research has demonstrated that there is some truth to both the social psychological and rational choice accounts of partisan attachments. Individuals vary in the degree to which their partisan identities serve as an instrumental or an expressive purpose (Huddy, Mason, and Aarøe, 2015). Some individuals behave as if their partisan identity is more or less a running tally of positive and negative evaluations, while others treat it like an affectively rooted social identity. In addition, not all partisans share uniformly positive sentiments toward their party. Some individuals are actually ambivalent about their party – holding both positive and negative views about it – and these "ambivalent partisans" are more open to changing their partisan identity to reflect their issue positions (Lavine, Johnston, and Steenbergen, 2012). Groenendyk (2013) links stability of partisan identity, or lack thereof, to the tension between the motive to be loyal to one's party and the motive to justify one's reasons for being loyal to that party. If people encounter a stream of negative information about their party, it becomes difficult to justify their loyalty to that party, increasing the probability that they change their partisan identity.

As we noted in Chapter 2, we believe that the Intuitionist Model of Political Reasoning dovetails with this emerging line of research on partisan identity and offers a unifying framework that squares social psychological and rational choice theories of partisan stability. In our model, people's affective attachments (both positive and negative) shape their intuitions about political issues and evaluations. Critical reflection encourages individuals to second-guess their intuitions and, thus, potentially override them to arrive at a conclusion that is at odds with their partisan convictions. If critical reflection leads individuals to override their partisan intuitions on numerous occasions – say they encounter a stream of negative information about their party – it will reduce the ratio of positive to negative sentiments about their party, causing them to become more ambivalent and less able to justify their continued loyalty to that party. Consequently, when the political environment delivers a stream of negative news about one's party, the propensity to be reflective will cause people to view their partisan identity in less expressive terms and increase the probability that they shift away from their party as the rational choice model predicts. In contrast, less reflective individuals will be more likely to resist the pull of negative information (i.e., fail to override their partisan intuitions), continue justifying their partisan loyalty, and maintain their partisan identities as the social psychological model predicts.

The 2012 Campaign Study provides some leverage to investigate the claim that reflection makes people more open to shifting away from their partisan identity. The survey interviewed participants three times across the 2012 campaign: December 2011, the last week of October 2012, and right after Election Day (November 6, 2012). Participants revealed their partisan identity on a seven-point scale that ranged from strong democratic to strong republican in December 2011 as well as after the election, giving us a before-and-after-the-campaign measure of each participant's partisan identity. To simplify the analysis that we report below, we placed participants in one of three categories: (1) partisan identity weakened over the campaign (e.g., a strong democrat becoming a weak democrat), (2) partisan identity stayed the same over the campaign, or (3) partisan identity strengthened over the campaign (e.g., a weak democrat becoming a strong democrat). We measured need for affect and need for cognition on the October survey, providing us with measures of reflection.

These are observational data. Unlike in the experiments reported in the previous section, we did not manipulate the information that study participants encountered over the course of the 2012 campaign. Nonetheless, we can safely assume that the 2012 elections increased the likelihood that individuals encountered negative information about their party's candidates for elected office – be it in the news, campaign advertisements, or political discussions in their social networks. Negativity is a staple of competitive political campaigns, as it is the primary vehicle through which candidates can draw support away from their opponents (Geer, 2006), and the 2012 campaign had its fair share of negativity (Sides and Vavreck, 2013). Consequently, as reflection increases, we would expect to see evidence of people's partisan identities weakening. In contrast, individuals who are less motivated to be reflective should behave in line with the social psychological model, which predicts that people maintain (and perhaps even strengthen) their partisan identities in the face of negative attacks.[4]

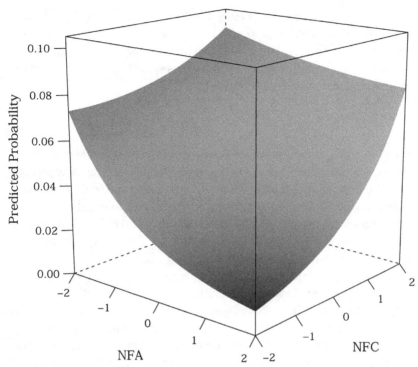

FIGURE 4.3. The Relationship between Weakening Partisan Identity and Need for Affect and Need for Cognition, 2012 Campaign Study

Note: The y-axis reports the probability that participants' partisan identity weakened over the course of the 2012 campaign.

The results of our analysis are summarized in Figure 4.3, where we plot the probability that participants' partisan identity weakened over the course of the 2012 campaign over the joint ranges of need for affect and need for cognition. We exclude pure independents from this analysis, since our model has no prediction for how independents should respond to negative information about the two political parties. As we expected, less reflective individuals (i.e., those high in need for affect and low in need for cognition) were exceedingly unlikely (roughly 1 percent chance) to shift away from their partisan identity during the 2012 campaign. In contrast, more reflective individuals (i.e., those low in need for affect and high in need for cognition) were nearly ten times more likely (about 9.6 percent chance) to register a shift away from their partisan identity between December 2011 and November 2012. We further note the striking similarity between these results and the theoretical predictions shown in Figure 2.4. These results underscore how both rational choice and social psychological models of partisan stability have merit, once we consider individual differences in people's psychological motivations to process political information critically.

4.5 SUMMARY

When it comes to politics, people have attitudes, not preferences. Some people reliably behave as if they have preferences insofar as a political worldview structures and constrains how they form policy attitudes, whereas other people do not. In the absence of crystalized attitudes to guide people's opinions about specific policy proposals, many rely on partisan cues as their guide. This finding is consistent with previous research (e.g., Arceneaux, 2008; Bechtel et al., 2015; Slothuus, 2010). In addition, we find that when people confront political arguments about low salience issues from partisan sources, cognitive reflection helps motivate people to second-guess their partisan reaction and ensure that their opinion is consistent with their political worldview. Data from the 2012 campaign provides circumstantial evidence that reflection makes people more open to shifting away from their partisan identities. In the absence of reflection, people simply toe the party line on low salience issues. As the low salience issue experiment shows, less reflective partisans were fine with diametrically opposed approaches to protecting the environment as long as the proposal came from their party. Parties appear to lose this leverage over voter positions in the domain of high salience issues.

What should we make of these findings? One reaction would be to minimize their importance by focusing on the limits of partisan cue effects. Political parties do not have a free reign on moving people's policy attitudes around. They only appear to be able to do so among particular individuals on low salience issues. While we appreciate the silver lining here, we do not believe that this is reason to celebrate. After all, many consequential issues are low salience, and almost all issues were low in salience before they were not. These results, then, imply that political parties can have a great deal of leeway on important and consequential political questions among a considerable segment of the population.

These results also imply that when political parties take a position on a low salience issue, it causes a number of party adherents to adopt the issue position for no other reason than their party says that they should. Real world evidence bears this out. Gabriel Lenz (2012) shows that when specific issues rise to the top of the agenda in the United States and other industrialized democracies, citizens are more than willing to change their attitudes so that they align with the public stances taken by prominent members of their party. When an interest group in the United States attempted to convince republican women to support a Democratic candidate in a Pennsylvania statehouse election by raising a new issue, access to birth control, the gambit completely backfired. Rather than attracting new voters with a wedge issue, the group succeeded in bolstering the women's support for the Republican candidate and polarized their attitude on birth control along partisan lines (Arceneaux and Kolodny, 2009a,b).

Another reaction would be to point out that most Americans do not have well-formed political ideologies (Converse, 1964; Lewis-Beck et al., 2009). In the absence of an overarching belief system to structure policy attitudes, the argument might go, we should be happy that citizens can at least rely on political parties to do the job for them. We do not fully accept the premise on which this reaction is based, and even if we did, the normative conclusion strikes us as unfounded. With respect to the premise, it is certainly true that most citizens lack a principled political philosophy. Yet people do possess deep-seated values and predispositions that differentiate liberals from conservatives (e.g., Feldman, 1988; Haidt, 2012; Hibbing, Smith, and Alford, 2013; Jost et al., 2003; Schwartz et al., 2012), and these values are not simply a product of attentiveness to politics or possessing a clearly articulated political philosophy (Goren, 2001). With respect to the normative conclusion, as we noted at the beginning of the chapter, toeing the partisan line for the sake of toeing the partisan line undermines a crucial pillar on which theories of democratic accountability rest. Citizens cannot hold politicians accountable for their policy positions if they let them take whatever policy position they want as long as the politician shares the voters' partisan identity. In addition to undermining democratic accountability, it is also a recipe for creating partisan polarization, as citizens follow their party to its respective corner (Ansolabehere, Rodden, and Snyder, 2008; Levendusky, 2010), even if those differences are unconnected to citizens' underlying values.

Nonetheless, we do find it heartening that when political messages do touch on salient issues, people are capable of resisting partisan cues. Although this only applies to the subset of issues on which citizens have crystalized opinions, it implies that parties face some constraints when it comes to changing policy positions on an issue for which they have already taken a clear position. When parties do switch sides on highly salient issues, it forces people to make a choice: stay with the party and ignore the issue conflict, stay with the party and change their attitude, or maintain their preexisting attitude and leave the party. As such, the Intuitionist Model of Political Reasoning does not predict that people always blindly follow their party. Some might, but others will not. As history teaches us, partisan realignments are possible but rare, which is exactly what our model would predict and what is less clear from preexisting models of public opinion, such as Zaller's (1992) RAS model and Lodge and Taber's (2013) JQP model. Both of these models do not explain the conditions under which citizens are able to resist messages delivered by their party, and as such, they do not anticipate the evidence reported here that they can.

5

Throwing the Rascals Out: Partisan Identities and Political Evaluations

Although no longer a household name, Alben William Barkley enjoyed an accomplished political career. He began as an elected county prosecutor in Kentucky at the age of 29. Six years later he was elected to the US House of Representatives. After seven terms, he was elected to the US Senate, where he would go on to serve in the leadership, and in 1948 he was chosen to be President Truman's running mate and subsequently served as the nation's thirty-fifth vice president. Barkley was fond of telling a story in his campaign stump speeches about a farmer who lived in the county where his political career began. The farmer had long been a loyal supporter, so Barkley was surprised to learn that he was thinking of voting for his opponent in an upcoming election and called on him. He reminded the man of all of the things he had done for him as a county prosecutor, representative, and senator. It was a mighty long list, and after reciting it, Barkley implored, "How can you think of voting for my opponent? Surely, you remember all of the things I have done for you." The farmer replied, "Yeah, I remembered. But what the hell have you done for me lately?" (Barkley, 1954, 165).

Barkley's story speaks to the heart of what democratic accountability is all about at the level of the individual voter. Elections give individual voters the opportunity to punish incumbent politicians when they behave like rascals. There are two avenues by which people can accomplish this task. The first involves choosing the candidate offering to enact policies that fall closest to the voter's ideological position on the left/right continuum (Downs, 1957; Kramer, 1977; McKelvey, 1975). We have already discussed a significant obstacle in this pathway. For many voters, their ideological "preferences" are endogenous to their partisan loyalties, which gives politicians from their party leeway to take positions that they prefer even at the expense of their constituents. In addition to the problem of endogenous preferences, Ferejohn (1986) offers another downside to issue-based voting. Even if we assume the best-case scenario – people have coherent ideological preferences and partisan identities are inconsequential – the fact that incumbents must reveal their policy positions in office means that challengers can always offer a set of policy positions that defeat the incumbent. Being able to figure out that their defeat is certain, incumbents should simply follow their own wishes in office and ignore the wishes of their constituents.

Of course, we know that we do not live in a world where everyone has coherent ideological preferences and partisan identities are inconsequential, but Ferejohn's thought experiment offers insight into a second avenue voters can take to achieve democratic accountability. Rather than selecting candidates on the basis of what they say they are going to do in the future, one should simply evaluate incumbent office holders on the basis of how they performed while in office and sanction those who perform poorly by voting for their opponents. To make this determination, voters should look to policy outcomes. Is the economy growing, are the potholes filled, is the country mired in a disastrous war, and so on? As *retrospective voters*, citizens look to recent policy performance much like Alben Barkley's constituent. It is immaterial if the incumbent performed well five years ago. In every election the question is the same: "What the hell have you done for me lately?" Knowing this, incumbent officials have an incentive to choose policies that produce outcomes their constituents desire.[1]

Ferejohn's model moves consideration away from people's attitudes on position issues to how people evaluate their incumbents' performance on valence issues. Position issues fall on the left-right dimension and divide voters into pro and con camps, whereas valence issues are those on which most voters share preferred outcomes (Stokes, 1963). People may disagree on whether the federal government should champion free trade with other countries or erect protectionist barriers to foreign goods, but pretty much everyone wants the economy to be healthy and unemployment low. People may disagree on the merits of the death penalty, but everyone wants to live in safe neighborhoods with low crime. If we doubt that people have coherent preferences over position issues, we can be sure that they know what they want on valence issues.

An optimistic take on Ferejohn's model of democratic accountability is that it lowers the bar voters need to clear to behave in a manner consistent with rationality. We no longer need to assume that people possess coherent and exogenous preferences on position issues because we can safely assume that people's preferences on valence issues are exogenous. After all, it is unlikely that people can be persuaded by a politician from their party that high crime and declining wages are desirable. Moreover, people need only observe the world around them to know how things are going to vote on the basis of valence issues. In good times, vote for the incumbents, and in bad times, throw the rascals out. All well and good, the pessimists retort, save for the fact that people are motivated to view the world around them through their own worldview-affirming screen. Preferences on valence issues may be exogenous, but performance evaluations need not be. Partisan identities distort how people evaluate plain facts, undermining yet again voters' ability to hold politicians responsible. As may be familiar by now, we take a different view that recognizes some degree of validity in both optimistic and pessimistic accounts and seek to understand the conditions under which people are capable of pushing beyond their partisan screens. Consistent with the Intuitionist Model of Political Reasoning, we find that people who are predisposed to be reflective are less likely to filter their performance evaluations through a partisan lens.

5.1 ARE FACTS IN THE EYE OF THE BEHOLDER?

The retrospective model of democratic accountability requires citizens to update their beliefs about the state of the world – economic performance, crime rate, level of pollution, and so on – in light of the facts and then connect those beliefs to their evaluation of incumbents. Not all facts are created equally, of course. Perhaps we should give more weight to a report about unemployment rigorously researched by the Bureau of Labor Statistics than to the fact that a cousin's friend's mother just lost her job. Rational choice models typically assume that people sort out facts using Bayes' Theorem (Bullock, 2009; Chong, 2013). The theorem can be summarized as the following equation:

$$Pr(S|E) = \frac{Pr(E|S)Pr(S)}{Pr(E)} \qquad (5.1)$$

where S refers to the state of the world in some respect (e.g., economic performance) and E corresponds to an event that relates to S (e.g., the unemployment rate reported in the news). S and E are enclosed in $Pr(\cdot)$ to indicate the argument's probability of occurrence, and the vertical line literally means "given that." Thus, $Pr(S|E)$ should be read as "the probability that S is true given that E happened." $Pr(S)$ is the probability that a particular state of the world is happening or will happen (e.g., it will rain tomorrow). This probability communicates both what we think will happen and how certain we are that it will take place. In the absence of further considerations, if we believe that there is a 100 percent chance that it will rain tomorrow, we should choose to go to the beach on a different day, whereas if we think there is no chance it will rain tomorrow, we should pack our beach bag. $Pr(E)$ is the probability associated with observing the event that relates, in some fashion, to the state of the world (e.g., a drop in barometric pressure). $Pr(S)$ is often referred to as the prior probability – or just prior – as it represents what we believe about the state of the world before encountering E. Once we encounter E, we adjust our priors as a function of two things: (1) how likely it is that this event occurred if the particular state of the world exists ($Pr(E|S)$) and (2) the probability that the event itself occurred ($Pr(E)$). In doing so, we generate a posterior probability ($Pr(S|E)$) that reflects our belief about the state of the world in the light of the event-based information received.

As long as an event has some credence, a Bayesian analysis should lead people's posterior probability to move in the direction of that information. If Susan thinks it is going to be sunny in the afternoon and then notes a significant drop in barometric pressure, she should update her belief away from it being sunny and toward it being cloudy. Of course, if she knows that her barometer is too sensitive, she might not move quite as far (e.g., partly cloudy). In politics, Bayesians would assign a probability to how their elected officials are doing in office and then update this probability in light of the relevant facts they observe. If the elected official is responsible for economic policy, a Bayesian would update in a positive direction when unemployment goes down and in a negative direction when unemployment goes up. Just like the sensitive barometer, one need not treat all facts equally. Systematically collected data reported by the Bureau of Labor Statistics are more reliable indicators of unemployment than an unsystematic survey of one's friends, and a Bayesian analysis would take that into account by giving more weight to government statistics than to unscientific polls.

Optimists and pessimists debate the degree to which partisan identities frustrate Bayesian updating with respect to policy performance and, ultimately, evaluations of incumbents. Alan Gerber, Donald Green, and colleagues contend that although partisans consistently rate their party more positively than the opposing party, their evaluations tend to move in a parallel fashion, which suggests that they update their evaluations in light of facts in an unbiased way (Gerber and Green, 1999, 1998; Green, Palmquist, and Schickler, 2002). In contrast, a number of other scholars take a different view. First, they contend that a Bayesian analysis requires partisans to converge in their evaluations when confronting the same facts (Bartels, 2002; Grynaviski, 2006; Redlawsk, 2002). Second, they note that partisans' political evaluations often diverge from one another and polarize, which they interpret as substantial evidence that rather than updating their evaluations in accordance with Bayes' Theorem, partisans are biased reasoners who ignore facts they do not like and unquestioningly accept those that they do (e.g., Bartels, 2002; Duch, Palmer, and Anderson, 2000; Bisgaard, 2015). Somewhere between these positions stands the argument that the Bayesian framework permits variation across individuals in terms of what constitutes evidence and how they assimilate it (Bullock, 2007, 2009; Hill, forthcoming).

Brian Gaines and colleagues offer a useful way to understand why the same facts might cause people to make radically different evaluations (Gaines et al., 2007). They offer the following updating model:

$$\text{Facts} \rightarrow \text{Beliefs} \rightarrow \text{Interpretations} \rightarrow \text{Evaluation}$$

The Bayesian model really focuses on the first arrow. Facts influence people's beliefs about reality. Whether beliefs influence evaluations depends on how people interpret their beliefs. Interpretations can be thought of as giving one's factual beliefs meaning. They provide reasons for why particular things happened (or failed to happen). It is at the interpretation phase that partisan bias can creep into people's reasoning. To illustrate how interpretations link beliefs to political evaluations, Gaines and colleagues (2007) interviewed the same group of students multiple times between October 2003 and December 2004. Republican President George W. Bush ordered the US military to invade Iraq in March 2003 on the pretext that its leader, Saddam Hussein, possessed weapons of mass destruction and posed a grave threat to American interests. The war deeply divided democrats, who largely opposed the war, and republicans, who largely supported it. Over this time period, casualty rates of American soldiers mounted precipitously, and by the end of the study, well over 1,000 soldiers had been killed in combat. Gaines and his collaborators found that among respondents in their sample, partisans accurately updated their beliefs about the number of American casualties. Democrats did not overestimate the number of soldiers killed, and republicans did not underestimate them. Nonetheless, democrats' and republicans' evaluations of President Bush remained stable and polarized over the period. Republicans, despite knowing the casualty rate, did not become less supportive of Bush.

Gaines and colleagues concluded that partisans' sticky evaluations of President Bush could be attributed to the way democrats and republicans interpreted facts about the Iraq war. Democrats overwhelmingly said that the number of soldiers killed was "very large," while republicans minimized the magnitude of American casualties. Scholars have found similar patterns in how people connect their beliefs about the economy to their evaluations of incumbents. For the most part, partisans accurately update their beliefs about the state of the economy but interpret those facts differently depending on whether their party is in power or not (Anson, forthcoming; Bisgaard, 2015; Brown, 2010; Rudolph, 2003; Tilley and Hobolt, 2011). If their party is in power, something or someone else is to blame for poor economic performance, while their party clearly deserves the credit for a good economy. If the other party is in power, it gets the blame for a bad economy but none of the credit for a good one.

So, even if facts are not necessarily in the eye of the beholder, interpretations can be. The degree to which people can use interpretations as a way to preserve their preexisting attitudes and beliefs depends on the context. Robert Abelson (1986) makes a valuable distinction between *testable* and *distal* beliefs that we think applies to interpretations. When people observe and experience feedback about their interpretations, those interpretations are put to a test. Given sufficient negative feedback, they can be refuted. Having dismissed our barometer as overly sensitive as we observed its barometric reading drop, we would be forced to revise that interpretation as rain falls on our heads at a deserted beach. Yet in politics, people's beliefs and, therefore, interpretations are often about things that are distal and remote to personal experience. While one can experience being unemployed, one does not experience the macroeconomic phenomenon known as the unemployment rate. Connecting one's individual experience to beliefs about the national economy allows for an array of interpretations. For instance, if an unemployed individual wants to maintain a positive view of his or her party's economic policies, he or she need only find another outlet to blame for his or her predicament. Perhaps it is the lingering effects of the opposing party's policies or the product of global economic forces outside of his or her party's control.

In Abelson's reckoning, distal beliefs are like possessions. People hold them to serve particular functions in the same way that clothes, food, and furniture do. Models of democratic accountability presume that distal beliefs about policy performance serve an instrumental function. They help citizens sort out whether they should support the incumbent. From this perspective, distal beliefs are treated as "… products of mental skill," and "[i]deally, we are supposed to scrutinize them, to shape them, to be skeptical of them, to debate them" (Abelson, 1986, 229). Yet, like possessions, distal beliefs can serve other purposes, such as rationalizing and defending partisan identities.

5.2 THE ROLE OF REFLECTION IN POLITICAL EVALUATIONS

The hallmark of reflection is being skeptical of one's own preconceived notions and a willingness to surrender cherished beliefs to the facts. It would be tempting to say that being reflective is analogous to being Bayesian. Although we believe that the Bayesian model is useful for conceptualizing how people update their political beliefs – as we explain in greater detail below – we resist making that analogy for a simple reason. Bayes' Theorem does not require people to be skeptical of their priors. People can hold beliefs with a high degree of certainty and weight the facts according to their own values. Bayesian updating is not the same thing as being "reasonable" (Bullock, 2009, 1123). One could follow Bayes' Theorem to the letter and hold on to cherished beliefs in the face of contradictory evidence long after a point that could be deemed reasonable by most people. The Bayesian model of updating does not prevent strong partisans from sticking by their party even when they confront negative information about its performance. Consequently, we do not accept the presumption – on which many optimists and pessimists seem to agree – that Bayesian updating always facilitates democratic accountability.

Instead of focusing on the algorithmic manner in which people update their beliefs, we focus on the normative yardstick offered by Bartels (2002, 125–126). When it comes to evaluating policy performance and, ultimately, politicians, voters should exhibit "rationality in the sense of plain reasonableness." People should not engage in mental gymnastics to defend the indefensible, for instance, just because the bad actor was a member of their party. By the same token, one should be willing to give credit where credit is due, even if it goes to a politician from the opposing party. When the facts warrant it, people should be willing to withdraw support from their party and give it to the other.

From the standpoint of "plain reasonableness," the Intuitionist Model of Political Reasoning offers a more fruitful approach than a Bayesian one. Bayes' Theorem is simply an algorithm for processing information. The inputs – people's priors and subjective assessments of facts – are exogenous to the Bayesian model. Our model offers an explanation for how people form those inputs. Priors can be thought of as people's intuitions. Strong priors (i.e., those held with a high degree of certainty) are akin to strong intuitions. The degree to which people down-weight evidence that is inconsistent with their priors (i.e., $Pr(E|S)$) is a function of reflection. The more reflective people are, the more likely they are to consider evidence that is contrary to their priors.

Extending this logic to the question at hand, strong partisans tend to have strong priors and a desire to evaluate evidence about policy performance in a way that sheds the best possible light on their party and the worst on the opposing party. If that means accepting interpretations that explain away bad news, then so be it. In this context, being reflective corresponds with being reasonable, with striving to fashion objective interpretations of the available data. If that leads one to have a lower opinion of a party leader, then so be it. In short, reasonable partisans do not give the benefit of the doubt to their politician, while holding the other politician to a higher standard.

Individual differences in reflection should predict which partisans update in the direction of facts, even those that cast their party's leaders or policies in a negative light, and which partisans only update in the direction of facts that are congenial to their party. In our initial work on this project, we found evidence consistent with the expectation that reflective partisans are reasonable partisans (Arceneaux and Vander Wielen, 2013). We presented subjects in an experiment with actions taken by either the Democratic or Republican Party in a recent session of Congress. We chose instances in which the parties took unpopular positions for strategic political reasons, such as the Democrats blocking food safety legislation out of concern for its impact on the container industry and the Republicans supporting Wall Street banks even in the aftermath of the 2008 financial collapse. Some study participants read about unpopular positions taken by their party, while others read about unpopular positions taken by the opposing party. Participants who were less reflective (i.e., high need for affect and low need for cognition) held the opposing party to a higher standard than their own, while participants who were more reflective (i.e., low need for affect and high need for cognition) held both parties to the same standard.

Although these findings are consistent with the notion that reflection causes partisans to update their political evaluations in a reasonable fashion, they only offer suggestive evidence on this score. First, the congressional actions that we chose, while generally unpopular, were nonetheless linked closely to position issues. As we showed in the last chapter, it could simply be that less reflective individuals were more willing to give their party leeway on the positions they took in congressional battles. Second, we only offered participants negative information about their party or the other party. It would be helpful to observe how individual differences in reflection influence reactions to both positive and negative information. Finally, this study did not measure updating, or how participants' evaluations *changed* in response to new information. We address these limitations in the next section with a canonical experimental design to study updating.

5.3 THE BELIEF PERSEVERANCE EXPERIMENT

In the early 1970s, a team of psychologists conducted a novel, if somewhat macabre, experiment. Ross, Lepper, and Hubbard (1975) recruited students to participate in a study on sorting out real suicide notes from fake ones. The students were divided into two groups – one group read and categorized suicide notes as real or fake, while the other group observed the categorizers. After categorizing each suicide note as real or fake, experimenters fed the participants false information. Categorizers and their observers were essentially told at random whether they succeeded or not at the grim task. At the end of the study, the experimenters set the record straight for a subset of subjects, telling them that the feedback was fake. Nonetheless, the fake feedback continued to influence both categorizers' and observers' performance evaluations. These results suggest that people do not fully update their beliefs and that even false beliefs can persevere in the face of straightforward corrections.

Recent work extends the belief perseverance experiment to politics. Bullock (2007) told subjects that a Republican candidate running for the US Senate took a number of unpopular positions and then later supplied them with correct information. Despite receiving the correction, participants – particularly Democrats – continued to hold negative views toward the candidate. Cobb, Nyhan, and Reifler (2013) extended Bullock's work by falsely attributing a positive act to a politician – sponsoring a popular bill – and then correcting the information. In this instance, they found that people's positive beliefs do not persevere in the way that negative beliefs did in Bullock's study. Instead, people tended to come to a less favorable view of the politician, which Cobb et al. interpret as the product of people overcorrecting a perceived bias.

We build on the Bullock (2007) and Cobb, Nyhan, and Reifler (2013) studies by presenting subjects with inaccurate positive or negative information about the actual governor of their state with respect to his or her involvement in an unpopular action. We restricted the study to individuals who *shared* the same partisan identity as their governor (i.e., republicans in states with Republican governors and democrats in states with Democratic governors). Briefly described in Table 3.3 and in greater detail in Section 1 of the Appendix, participants in the Governor Evaluation Study were recruited from an online sample in the spring of 2013. Based upon the geolocation of the computer accessing the survey (using IP addresses), we presented respondents with hypothetical information regarding their governor, which they were led to believe came from media reports.[2] Respondents were randomly assigned to read and react to a fictional report, shown in Table 5.1, that either depicted their governor as a loyal or disloyal (i.e., shirking) agent. The fictional report indicated that the governor either advocated or opposed severe reductions to funding for public safety. We borrow this scenario from a seminal experimental design employed by McGraw (1990), which establishes public safety as a valence issue on which there is a broad bipartisan consensus regarding what constitutes (dis)loyal behavior. To ensure that spending cuts would be viewed as uniformly objectionable across democrats and republicans, we noted that the cuts to public safety would *not* reduce gross spending (i.e., the cuts would be offset by other expenditures).

After reading the assigned (loyal or shirking) item, respondents were asked to evaluate the statement, "If there were an election today, I would vote for Governor *Name*," along a discrete scale ranging from 0 (strongly disagree) to 100 (strongly agree). Following the belief perseverance protocol, we then asked participants to answer a number of questions unrelated to their governor to create some distance between the false information and the disclosure. At the close of the study, we told respondents, "The item you read above about Governor *Name* was created for the purpose of this study. The events described were fictional and did not happen." They were then asked to reassess the governor, using the identical statement of evaluation and scale. Since all subjects shared their governor's partisan affiliation, the correction offers *positive* information in the aftermath of the shirking item (hereafter the "positive

TABLE 5.1. *Text of Stimuli in Belief Perseverance Experiment*

Shirking Treatment

Governor *Name* (*State – Party*) cut millions of dollars in state funding for public safety. As a result, the number of fire safety, police, and other criminal justice personnel will be severely reduced, and the purchase of new safety equipment will decline significantly. The governor supported these cuts so that spending could be raised in other areas.

Loyal Treatment

Governor *Name* (*State – Party*) refused to sign into law a bill that would cut millions of dollars in state funding for public safety. The governor's opposition to the bill will protect against severe reductions in the number of fire safety, police, and other criminal justice personnel, and will ensure that local governments can purchase new safety equipment. Instead, the governor advocates cutting spending in other areas.

disclosure" treatment) and *negative* information in the aftermath of the loyal item (hereafter the "negative disclosure" treatment).

We are ultimately interested in how people's evaluations of their governor changed between their initial evaluation and their evaluation following the disclosure, which can be easily measured by taking the difference between the two (second evaluation *minus* first evaluation). We analyze how need for affect and need for cognition influenced the effect of information (positive or negative) on participants' change in evaluation (see Section 2 of the Appendix for a discussion of the statistical model and Section 6 for the full results). Figure 5.1 reports the results among individuals that fall at either end of the reflection spectrum (high need for affect/low need for cognition and low need for affect/high need for cognition). The dots represent the average change in evaluation, and the horizontal lines represent 90 percent credible intervals.[3]

The results are consistent with our expectation that reflection reduces motivated reasoning. Irrespective of the type of disclosure, less reflective individuals (i.e., those high in need for affect and low in need for cognition) developed a more positive view of their party's governor. In response to the negative disclosure, less reflective participants responded defensively by bolstering their initial opinion. In contrast, more reflective individuals (i.e., those low in need for affect and high in need for cognition) always update in the direction of the correction. Unlike their less reflective counterparts, they display a willingness to adjust downward

Throwing the Rascals Out

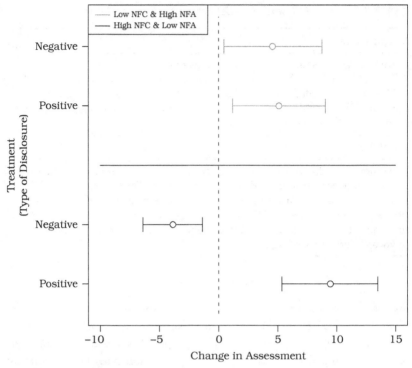

FIGURE 5.1. Predicted Change in Evaluation of Governor by Low-NFC/High-NFA and High-NFC/Low-NFA Participants, Governor Evaluation Study

their evaluation of their party's governor after being told that he or she had actually not done something positive. Therefore, these findings suggest that the results reported by Cobb, Nyhan, and Reifler (2013), who found that people tend to lower their evaluations of politicians when told that positive information was false, are sensitive to the manner in which recipients of these messages process information. We find support for their results among more reflective individuals but not among those who are less reflective. More importantly, our results suggest that reflection is an important attribute in order for partisan identifiers to punish elected officials from their party when they make bad decisions.

5.4 THE ECONOMY AND PRESIDENTIAL EVALUATIONS

The results from the belief perseverance experiment illustrate that reflection leads people to behave in ways that would fit the everyday meaning of "reasonable." If an incumbent member of our party really did not take that heroic stand that we had given him or her credit for, then we should adjust our evaluation of the incumbent downward. To respond to such information by essential saying, "Oh, yeah? Well, that just makes me like the person even more," strikes us as the very definition of being unreasonable. If people were to behave this way in the real world, it would be at variance with a central premise of the textbook model of democratic accountability, which raises an important question: Are the experimental findings actually indicative of something that would happen in the real world? What if reflective individuals are just better at figuring out the point of our experiment and they really are not so reasonable when it matters? What if less reflective individuals are only defensive when some researcher puts them on the spot but are more reasonable when it matters?

To address these concerns, we look to how people actually behave in the real world in the remainder of this chapter. In this section, we return to a question that lies at the heart of the retrospective voting literature: Do shifts in macroeconomic performance influence how voters evaluate incumbent politicians, particularly the president (or prime minister in parliamentary systems)? Individual voters, it seems, are not reliably influenced by the macroeconomy (e.g., Fiorina, 1978), and partisanship is part of the explanation (Wlezien, Franklin, and Twiggs, 1997). Figure 5.2 offers a stylistic illustration of the problem. These data come from the American National Election 2000-2002-2004 panel study in which survey respondents were re-interviewed in those years. The survey asks respondents whether they believe the national economy has gotten better, stayed the same, or gotten worse over the previous year. We categorized shifts in economic perceptions from the 2000 to 2004 presidential elections into five categories. Some individuals thought the economy had been good in 2000 and worse in 2004 (got worse), some thought that the economy wasn't so great in 2000 but had improved in 2004 (got better), some thought the economy was bad in both years (stayed bad), some thought the economy was good in both years (stayed good), or some thought that it had simply stayed the same. We aggregated the responses by partisanship and, as Figure 5.2 makes abundantly clear, found that democrats were nearly three times more likely than independents and four times more likely than republicans to say that the economy had soured over those four years. Meanwhile, republicans were four times more likely than independents and nearly seven times more likely than democrats to say that the economy had improved since 2000. Unemployment had actually increased between 2000 and 2004 but remained at a low rate (around 5.5 percent) in 2004. The economy had also continued to grow.

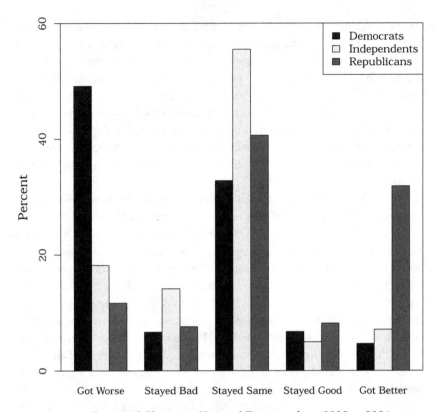

FIGURE 5.2. Shifts in Economic Perceptions from 2000 to 2004, American National Election Panel Study

So, why would democrats and republicans have such divergent views on the economy? Although it is possible that democrats and republicans simply experience the economy differently, we observe the same patterns even after accounting for income, education, political knowledge, and other key demographic variables (see Section 6 of the Appendix for the full results). A more likely explanation is that a Democrat sat in the White House in 2000, whereas a Republican occupied the Oval Office in 2004.

In an influential essay on the effect of the economy on political evaluations, Kramer (1983) argues that it is possible to attenuate the bias in economic perceptions created by partisan rationalizations that exist at the individual level by examining the aggregate relationship between the macroeconomy and political evaluations *over time*. The argument is that aggregate evaluations of the economy shift up and down depending on changes in economic performance, despite the healthy degree of noise in economic perceptions at the individual level. It turns out that there is a robust correlation between shifts in the macroeconomy and shifts in presidential approval in the aggregate. As the economy improves, the president tends to become more popular, and as the economy sours, the president tends to become more unpopular (e.g., Beck, 1991; Brace and Hinckley, 1991; Hibbs, Rivers, and Vasilatos, 1982; MacKuen, Erikson, and Stimson, 1992; Monroe, 1978; Mueller, 1970; Norpoth, 1984). As we noted at the outset of the chapter, optimists often point to these aggregate regularities as evidence that democratic accountability is healthy in the United States and other advanced democracies.

Recent work challenges this argument by empirically demonstrating that partisan bias also contaminates aggregated economic perceptions (Bisgaard, 2015; Duch, Palmer, and Anderson, 2000). As Figure 5.2 illustrates, many individuals' partisan identities systematically shape how they evaluate economic performance. These systematic biases do not always cancel out. Depending on the distribution of partisan biases, the aggregate relationship between economic performance and incumbent evaluations could be overestimated or underestimated, making it difficult to know what inferences to draw from aggregate analyses about the health of democratic accountability. Fortunately, our theoretical framework gives us a way to separate citizens who update their political evaluations in light of facts, like the macroeconomy, from those who do not.

The Intuitionist Model of Political Reasoning predicts that less reflective individuals should account for much of the partisan bias in the aggregate relationship between the economy and evaluations of incumbent politicians, such as the president, while more reflective individuals drive the signal through the noise. Partisans who are high in need for affect and low in need for cognition should be most likely to interpret economic performance in self-serving ways – rejecting good economic performance as evidence of good governance when the opposing party is in power, while making the exact opposite conclusion when their party is in power.

Although there are numerous national-level surveys that measure how the public evaluates the president of the United States, these surveys do not include measures of people's predisposition to be reflective. Fortuitously, the full batteries for need for affect and need for cognition were included on The American Panel Survey (TAPS) conducted by the

Weidenbaum Center at Washington University in St. Louis. In ongoing research with Daniel Butler, we analyze how need for affect and need for cognition shape the relationship between economic performance and presidential evaluations. We summarize the most pertinent aspects of that research here. TAPS has been collecting measures of presidential approval just about every month since December 2011, and we possess data up through July 2015. We aggregated monthly presidential approval by four subgroups: less reflective democrats, less reflective republicans, more reflective democrats, and more reflective republicans. We categorized respondents as less reflective if they scored high on the need for affect scale (above the seventy-fifth percentile) and low on the need for cognition scale (below the twenty-fifth percentile), and we categorized respondents as more reflective if they scored low on the need for affect scale (below the twenty-fifth percentile) and high on the need for cognition scale (above the seventy-fifth percentile).[4] Next we examined the relationship between macroeconomic performance, as measured by change in unemployment, and approval of President Obama.

The results are shown in Figure 5.3. The x-axis represents the lagged change in unemployment across the two previous months, and the y-axis represents the change in presidential approval from the previous month. We focus on unemployment as an indicator of macroeconomic performance for three reasons. First, previous research finds a robust relationship between changes in unemployment and presidential approval. Second, the financial meltdown of 2008 caused eight million Americans to lose their jobs and doubled the unemployment rate from 5 percent to 10 percent by mid-2009, making job creation a central focal point (rhetorically, at least) of both Democratic and Republican economic plans. Third, inflation rates – which have also been linked to presidential approval – remained historically low between 2008 and 2015. In short, the depth and breadth of unemployment created by the Great Recession elevates its salience as an indicator of policy performance.

The unemployment rate in December 2011, when TAPS began collecting data, was 8.5 percent. It shrank to 5.3 percent by July 2015, which is the most recent data to which we have access. Nonetheless, the secular decline in unemployment occurred in fits and starts from month to month. Some months saw unemployment decline by as much as 0.5 percentage points, some saw no change, and a few months (up until the end of data collection) saw a small increase in the unemployment rate by 0.1 percentage points (the mean change in monthly unemployment during the period of analysis was −0.09 percentage points). How

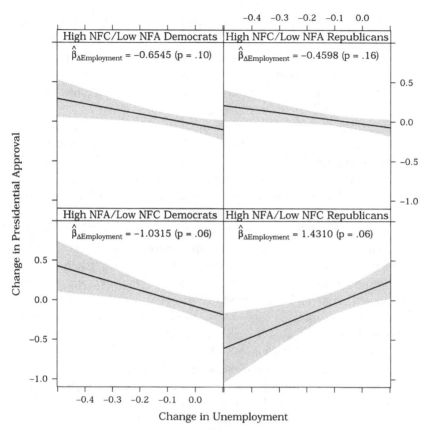

FIGURE 5.3. The Effect of Shifts in Monthly Unemployment on Change in Approval of President Obama, The American Panel Survey 2011–2015

Note: This analysis is part of a larger, ongoing project in collaboration with Daniel Butler.

do monthly shifts in unemployment influence evaluations of President Obama? It depends on both partisanship *and* one's predisposition to be reflective. More reflective democrats and republicans responded to shifts in unemployment in practically identical ways. These results, displayed in the top two panels of Figure 5.3, show that as unemployment decreases (moving from right to left along the x-axis), more reflective democrats and republicans adjust their assessment of President Obama upward by roughly the same magnitude. Reflective democrats appear to be a bit more receptive to good news than reflective republicans, but the difference is small and statistically insignificant. Meanwhile, less reflective democrats and republicans behave in strikingly different ways. As the bottom panels of Figure 5.3 illustrate, less reflective democrats respond strongly to good news, updating their assessment of Obama more positively than more reflective democrats and republicans. In contrast, less reflective republicans actually developed a more *negative* view of Obama as unemployment improved.

These findings line up nicely with the results we observed in the belief perseverance experiment. Reflective partisans update in the direction of the information provided, even if that means resisting the pull of one's partisan leanings. Reflective republicans could have dismissed the good news about declining unemployment and continued to hold President Obama in low regard, but they did not. Less reflective partisans, on the other hand, update in ways that bolster their preexisting attitudes, even when faced with contradictory information. The better the news about the economy, the more polarized less reflective partisans became on the question of Obama's performance. In particular, less reflective republicans seem to have behaved defensively, whereas less reflective democrats were especially eager to reward the president for improvements in the economy.[5] As we discussed above, this behavior need not be at odds with algorithmic definitions of rationality (e.g., Bayes' Theorem), but it certainly violates commonsense notions of reasonableness. It also weakens the basis on which democratic accountability is built, which is an issue we address more directly in the next section.

5.5 WHO VOTES THE PARTY LINE?

Thus far we have demonstrated that the predisposition to be more or less reflective influences how people update their evaluations of incumbents in light of facts about their performance. Although politicians may respond to aggregate shifts in how the public evaluates them, and there is evidence that the president of the United States does (Canes-Wrone, 2005), most incumbents do not have access to a steady stream of public opinion polls about how much the public approves of them. As a result, the ballot box remains the most effective way for the public to make itself heard for most elected offices. Studies of performance evaluations presume that they ultimately translate into votes (Beck, 1991), yet there is no guarantee that this is the case.

In this section, we investigate whether individual differences in reflection influence voting behavior. The most straightforward approach would be to see if need for affect and need for cognition condition the correlation between performance evaluations and voting decisions. Unfortunately, this approach makes the untenable assumption that people's voting decisions do not influence how they answer questions about performance. As we have demonstrated in the previous two sections, some partisans (especially less reflective ones) are more likely to give politicians of their party high marks even when they do not deserve it. Consequently, the correlation between performance evaluations and voting decisions would actually be higher among less reflective individuals, offering another example of the dictum that correlation is not necessarily causation.

We take a more indirect approach to establishing the influence of need for affect and need for cognition on voting behavior. The structure of American government gives voters multiple opportunities to hold politicians accountable. At the federal level, citizens get a chance to vote for president every four years, their senators every six years, and their House representative every two years. The offices are responsible for overlapping and non-overlapping issue areas. Both the president and Congress must work together to pass the federal budget, for instance. Nonetheless, the president is generally seen as a national representative, while senators and representatives are also expected to tend to state and local matters as they relate to the federal government (e.g., capital construction, helping constituents navigate the federal bureaucracy, etc.). Accordingly, voters' evaluations of the president, their senators, and their representative are likely to be related but distinct. For instance, one can give President Obama, a Democrat, high marks for his stewardship of the economy while also giving one's Republican representative in Congress high marks for steering resources to one's community. More reflective partisans should be more likely to engage in nuanced evaluations of these kinds, and, therefore, they should be less likely to cast party-line votes across the three offices.

The 2012 Campaign Study (which was part of the Cooperative Campaign Analysis Project) asked respondents on the post-election survey whom they voted for in all federal elections (president, Senate, and House). Among the 1,000 respondents who participated in the survey, 474 lived in states where they had an opportunity to vote in all three (and provided the requisite information on additional covariates for inclusion in the analysis). Figure 5.4 shows the joint influence of need for affect and need for cognition on straight-ticket voting in the 2012 election. The y-axis reports the probability that a respondent voted for his or her party in the 2012 presidential race and congressional races. In line with our expectations, at high levels of need for affect and low levels of need for

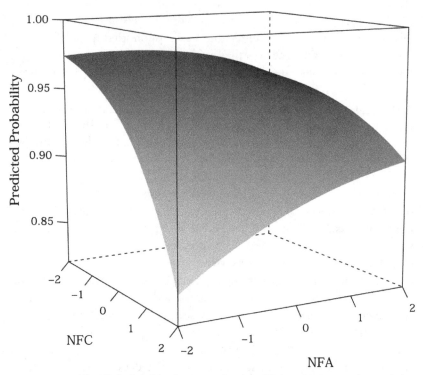

FIGURE 5.4. The Relationship between Straight-Ticket Voting and Need for Affect and Need for Cognition, 2012 Campaign Study

cognition, individuals exhibit a high degree of party-line voting in federal elections. There is a 95 percent chance that these less reflective individuals voted for the same party in all three elections. In contrast, more reflective individuals (those with low levels of need for affect and high levels of need for cognition) were about 84 percent likely to vote for the same party in all three. Although this remains a high degree of party-line voting, it nonetheless represents a noteworthy drop in straight-ticket voting relative to less reflective individuals.

Of course, as we have already noted, this represents an indirect test. We do not possess objective information about how various senators and representatives performed while in office, and given the overlap in responsibilities at the federal level, casting a straight-ticket vote is not, definitionally, evidence that an individual's behavior was unreflectively partisan. Consequently, we cannot take a normative position about what level of straight-ticket voting should be considered "too much." However, this evidence suggests that some degree of reflection is at least partially responsible for the small but substantively meaningful percentage of voters who choose to defect from their party in at least one federal election. Note that this offers a relatively weak test. Had we been able to include offices at the state and local levels, where functional responsibilities are more distinct from the federal government, we would have had more opportunities to observe reflective behavior.

5.6 SUMMARY

In this chapter we concerned ourselves with assessing how reflection influences the ways in which voters evaluate politicians. Under a minimalist model of democratic accountability, voters are expected to behave in a reasonable fashion – where reasonable is defined as a willingness to evaluate one's party negatively and the opposing party positively when the facts warrant it. Across an array of experimental and observational data, we showed that reflection, as measured by need for affect and need for cognition, makes people more reasonable. More reflective partisans update in the direction of the information provided, irrespective of the partisan implications, whereas less reflective partisans behave like partisan cheerleaders.

Recalling Abelson's (1986) distinction between testable and distal facts, these findings suggest that reflection helps people link distal facts to political evaluations in a way that minimizes the human urge to interpret facts in the most favorable light. Reflective Republicans, for instance, could have chosen to interpret the good news about the economy as the result of something other than President Obama's policies, as their less reflective counterparts appear to have done. Because political facts tend to be distal facts, people rarely have an opportunity to directly observe the effects of policies generated by their party or the other party. A tax cut, for instance, may marginally increase people's personal incomes, but we leave it to the world of economists and statisticians to say whether a particular tax cut boosted the macroeconomy overall. Given the human urge to hang onto beliefs about distal facts, reflection plays an important role in a democratic polity, getting people to be a bit more honest with themselves and a bit less possessive of their own worldview affirming beliefs.

In short, reflection facilitates democratic accountability, at least according to the minimalist definition. However, it should be noted that not all scholars believe that the minimalist model of democratic accountability, drawn from Ferejohn (1986), is sufficient for ensuring accountability and responsiveness. If voters are too myopic, punishing or rewarding incumbents on the basis of their most recent performance, they risk holding politicians accountable for random events. In fact, there is evidence that some voters do engage in this kind of blind retrospective voting, with events as random as shark attacks (Achen and Bartels, 2016) and how well the local college football team recently played (Healy, Malhotra, and Mo, 2010) influencing election outcomes. Although we do not possess the data to consider whether reflective voters are less likely to be myopic voters (and that less reflective voters are more likely to be susceptible to myopic voting), we are comfortable asserting that this should be the case from the perspective of the Intuitionist Model of Political Reasoning.

Finally, we reiterate the point that the effects of need for affect and need for cognition that we report in this book represent a kind of general equilibrium. People's predispositions to be more or less reflective are behavioral tendencies. They are defaults that point to how people behave on average, rather than how they should behave in every context. Clever experiments, in fact, demonstrate that people can be induced to behave in more reflective, and thus less partisan, ways. By paying people small amounts of money to provide accurate factual answers on surveys, researchers have been able to reduce partisan bias in economic perceptions (Bullock et al., 2015; Prior, Sood, and Khanna, 2015). Although paying people to be less partisan is unlikely to be a realistic strategy to improving democratic accountability, these studies do show that individuals can be induced to be more reflective and less partisan. We return to the implications of this point in the conclusion.

6

Can't We Disagree without Being Disagreeable? The Role of Reflection in a Polarized Polity

On September 9, 2009, President Obama spoke at a joint session of Congress about his proposal to expand health care insurance. The issue had deeply divided Democrats and Republicans in Congress as well as within the electorate. About midway through the speech, Obama noted that his proposal would not extend coverage to individuals living in the country illegally, despite concerns voiced by Republicans to the contrary. The claim was too much to take for Joe Wilson, the Republican representative of South Carolina's second congressional district. From the back of the chamber he shouted, "You lie!" It was an extraordinary breach of decorum. Presidential addresses to Congress are generally only interrupted by applause, rather than name calling. Yet Wilson's outburst is not an isolated story in today's divisive political climate. Discourse among members of Congress has become less civil (Ahuja, 2008), and members from both parties have increasingly resorted to calling members from the other side names (Annenberg Public Policy Center, 2011). Partisan incivility extends beyond Congress, as well. Partisan talk show hosts on the radio and television routinely minimize those who disagree with them as idiots, pinheads, and just plain stupid (Sobieraj and Berry, 2011). It also reaches down to discourse among citizens. In a study of exchanges in the comment section of newspapers, Coe, Kenski, and Rains (2014) find that over a half include uncivil words.

The rise in partisan incivility tracks with increasing levels of polarization in Congress. Since the 1970s, Democrats and Republicans in the US House of Representatives as well as the US Senate have become steadily more likely to take ideologically divergent positions on issues and vote along party lines (McCarty, Poole, and Rosenthal, 2006). The passage of Medicare in 1965 and the passage of the Affordable Care Act in 2010 illustrate this profound transformation in Congress. Both count as landmark pieces of legislation that expanded health care coverage in the United States. Denounced as "socialized medicine" by opponents, both sparked controversy that divided the electorate (Klein, 2010). Despite the similarities in the prevailing opposition to these programs, half of the Republican caucus supported the passage of Medicare, while not one Republican voted for the Affordable Care Act (Herszenhorn and Pear, 2010; Social Security History, 2014). The key difference between 1965 and 2010 was the disappearance of moderate and liberal Republicans (as well as moderate and conservative Democrats). As the moderates departed, so too did the peacemakers who worked across party lines and preserved an atmosphere of comity. In their place, ideologues refashioned the Democratic and Republican parties as ideologically coherent teams that would rather shout at one another than work together.

These trends highlight two varieties of partisan polarization that echo the tension between economic and psychological explanations of partisanship that we have confronted in previous chapters. One occurs along the left/right ideological dimension. It fits well within the rational choice model of democracy articulated by Anthony Downs (1957). Ideologically disciplined parties articulate ideological divisions that arise from a bimodal electorate. The other occurs on an affective dimension. It is more consistent with the social psychological model of partisanship articulated by the Michigan School in *The American Voter* (Campbell et al., 1960). As should be familiar by now, people's support of parties in the social psychological framework has less to do with their ideological preferences and more to do with their affective attachments to socially constructed groups.

These varieties of polarization generate different implications when it comes to the textbook model of democratic accountability. The Downsian variety of polarization does not necessarily undermine democratic accountability. As long as voters are willing to remove support from politicians who perform poorly or stray from their preferences, it does not matter if parties take ideologically divergent positions. In fact, it could be argued that ideologically distinct parties can help voters assign credit and blame for policy outcomes and, thus, enhance democratic accountability (Anderson, 2000). In contrast, the affective variety of polarization envisioned by the Michigan School model frustrates democratic accountability because it motivates voters to be partisan cheerleaders who support their team no matter what.

In the preceding chapters, we have shown how partisan cheerleading undermines the assumptions that lie at the heart of the textbook model of democratic accountability. In this chapter, we consider the genesis of partisan cheerleading – people's affective attachments to the major political parties. When party elites behave as a coherent team, it induces partisans in the electorate to view political competition as a battle between us and them and, in doing so, develop a deep dislike for the other side. Disliking the opposition makes it difficult to listen to the other side, much less vote for them when the facts warrant it. We contend and offer evidence that reflection abates the affective aspects of partisan polarization. It helps people disagree without being so disagreeable.

6.1 US VERSUS THEM: THE AFFECTIVE ROOTS OF POLARIZATION

As deep as the partisan divide seems today, scholars in the 1980s and 1990s actually puzzled over the steady rise of Americans who identified as independent – or unaffiliated with a political party – since the 1960s. When *The American Voter* was published in 1960, around 10 percent of Americans did not identify (or even lean toward) one of the two major parties, while over one-third considered themselves to be a strong democrat or republican. By 1980, 15 percent of the electorate did not identify with a party, while strong partisans had declined to a quarter of the electorate. Although scholars disagreed over the extent to which Americans had become dissatisfied with the two major parties or just merely indifferent to them (Craig, 1985; Nie, Verba, and Petrocik, 1976; Konda and Sigelman, 1987; Wattenberg, 1998), there was a consensus that political parties and partisan identities were no longer as important as they once were. Some even went so far as to announce the death of the "traditional partisan regime" (Burnham, 2013, 89). Parties were now irrelevant to voters, who were more educated than they were in the 1950s and 1960s. It would seem that the Michigan School model of partisanship was a time-bound phenomenon, as Americans moved inexorably into the era of partisan "dealignment."

Of course, it is usually a mistake to presume that trends will go on without end. Just as stocks cannot go up forever, trends in partisanship are unlikely to move in one direction only. Rather than a permanent dealignment of partisan identities, it turns out that the apparent weakening of partisan identities in the 1970s and 1980s was actually a rejiggering of partisan loyalties. By the late 1990s, political scientists noted an uptick in partisanship within the mass electorate (Bartels, 2000) and connected it to the increasing levels of polarization among political elites (Adams, 1997; Ansolabehere, Rodden, and Snyder, 2008; Hetherington, 2001; Rohde, 1991). As the Democratic and Republican parties became more ideologically coherent, so too did partisans within the electorate.[1] Matt Levendusky (2009) identifies two mechanisms through which partisans became more ideologically coherent. Some ideologically misaligned partisans – conservative democrats and liberal republicans – simply brought their political attitudes in line with their partisan identities, while other misaligned partisans switched parties in order to bring their partisan identities in line with their political attitudes. In addition to inducing partisans to be more ideologically consistent, ideologically disciplined parties gave independents stark choices from which to choose in elections, making the party affiliations of politicians more salient and inducing them to choose sides (Hetherington, 2001).

Until recently, there has been an overwhelming tendency to think of partisan polarization in terms of where rank-and-file democrats and republicans fall on *position issues* – the controversies that divide people along the left/right ideological continuum (Stokes, 1963). Yet disagreement over position issues is unlikely the sole driving force behind partisan polarization in the electorate. Although democrats and republicans have become more ideologically coherent, many still hold a mix of liberal and conservative policy opinions (Ahler and Broockman, 2016). Moreover, as we demonstrated in Chapter 4, many partisans are more than willing to depart from the ideological doctrine of their party if party elites merely take a different position. For many voters, their opinions on position issues are largely the *consequence* of their partisan identity, rather than the cause. So, what else explains why democrats and republicans seem so deeply divided?

The answer for many partisans lies not in the Downsian conception of partisanship but in the Michigan School model of partisanship. Political parties are not simply vehicles for making public policy. They are also teams that compete in head-to-head competition every election as well as within the halls of power. To be a part of a team, to root for a team, makes one part of a social group. Seen from this angle, democrats are not simply democrats and republicans are not simply republicans because they agree on the major issues of the day. In fact, many do not. Rather, some democrats are democrats because they want to beat those republicans, and the same goes for many republicans – they may not all agree on trade policy, but they can pretty much all agree that the country would be better off if they beat the other side.

In a series of influential articles, Shanto Iyengar and his colleagues have reconceptualized partisan polarization from the standpoint of social groups (Iyengar, Sood, and Lelkes, 2012; Iyengar and Westwood, 2015). In this telling, the divisions among democrats and republicans arise from the us-versus-them mentality created by electoral competition. Policy disagreements are an articulation of this competition, of course, but that drives partisan polarization less than the dislike that many partisans have for members of the opposing party. This affective dimension of polarization manifests in how people *feel* about opposing partisans rather than how they *think* about public policy. So, even though divisions among partisan elites have largely been about policy disagreements, many rank-and-file partisans have internalized the shrill policy debates that animate elite discourse in affective terms. And, as elected representatives in Congress and state houses have become more disciplined partisans – voting in lock step with their party and consistently against the opposing party – partisans in the electorate have become more affectively polarized. In the less polarized era of the early 1970s, people liked their party more than the other party, but they still had relatively positive feelings toward the other party. That is no longer true today. Not only do partisans say they feel rather cold toward members of the opposing party, but they are also more likely to ascribe negative personality traits to the other side – being unintelligent and selfish – than they were 50 years ago (Iyengar, Sood, and Lelkes, 2012).

6.2 REFLECTION AND POLARIZATION

We believe that the Intuitionist Model of Political Reasoning provides some insight into whether the Downsian or the Michigan School model of partisanship best describes polarization. As the evidence in Chapter 4 demonstrates, as people become more reflective, their political attitudes are more likely to reflect ideological considerations and less likely to be tied to the affective pull of their partisan identities. In contrast, less reflective individuals are more likely to rely on the affectively rooted intuitions that are guided by their partisan identities. Accordingly, we anticipate that less reflective individuals are more likely to treat their partisan identity as a social identity and behave more in line with the group-centric Michigan School model, while more reflective individuals should be more likely to behave in line with the Downsian model.

If we could observe the evolution of partisan polarization among more and less reflective individuals from the 1970s to today, we believe we would see that as the Democratic and Republican parties became more ideologically coherent, more reflective individuals would have sorted themselves into the party that aligned with their ideological preferences. Meanwhile, we would predict that less reflective individuals would stick with their party and that, when it becomes necessary to take a position on a controversial issue, they would bring their policy attitudes in line with their partisan identification. We suspect that both more and less reflective partisans were susceptible to the forces of affective polarization. It is human, after all, to have some dislike for people who disagree with you. However, the Intuitionist Model of Political Reasoning would predict that less reflective partisans should be more affectively polarized than more reflective partisans. Insofar as reflection causes people to second-guess their affectively rooted intuitions, it should also lead them to take a more thoughtful and less knee-jerk, group-centric approach to fashioning attitudes about opposing partisans.

Unfortunately, we do not possess the sort of data we would need to chart the political attitudes of more and less reflective individuals over the past forty-five years. These data simply do not exist. Instead, we only possess data about the political attitudes of more or less reflective partisans at this slice in time. Nonetheless, these data do give us some leverage to evaluate our claim that reflection influences the ways in which people are polarized. When it comes to issue polarization, more reflective partisans should exhibit higher levels of polarization than less reflective partisans. Nevertheless, we do not expect the differences to be stark. After all, party elites are quite polarized, and less reflective partisans – as shown in Chapter 4 – do square their issue attitudes with their party's positions when exposed to party cues. Therefore, even less reflective partisans should be polarized on the left-right ideological dimension to some extent. It is affective polarization where we expect to find clearer differences.

6.2.1 Issue Polarization

We draw on two data sources to evaluate the relationship between reflection and issue polarization. The 2012 Campaign Study included eight questions about controversial issues that clearly divide party elites: abortion, affirmative action, climate change, same-sex marriage, government regulation, health care, immigration, and taxation. We recoded respondents' responses to these questions such that higher values indicate agreement with their party's positions on these issues. For example, republicans scored higher values if they opposed abortion, affirmative action, same-sex marriage, and high taxes as well as believed that climate change was not influenced by human activity, that there should be less government regulation, and that the Affordable Care Act (known as Obamacare) should be repealed. Democrats were given higher scores if they took the opposite positions on these issues.

Because the questions on the 2012 Campaign Study tended to measure only the direction of people's preferences (e.g., support for or opposition to same-sex marriage) and not the intensity of their preferences (e.g., strongly oppose versus somewhat oppose same-sex marriage), we administered the Issue Polarization survey in the summer of 2015 to a nationally descriptive Internet panel that asked participants to register their opinions on fourteen controversial and partisan issues: abortion, regulating banks, increasing spending on public education, environmental regulations, reducing income inequality, government-funded health care, same-sex marriage, welfare, immigration, prayer in school, the death penalty, gun rights, increasing military spending, and taxing the rich. Participants indicated whether they supported or opposed these policies and to what extent (ranging from somewhat to strongly). We followed the same coding strategy that we used for responses to the items on the 2012 Campaign Study, such that higher values indicated stronger agreement with one's party on these issues.

For both studies, we combined all of the re-coded responses into a single-issue polarization scale, which ranges from 0 to 1. A score of 0 indicates that the respondent took the opposite position of his or her party on all eight or fourteen issues (for the 2012 Campaign Study and Issue Polarization Study, respectively). On the 2012 Campaign Study, only six individuals were severely misaligned with their party on these issues, while there were no instances in which respondents strongly disagreed with their party's position on all fourteen items in the Issue Polarization Study. A score of 1 indicates that the individual agreed with his or her party on all issues. Roughly 23 percent of partisans fell in this category in the 2012 Campaign Study. Because the Issue Polarization Study included more issues and allowed participants to register the intensity of their attitudes, only three participants strongly agreed with their party on all fourteen issues.

Figure 6.1 aggregates these responses by level of reflection (after controlling for partisan identity and demographics). The results show that partisans are polarized on these controversial issues and that more

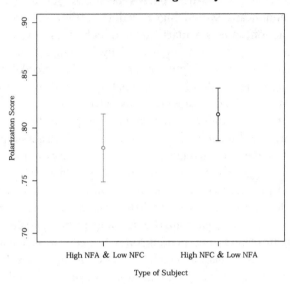

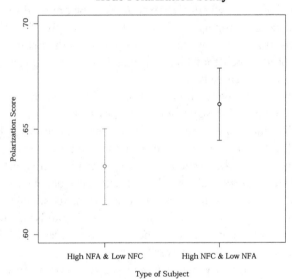

FIGURE 6.1. Reflection and Issue Polarization, 2012 Campaign Study and Issue Polarization Study

reflective individuals exhibit slightly higher levels of issue polarization. As we suspected, these differences are not stark. For the 2012 Campaign Study, partisans who are high in need for affect and low in need for cognition scored a 0.78 on the polarization scale, while those who are low in need for affect and high in need for cognition scored a 0.81. This difference accounts for roughly one-seventh of a standard deviation on the partisan polarization scale, which is substantively quite small. For the Issue Polarization Study, partisans who are high in need for affect and low in need for cognition scored a 0.63 on the polarization scale, while those who are low in need for affect and high in need for cognition scored a 0.66. This rather small difference translates into one-fifth of a standard deviation on the polarization scale. In sum, both of these studies, which used different measurement approaches and were conducted three years apart, show remarkably similar substantive conclusions. In our polarized polity, the propensity to be reflective does little to predict the level of partisan polarization on controversial issues. As we show in the next section, individual differences in reflection tell us more about partisans' level of affective polarization.

6.2.2 Affective Polarization

In the Party Cues Study we included a number of items that mirror the analysis reported by Iyengar, Sood, and Lelkes (2012). We asked respondents to place the Democratic and Republican parties on a feeling thermometer that ranged from 0 to 100. We also asked them to identify the traits that best describe people who identify as republicans and democrats. They could select freely from a list of nine traits that included five positive traits (patriotic, intelligent, honest, open-minded, and generous) and four negative ones (close-minded, hypocritical, selfish, and mean). These questions get at how partisans feel about people who identify with their partisan ingroup and others who identify with their partisan outgroup.

Figure 6.2 shows the degree to which need for affect and need for cognition jointly influence how partisans feel toward members of their party and the opposing party. To be clear, both more and less reflective individuals feel more warmly about their party than the opposing party. However, less reflective partisans register more extreme feelings than more reflective partisans. As the top panel of Figure 6.2 illustrates, partisans who are high in need for affect and low in need for cognition place members of their party at a temperate 69 on the feeling thermometer scale

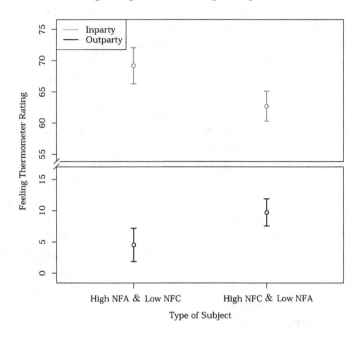

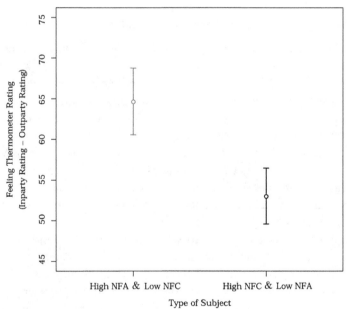

FIGURE 6.2. Reflection and Affective Polarization, Party Cues Study

while placing members of the opposing party at a frosty 5. Partisans who are low in need for affect and high in need for cognition view members of their party somewhat less warmly at a 63, while feeling a bit more warmly, though far from warm, toward members of the opposing party by placing them at 10 on the feeling thermometer scale. Therefore, variation in reflection leads to differences in the gaps between feelings toward the in- and outparty – by about twelve points (see the bottom panel of Figure 6.2) – that are both substantively and statistically significant.

We observe a similar pattern of results with respect to traits. Because there were five positive traits and four negative traits, we converted responses to the traits question to proportions and analyzed them separately (see Figure 6.3). Less reflective partisans are more likely to ascribe negative traits to opposing partisans while choosing to view their fellow partisans in positive terms. More reflective individuals, in contrast, are less likely to ascribe traits in such a knee-jerk partisan fashion. In fact, more reflective partisans are a bit more willing to see the positive in members of the opposing party. Looking at the top panel of Figure 6.3, we find that, on average, individuals high in need for affect and low in need for cognition select about 59 percent of the positive traits to describe their party and 66 percent of the negative traits to describe the opposing party. In contrast, individuals low in need for affect and high in need for cognition only select 52 percent of the positive traits to describe their party and 60 percent of the negative traits to describe the other party. Given that respondents were choosing from a constrained list (five positive traits and four negative traits), these differences are substantively meaningful – although it should be noted that these differences attain statistical significance in only the case of positive traits for which there was more possible variation. As the bottom panel of Figure 6.3 shows, when considering the balance of positive to negative terms used by partisans, less reflective individuals are statistically more likely to describe their party in positive terms and the outparty in negative terms than more reflective individuals are.

6.3 POLARIZING RHETORIC CONTRIBUTES TO AFFECTIVE POLARIZATION

We began this chapter with the story of Republican Congressman Joe Wilson attempting to shout down President Obama, a Democrat, in the middle of a prime-time televised address to a joint session of Congress as an extraordinary example of how shrill partisan rhetoric has become

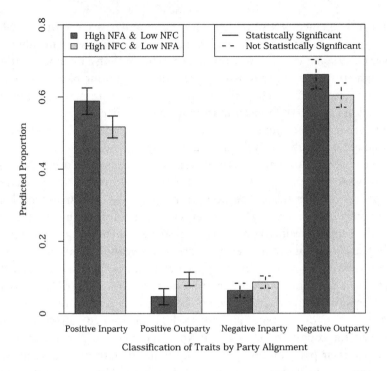

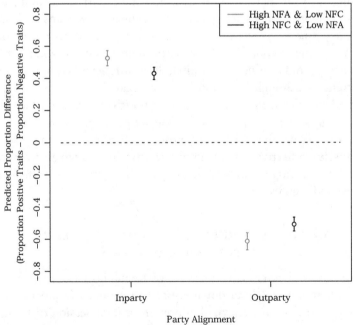

FIGURE 6.3. Reflection and Attribution of Personality Traits to Inparty and Outparty Members, Party Cues Study

in the United States. Although the extant literature draws a connection between the changing behavior of elites over the previous few decades and growing partisan polarization in the electorate (e.g., Adams, 1997; Hetherington, 2001; Iyengar, Sood, and Lelkes, 2012; Levendusky, 2009), these scholars rely on the correlation in the two time trends to make a circumstantial case – albeit a compelling one. Unfortunately, we do not have access to data that measures polarization and markers of reflection across decades. So, while we can show a connection between the propensity to be reflective and affective polarization in current-day America, we cannot make empirically grounded claims about this relationship in the past.

Nonetheless, it is possible to use the experimental method to simulate the shift in elite rhetoric from one of bipartisanship to the kind of shrill hyper-partisanship we have observed over the past decade. We embedded such an experiment in a survey that we administered to the participants in the Party Cues Study two weeks after they completed the initial survey, which included measures of need for affect and need for cognition as well as the affective polarization items that we analyzed in the previous section. We placed two weeks between surveys so that questions about affective polarization would not interfere with the way in which participants responded to the experiment that we present in this section. Of the 1,258 individuals who participated in the initial Party Cues Study, 840 agreed to participate in the follow-up survey (a healthy 66.8 percent re-contact rate). Participants' need for affect, need for cognition, and level of affective polarization does not predict whether they participated in the follow-up study, suggesting that the re-contact sample is similar to the initial sample along relevant dimensions.[2]

Table 6.1 shows the stimuli for the polarized rhetoric experiment. Half of the participants were randomly assigned to read the *bipartisan rhetoric treatment* in which President Obama and the Republican leadership in Congress agree on the need to work together to create more on-the-job training programs. The remaining half of participants were assigned to read the *polarized rhetoric treatment*, which described how the Republican leadership in Congress filed a lawsuit against President Obama accusing him of violating the constitution and how Obama dismissed this lawsuit as a shallow stunt. Although we took some liberties with the facts, these stimuli were inspired by actual events. The Republican leadership in Congress did, in fact, file a lawsuit against President Obama in 2014, and it also sent a letter to President Obama that indicated their agreement with his call for more on-the-job training

TABLE 6.1. *Text of Stimuli in Polarized Rhetoric Experiment*

Bipartisan Rhetoric Treatment

Recently, the Republican leadership of the United States House of Representatives wrote a letter to President Obama saying that they agree with his proposal to reform job training programs so that more Americans can get the training they need for today's jobs.

President Obama asked the vice president to work with both Democrats and Republicans in Congress to create an across-the-board reform package – one that will create more on-the-job training and connect companies to colleges.

Polarized Rhetoric Treatment

Recently, the Republican leadership of the US House of Representatives filed a lawsuit against President Obama, accusing him of overstepping his authority and violating the constitution for making executive decisions on his own.

President Obama dismissed the lawsuit as a partisan stunt and said that Republicans in Congress were just mad at him for taking actions that help Americans. He said that if the Republicans would work with him, he would not have to take action on his own.

in his 2014 State of the Union address (although it should be noted that the letter was ultimately critical of President Obama's plans to achieve this goal). We chose to root our stimuli in actual events to lend them verisimilitude and increase the credibility of the vignette. In doing so, we constructed a bipartisan example that looks like the kinds of bipartisan deals that congressional leaders and the president used to hammer out. It focused on an issue that attracts broad support and benefits many people. We also shied away from recreating a polarizing example as viscerally partisan as Congressman Wilson's outburst, opting instead for the type of partisan bickering that has become commonplace. Americans regularly encounter stories of Republicans and Democrats sniping at one another with language that thinly veils their contempt for the opposition, rather than outright name calling.

After reading the vignette, participants were told, "We are interested in getting your reaction to this exchange," and then they were provided with a list of emotional terms, two of which were chosen to gauge anger (*angry* and *disgusted*). These words were taken from the *Positive and Negative Affect Schedule* (Watson and Clark, 1994), which offers specific recommendations for measuring people's affective states using commonly

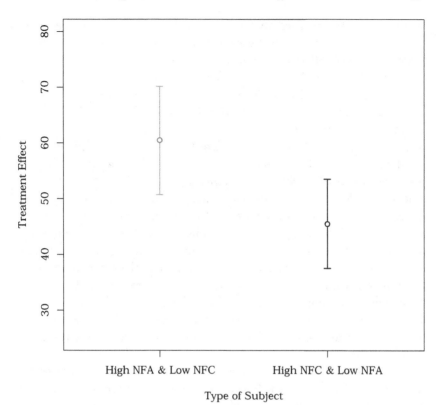

FIGURE 6.4. Reflection and the Effect of Polarized Rhetoric on Anger, Party Cues Study

understood English words. Participants registered their reactions to these emotional terms on a 101-point scale that ranged from 0 (did not feel this way at all) to 100 (felt this way more than ever before). We averaged participants' responses to *angry* and *disgusted* and investigated whether partisans (i.e., individuals who identify as democrat or republican) were more likely to register anger (the term we use to describe these emotions jointly) in response to the *polarized rhetoric treatment* as well as whether need for affect and need for cognition influenced the magnitude of their response.

The results of our investigation are summarized in Figure 6.4. The circles represent the effect of the *polarized rhetoric treatment* on partisans' anger reactions. We estimated this effect by taking the mean self-reported level of anger among participants assigned to the *bipartisan rhetoric treatment* and subtracted that number from the mean anger response of participants assigned to the *polarized rhetoric treatment*. A positive number indicates that partisans who read the polarized vignette were angrier than those who read the bipartisan vignette. We found that, on balance, the polarized vignette provoked quite a bit of anger among our respondents. Moreover, when we separate out the effect of the polarized rhetoric by the propensity to be more or less reflective, we observe a substantial difference between the two. Less reflective individuals (high need for affect and low need for cognition) who read the polarized vignette placed themselves 60.5 points higher on the anger scale than did less reflective individuals who read the bipartisan vignette. More reflective individuals (low need for affect and high need for cognition), in contrast, exhibited less extreme responses, on average. More reflective individuals who read the polarized vignette placed themselves 45.5 points higher on the anger scale than did more reflective individuals who read the bipartisan vignette. This fifteen-point difference is substantively meaningful, accounting for nearly half of a standard deviation on the anger reaction measure. However, we do note that this difference just misses statistical significance.[3] Consequently, we think of these results as highly suggestive.

These results offer some evidence that reflection mutes – although it does not obviate – partisans' negative emotional reactions to polarized rhetoric. These findings also provide suggestive evidence for the claim that the polarized context in which Americans live fuels their hostility toward the other side. It appears that being reflective does not insulate individuals from feeling angry or hostile, but it does curb these responses to some extent. Taken together, the analyses in this section and the foregoing one offer some clues for why more reflective partisans behave less like knee-jerk cheerleaders than less reflective partisans do.

6.4 SUMMARY

In a polarized polity, partisans do not simply disagree with each other; they tend to dislike each other as well. More reflection helps reduce affective polarization among partisans. Despite disagreeing with the other side, reflective partisans view opposing partisans in somewhat more positive terms as well as their own party in less effusive terms. We do not want to overstate our findings. Reflective partisans do like their fellow partisans more than the members of the opposing team. It is simply the case that the affective gulf between in- and out-partisans is substantively smaller for more reflective partisans than it is for less reflective partisans.

We believe that the differences in affective polarization between more and less reflective individuals corroborate a key assumption in the Intuitionist Model of Political Reasoning, while also providing some insight into why less reflective partisans hold elected officials from their own party to a lower standard than they do elected officials from the opposing party. We show that all partisans tend to like their party more than the other party, which is why reflection is necessary to overcome affectively rooted intuitions. But more than simply helping people override their intuitions, reflection also helps individuals be a bit less knee-jerk partisan in their *affective* evaluations. As a result, reflection creates a double benefit. It helps people override their intuitions, and it reduces to some extent the strength of those intuitions.

The political context plays an important role, too. In a polarized polity where the major political parties are ideologically disciplined and distinct, political debate among elites has the potential to engender animosity among partisan groups within the electorate. Reflection helps blunt this process, but it does not prevent it from happening. Even reflective people are only human. Consequently, polarized polities may evince lower levels of democratic accountability relative to less polarized polities because it makes partisan identities more difficult to overcome across all individuals.

7

Reflections on the Role of Reflection in Democracies

We end where we started by considering the most fundamental question in democratic theory: Are the people capable of self-governance? Rule by the people is a core tenant of democracy in all of its ideal forms (Dahl, 1989). If "the people" are not up to the task, then democracy is inherently impossible in practice. In electoral democracies, self-governance requires that voters are willing and able to hold elected officials accountable for their actions. The empirical study of democratic accountability is rich and replete with reasons for optimism and pessimism. In this book, we tackled what many scholars and observers see as a formidable threat to democratic accountability: partisan-motivated reasoning. If people are more interested in cheerleading their political party than they are in holding elected officials accountable, then it frees elected officials to pursue their own goals even at the expense of their constituents.

To get a handle on this question, we began by articulating a model of political reasoning that builds on recent advances in cognitive psychology and neuroscience and, we believe, extends and updates preexisting models of political attitude formation. Our Intuitionist Model of Political Reasoning starts with the same foundation that contemporary models of motivated reasoning do. People initially process information (political or otherwise) outside of conscious awareness in a way that is heavily guided by emotions (i.e., System 1 processing). The intuitions that result from these System 1 processes nudge people in the direction of a particular decision. In the domain of politics, people's partisan identities shape their intuitions, leading them to root for their team even when they should not. The Intuitionist Model of Political Reasoning departs from the standard partisan-motivated reasoning framework in how it treats cognition. In the standard framework, thinking is for rationalizing. To the extent that partisans bother to think about their political decisions, they take a biased approach that discounts evidence that calls their intuitive response into question while latching onto evidence, no matter how weak, that lends support. In contrast, the Intuitionist Model allows people to be reflective – to use cognition (i.e., System 2 processing) as a way to critically evaluate their intuitive responses.

Whether people choose to use System 2 processes to engage in reflection depends on psychological motivations that vary across individuals, space, and time. The core prediction of the Intuitionist Model of Political Reasoning is that individual differences in the forcefulness of System 1 intuitions and the willingness to engage cognitively taxing System 2 processes predisposes people to be more or less reflective, on average. As System 1 forcefulness increases, people's intuitions are strongly felt and powerful. Partisan identifiers who possess powerful intuitions and little inclination to engage System 2 processes will tend to be less reflective and behave more in line with standard models of partisan-motivated reasoning. In contrast, partisan identifiers who tend to have less forceful System 1 intuitions and a strong motivation to engage System 2 processes are more likely to be reflective and behave more rationally and reasonably.

In order to provide crucial empirical tests of the Intuitionist Model, we needed to first find a way to measure System 1 forcefulness and System 2 engagement. We did so by recruiting two measures of cognitive style developed by social psychologists to tap people's psychological motivations to seek out strong emotions – need for affect – and to engage in effortful cognition – need for cognition. Numerous tests, across a diverse set of studies, showed that need for affect and need for cognition do an adequate job measuring people's propensity to engage in reflection outside of the political domain and that these measures are not merely proxies for education, political awareness, or other measures of personality (e.g., one's openness to experience). With these measures in hand, we found substantial empirical support across a suite of observational and experimental studies for the Intuitionist Model's general prediction that reflection minimizes partisan reasoning and promotes democratic accountability. More reflective individuals tend to rely on policy information rather than partisan cues, whereas less reflective individuals rely more on partisan cues even when it leads them to adopt policy positions that are inconsistent with their ideology. More reflective individuals update their evaluations about politics in reasonable ways that reflect the balance of the facts, while less reflective individuals behave more like partisan-motivated reasoners who side with their team regardless of the facts. In a polarized political context, reflection also helps individuals maintain cooler heads, even in the face of ugly political rhetoric. Consequently, more reflective individuals are more likely to vote against their party, while less reflective individuals stick with their party's candidates. These effects of reflection on political attitude formation and behavior remain even after accounting for standard explanations of political sophistication (e.g., political awareness, education, and other demographic characteristics) as well as personality traits that lead people to be more open to new experiences.

In sum, we offer compelling evidence that the Intuitionist Model of Political Reasoning unifies rational choice and social psychological approaches to studying the effects of partisanship. Some individuals treat their partisan affiliation as a running tally of the policy positions that political parties take and how the parties perform in office, while some individuals treat their partisan affiliation as a social identity that acts as the unmoved mover of their political decisions. The willingness to second-guess one's intuitions – to be reflective – is key to understanding why people tend to take one path or the other.

By accounting for variability in people's proclivity to be reflective, our theoretical model builds upon and extends existing models of political attitude formation in a way that philosopher of science Imre Lakatos (1970) calls a "progressive problemshift." That is, we explain the things that previous models explain while also explaining the things that they do not. Zaller's (1992) RAS model, for example, does not provide an explanation for when or why individuals resist accepting political messages from their party's elites, even though an accumulation of evidence shows that individuals are sometimes capable of doing so. Our model offers an explanation. The RAS model considers how individuals differ in political awareness to be the quintessential indicator of political sophistication. However, evidence shows that political awareness does not consistently predict whether people engage information in ways that are consistent with Converse's (1964) conceptualization of political sophistication – namely, the ability to place their ideological belief system before their partisan attachments (e.g., Weisberg and Nawara, 2010). Again, our model offers a way forward by pointing to individual differences in reflection as a crucial variable. The Intuitionist Model also refines models of motivated reasoning, such as Lodge and Taber's (2013) JQP framework or Kahan's (2012) Cultural Cognition theory, which explain why people often resist changing their opinions even in the face of factual evidence, but offer less insight into why some people do change their minds. As our model predicts, and the evidence we offer demonstrates, people can use thinking to be reflective, not just for the purpose creating rationalizations.

With the specific theoretical and empirical contributions of the Intuitionist Model in place, we devote our attention in this chapter to pondering its broader implications. We begin by considering the larger objective that motivated the research reported in the previous chapters – the linkage between reflection and democratic accountability. Up to this point, we have demonstrated that reflection minimizes partisan biases in how people answer questions on surveys. Recent research demonstrates that some survey respondents answer questions in ways that reveal partisan bias (e.g., the economy is doing terribly because the other party is in power) even though they privately hold a different attitude (e.g., the economy is doing better than before) (Bullock et al., 2015; Prior, Sood, and Khanna, 2015). It is entirely possible that less reflective individuals only behave in a more partisan fashion when they are answering survey questions, while they cast ballots that actually hold elected officials accountable. Even if that were true, how people respond to surveys can have meaningful effects on the decisions that elected officials make (Butler and Nickerson, 2011). Nonetheless, the implications of reflection for democratic accountability would surely be less important if its effects were limited to explaining differences between people's attitude expression and behavior.

In the next section, we take a preliminary stab at empirically evaluating whether reflection shapes people's voting behavior and, ultimately, electoral outcomes. We find that it does, suggesting the reflection does in fact help people *behave* in ways that we would describe as rational and reasonable. We then address the scope and limitations of the Intuitionist Model of Political Reasoning. Although we believe that our model improves on current models of political reasoning, much work remains to be done. In the penultimate section, we reflect on our model's broader implications and sketch out avenues of future research. We then close with some concluding thoughts about what we have learned and our ambitions for where the field will go from here.

7.1 REFLECTION PROMOTES DEMOCRATIC ACCOUNTABILITY

We believe that by minimizing partisan reasoning, reflection promotes democratic accountability. Yet as we noted in Chapter 1, democratic accountability is a system-level concept. It hinges critically on whether individuals collectively cast votes in ways that reward and punish politicians for their actions. The Intuitionist Model of Political Reasoning is not a model of how voters behave in the aggregate; it is a model of how individual voters make decisions. Nonetheless, it holds insights for how the aggregation of individual voting decisions influences the health of democratic accountability. Under reasonable assumptions, it tells us that as the proportion of reflective individuals in the electorate increases, electoral outcomes are more responsive to elite behavior.

In addition to implying a relationship between the aggregate level of reflection and democratic accountability, the Intuitionist Model also helps resolve conflicting empirical accounts in which some studies reach more optimistic conclusions about whether elections hold politicians accountable for their actions and, thus, make them more responsive to the median voter (e.g., Canes-Wrone, Brady, and Cogan, 2002; Soroka and Wlezien, 2010; Stimson, MacKuen, and Erikson, 1995), while others reach more pessimistic conclusions about democratic accountability and responsiveness (e.g., Achen and Bartels, 2016; Healy, Malhotra, and Mo, 2010). Part of the reason that these studies are at odds – beyond the obvious fact that they arrive at opposite conclusions – is that they are premised on fundamentally incompatible theoretical accounts of voting behavior. To help explain this point, we formalize the model of voting behavior implied by these empirical accounts using the following equation,

$$V_{ji} = \alpha - \beta(P_j - P_i)^2 + \gamma G_i + \epsilon \qquad (7.1)$$

where V_{ji} is the utility received by voter i from voting for representative j, such that positive values result in support for the incumbent. P_j is the ideological position (i.e., ideal point) of representative j, and P_i is similarly the ideal point of voter i. G_i denotes the effect of government policies on voter i. The voters' partisan attachments are captured in this equation by the intercept α, and ϵ represents the effects of random shocks on voter i's behavior. The remaining parameters, β and γ, are weights assigned to ideological congruence and the effects of government policies, respectively.

Because these theoretical models presume that all voters make decisions in a uniform fashion – be it rationally or irrationally – the values for α, β, γ, and ϵ are fixed, while voters' ideological preferences (P_i) and the impact of government policy on them (G_i) can vary from voter to voter. According to rational choice accounts, where voters perfectly hold their elected leaders accountable, α would be close to zero (and actually a function of ideology and government policies), ϵ would be close to zero, and both β and γ would be large in absolute terms. That is, voters would vote not on the basis of partisan attachments or irrelevant random shocks, but rather on the basis of the ideological positions taken by their representative and the influence of government policies on their well-being. Rational voters prefer elected representatives who minimize the distance between their ideal point on the left/right ideological continuum and their representative's ideal point (this is why β is negative). Simply put, liberals prefer liberal representatives, and conservatives prefer conservative representatives, as the spatial voting model holds (Downs, 1957). Rational voters also reward incumbent politicians when government policies positively affect them (e.g., the economy is growing) and punish incumbent politicians when government policies negatively affect them (e.g., the economy is declining), as the retrospective voting model holds (Ferejohn, 1986). Optimistic empirical accounts are consistent with the rational ideal, while pessimistic accounts show that people behave as if α is large, β and γ are trivial, and ϵ plays a more pronounced role than one would like. In other words, people vote largely on the basis of their partisan identities, and when they do not, it is because something random and politically irrelevant puts them in a happy or foul mood – say, the success of the home football team in the most recent game (Healy, Malhotra, and Mo, 2010) or shark attacks off the coast of New Jersey in the election of 1916 (Achen and Bartels, 2016).

If voters behave uniformly, election outcomes should reflect either spatial and retrospective voting *or* fecklessness. Researchers have found evidence of both despite the fact that the underlying models of voting behavior cannot simultaneously be true. In contrast, our theoretical model offers a way to resolve these differences by allowing for a range of outcomes. In particular, it does not presume that people behave uniformly when they process political information and make voting decisions. Some people are more reflective than others, and thus more willing to down-weight their partisan identities and make decisions based on policy positions and policy performance. By the same token, some people are unreflective partisan cheerleaders who would rather walk on hot coals than vote against their party. Although we left it empirically unexplored, our model also predicts that unreflective nonpartisans would be more vulnerable to politically irrelevant events than reflective nonpartisans.

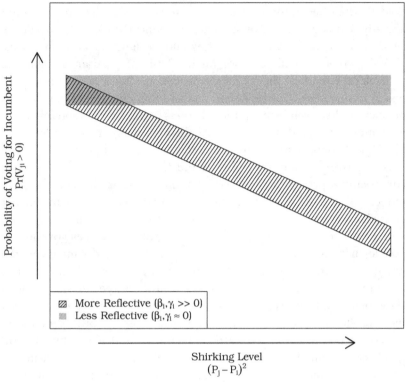

FIGURE 7.1. The Predicted Effects of Shirking on Support for Inparty Representatives among Reflective and Unreflective Partisans

In more formalized language, our model recasts Equation 7.1 as

$$V_{ji} = \alpha_i - \beta_i(P_j - P_i)^2 + \gamma_i G_i + \epsilon_i \qquad (7.2)$$

In contrast to the model presented in Equation 7.1, the values for α, β, γ, and ϵ are allowed to vary across voters, hence the subscripted i on these parameters. For reflective voters, β and γ are larger in absolute magnitude than α and ϵ. For unreflective voters, β and γ approach zero and are overshadowed by α and ϵ. For unreflective partisans, $\alpha > \epsilon$, whereas for unreflective nonpartisans, $\alpha < \epsilon$. To illustrate the implications of the Intuitionist Model, Figure 7.1 shows the comparative statics for unreflective and reflective partisans with respect to their support for an inparty incumbent representative across varying levels of shirking.[1] For the sake of generating this comparison, we define "shirking" as a voter's representative revealing policy positions that depart from the voter's preferred policy positions (i.e., $P_j \neq P_i$).[2] Therefore, shirking increases as $(P_j - P_i)^2$ increases.[3] These comparative statics show that as shirking increases, unreflective voters maintain their support for inparty incumbents, while reflective voters remove their support.[4] Importantly, they also stand in contrast to the extant literature, which largely suggests that we should find behavior consistent with one or the other, but not both, of the types of voters explored in this comparative statics exercise.

The implication of these comparative statics for the aggregate level is that the ratio of reflective to unreflective voters in the electorate shapes the degree to which elections facilitate democratic accountability and induce the government to be responsive to voters' preferences. The empirical evidence that we offer in Chapters 4 and 5 is consistent with this implication. After all, we find evidence that variation in the predisposition to engage in reflection at the individual level affects the extent to which people are willing to punish elected officials for shirking. Nonetheless, we did not take the extra step to show that the *aggregate* level of reflection in the electorate influences electoral outcomes, so we offer a preliminary effort at doing so here. We take advantage of the fact that the collective characteristics of voters – presumably including levels of reflection – vary across congressional districts in the United States, as does the behavior of elected representatives. We measure shirking in an indirect way. Recent research shows that many members of Congress vary their policy positions over the course of the two-year legislative term as a way to balance their personal goals against the needs and desires of their constituents (Lindstädt and Vander Wielen, 2013). By implication, the larger the variance in a representative's policy positions across the term, the more likely it is that the representative is casting votes that, at least at periods during the term, are inconsistent with his or her constituents' preferences (i.e., shirking). As for measuring aggregate levels of reflection, we were able to link participants in the Party Cues Study to US House districts and, thus, aggregate need for affect and need for cognition scores by congressional district.

We emphasize that this is a preliminary effort because we lack solid measures of shirking as well as unimpeachable aggregate-level measures of reflection. With respect to shirking, we do not have a direct measure of the correspondence between representatives' votes and their constituents' preferences, forcing us to rely on what we believe is a useful (but noisy) indirect measure. With respect to aggregate-level measures of reflection, the Party Cues Study draws on a nationally representative

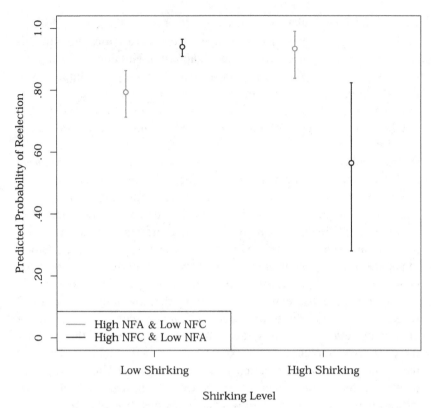

FIGURE 7.2. The Effects of Shirking and District-Level Composition of Reflective Voters on Support for Incumbent Representatives

sample, but not necessarily one that is representative of congressional districts. Consequently, we must assume that the participants in our sample are largely representative of other voters in their congressional district. Armed with these imperfect measures, we empirically evaluate whether the aggregate level of reflective voters (respondents who possess low levels of need for affect and high levels of need for cognition) and unreflective voters (respondents who possess high levels of need for affect and low levels of need for cognition) are predictive of incumbent representatives' electoral success.[5] Because the Party Cues Study was administered in 2015, we examined election outcomes in the 2014 US House elections, which were the most proximate available election results at the time of writing.

The results of this analysis, shown in Figure 7.2, are consistent with our individual-level findings. Notably, members of Congress who represent districts in which voters tend to possess high levels of need for affect and low levels of need for cognition do not face any discernible consequences for shirking. They tend to be reelected at high levels no matter what they do. Because voting in congressional races is largely a function of partisanship (democrats tend to vote for Democratic candidates, and republicans tend to vote for Republican candidates), we can infer that districts populated with less reflective partisans are less likely to punish inparty incumbents who shirk. The same is not true for members of Congress who represent districts in which voters tend to possess low levels of need for affect and high levels of need for cognition. In these districts, members who engage in high levels of shirking experience, on average, a drop in their likelihood of reelection by approximately 37.5 percentage points when compared to their more faithful counterparts, a decline that is statistically and substantively important. While admittedly somewhat crude, this preliminary analysis provides initial confirmation that the individual-level effects observed throughout the preceding chapters generate a measurable signal at the mass level. In short, this analysis shows that reflection does indeed promote democratic accountability.

Our crude analysis also offers some insight into why empirical studies of democratic accountability reach such disparate conclusions. From election to election, place to place, electorates can vary in the tendency to be reflective. Part of the reason for this variance may have to do with the fact that people choose to live around people who are similar to them, such that some neighborhoods may have more or less reflective people, on average, than others. We surmise that part of the explanation also has to do with the influence of political and social contexts. As we pointed out in Chapter 2, individual differences in the predisposition to be reflective are behavioral defaults, not unbending responses. Less reflective individuals *can* be reflective when there is a compelling reason, and reflective individuals *can* turn off their analytical mind from time to time. Perhaps major disruptions to the economy or civil order can jolt less reflective individuals to depart from their partisan defaults. It would certainly explain why electoral realignments do happen from time to time and, seemingly, in reaction to major exogenous shocks (Green, Palmquist, and Schickler, 2002). Likewise, intense partisan polarization, which generates heated political rhetoric that induces partisans to become angry, as we showed in Chapter 6, may lead some people who tend to be reflective to behave more like partisan cheerleaders.

Although it may be unsatisfying for those in search of definitive answers, we take neither an optimistic nor a pessimistic position on the broad question with which we began: Are people capable of self-governance? Our answer is that some people are and some people are not; self-governance hinges, then, on having a sufficient number of individuals who are capable of putting their partisan attachments – and other group attachments for that matter – to the side when evaluating the performance of elected officials. In this respect, we depart from scholars who take an overly rosy view of a rational public that can be counted on to do the right thing, on average (e.g., Key, 1966; Page and Shapiro, 1992; Soroka and Wlezien, 2010), as well as from those who take a decidedly pessimistic stand that elections fail to further responsive government (Achen and Bartels, 2016). We are not saying that these scholars are wrong. Sometimes elections work and sometimes they do not (Manza and Cook, 2002). Our point is that we should move past the understandable desire to come to a definitive answer on the question and instead dedicate our energy to investigating the conditions that make elections more or less likely to work.

The Intuitionist Model of Political Reasoning points to reflection as key to understanding who is and who is not up to the task that democratic theory places on our shoulders. We appreciate that we could be accused of being closet optimists given that the subtitle of our book is "How Reflection Minimizes Partisan Reasoning and Promotes Democratic Accountability," but it is important to emphasize that this statement is about individual voters. And while our aggregate analysis, reported above, suggests that variation in reflection has implications for aggregate outcomes, we cannot make any firm statements about how many voters in the electorate need to be reflective for democratic accountability to be achieved. We can certainly say, based on the data we have collected, that considerably less than a majority of Americans can be categorized as "predisposed to be reflective." Yet it is not clear to us that democracy requires *everyone*, or even a majority, to be reflective. In close elections, for instance, a small percentage of reflective or unreflective individuals could sway outcomes. We suspect that the threshold at which reflective voters are decisive as well as how reflective voters need to be to reach the right decision depends in no small part on the political and social context in which elections take place and the strategic calculations that elected officials make (Ashworth and Bueno de Mesquita, 2014). We hope that, if nothing else, we have opened avenues for future research to clarify the answers to these questions.

7.2 REFLECTION DOES NOT ALWAYS LEAD TO NORMATIVELY DESIRABLE OUTCOMES

We hope that we have driven home the point that one of the ways in which reflection promotes democratic accountability is by helping people align their voting decisions with their values. It may be tempting to view this feature of reflection as unambiguously good from a normative perspective. After all, if democracy is about matching public policy to public opinion, and reflection helps bring this about, then reflection leads to normatively desirable outcomes. If one's goal were merely to maximize popular sovereignty, then reflection would indeed be unquestionably "good," and no further conversation would be necessary. However, one cannot advance this claim from the standpoint of liberal democratic theory, which takes a more expansive definition of democracy that includes equality and liberty. Because nothing prevents a majority of the people from preferring outcomes that would be considered normatively "bad," such as depriving minorities of their liberties, majoritarian democratic institutions promote liberty and equality insofar as a majority of the people share liberal democratic values (Dahl, 1956). If people do not hold these values, then reflection may help voters select political candidates who would pursue policies that violate individual liberties and equality. In sum, reflection can lead to normatively undesirable outcomes when people hold normatively undesirable values.

To illustrate this point, we turn to the 2016 presidential election in the United States. The election pitted Democrat Hillary Clinton against Republican Donald Trump. Clinton advanced a conventional set of left-of-center policies that were largely in line with the Democratic Party platform, while Trump departed from Republican orthodoxy in a number of key respects. He opposed free trade, advocated isolationist policies, and at various points in the campaign expressed a desire to buttress social programs (e.g., Social Security). He took a harder line against immigration than most Republican Party elites, vowing to build a wall along the border between the United States and Mexico, deport undocumented individuals, and restrict immigration from Muslim countries. He also employed xenophobic rhetoric, such as painting a broad brush of Mexican immigrants as criminals and rapists. As a result, racial resentment was a key predictor of support for Donald Trump in the Republican primaries (Tesler and Sides, 2016).

To place our cards on the table, we consider white racial resentment and Donald Trump's xenophobic rhetoric to be repugnant because they undermine the core democratic principles of equality and liberty. We realize that this is a normative claim with which others may disagree. Yet if we are going to evaluate the normative implications of reflection, we must begin with a set of normative values. Not only is racial equality a normative value to which we are committed, but we also feel confident asserting that it is consistent with the normative framework that lies at the core of liberal democratic theory. Consequently, we view electoral outcomes as normatively undesirable if voters use racial resentment to guide their voting decisions.

Nonetheless, in a free society, people are free to hold repugnant views. One of the normatively troubling implications of the Intuitionist Model is that reflection should help individuals who hold repugnant views make political choices that are in line with those repugnant views. We are able to supply some evidence for this implication because it just so happens that we fielded a panel survey during the closing months of the 2016 campaign. We surveyed 818 individuals in the second week of September 2016, asking them to complete the need for affect and need for cognition batteries, along with a standard measure of racial resentment (Henry and Sears, 2002), their party identification, and their voting preference for the presidential election. We reinterviewed 485 of these participants in the first week of November 2016 and once again asked them their voting preference. Given that we are writing this conclusion in the days just after the 2016 presidential election occurred, we can offer a preliminary analysis of whether reflection played a role in reconciling the conflict between partisanship and racial values for democrats who scored high on the racial resentment scale. We find that it did. Among democrats with a high level of racial resentment who supported Clinton in the September wave of the survey, those predisposed to be less reflective (i.e., high need for affect and low need for cognition) had virtually no chance of switching to Trump in the second wave. In contrast, among racially resentful democrats who supported Clinton in the first wave survey, those predisposed to be more reflective (i.e., low need for affect and high need for cognition) had a 3.9 percent chance of switching to Trump by the second wave survey.[6]

These results push against the narrative that the outpouring of white nativism that helped propel Donald Trump to victory in the 2016 election was an unthinking and visceral response. For some racially resentful democrats, it appears, voting for Donald Trump was the result of reflection. It also illustrates how loyalty to one's party can guide people to make normatively desirable decisions, underscoring our point that the normative implications of partisanship are contingent. Yet the most important point we take away from this exercise is that the well-being of liberal democracy does not hinge on democratic accountability alone, and as a result, we cannot make the claim that reflection always leads to normatively desirable outcomes.

7.3 SCOPE AND LIMITATIONS OF THE INTUITIONIST MODEL

No theoretical model is without limitations, and the Intuitionist Model of Political Reasoning is no different. Some of these limitations are by design. A theory that attempts to explain everything ends up explaining nothing. A good theoretical model, then, is limited in scope. In some respects, the scope of our theoretical model is ambitious. We seek to explain how people form political attitudes and make politically consequential evaluative judgments. Yet in doing so, we leave the explanation for several important variables outside the scope of our theoretical framework. We do not offer an explanation for where people's partisan identities come from. We do not explain how people's associative networks are created and maintained. We do not offer an explanation for why people vary in their predisposition to be reflective. These explanations are worthy of pursuit, of course, and, it should be said, are under active investigation by other scholars. One scholar's burning question is another scholar's exogenous variable. From our perspective, we approach the question of political attitude formation – our burning question – by beginning with 60 years of research that establishes the power of partisan identities, and we marry it with an emerging line of research that shows the potential power of reflection.

Other limitations are not by design but rather are caused by the inherent gaps that exist in all theoretical models. We do not pretend to have nailed down every mechanism that lies within the scope of our model. Although we are also not going to pretend that we are capable of appreciating all of the gaps that exist, we intentionally left some aspects of the Intuitionist Model for future research. In making these decisions, we sought to focus on the most basic aspects of the model out of the belief that if we failed to find evidence for the model's most evident predictions, there would be little reason to consider a more elaborate version of the model. Now that we have offered considerable evidence that our model does explain important aspects of political attitude formation, we believe a useful next step would be to address key gaps in the model. One of those key gaps is the role that political and social context plays. We have already mentioned this and have made preliminary attempts to consider the effects of issue salience and polarizing political rhetoric.

Nonetheless, much work remains to be done to create a systematic framework that incorporates contextual influences into the Intuitionist Model. As it is currently stated, the Intuitionist Model averages across situational context to make predictions about how people who are predisposed to be more or less reflective *tend* to behave. The interactionist framework we took as a starting point in Chapter 1, which suggests that individuals' predispositions interact with their environment to shape beliefs, points the way forward. The interactionist approach provides an explanation for why people with different predispositions can sometimes form the same political attitudes, since the political environment can cause people to behave in similar ways. For instance, the 9/11 terrorist attacks caused people who possessed moderate levels of authoritarianism to see the world much like those high in authoritarianism did, leading them to support policies that enhanced security at the expense of personal freedoms (Hetherington and Weiler, 2009). At the same time, the interactionist approach also provides an explanation for why the same environmental context does not always induce people to behave in the same way. People with high levels of phobic fear react strongly to low levels of threat, while others do not, leading people with strong fear dispositions to adopt more negative outgroup attitudes (Hatemi et al., 2013). An interactionist account does more than simply say that the effects of predispositions and of the environment are contingent on one another. They are, to some extent, endogenous to one another as well. As Buss (1987) explains, predispositions affect which environments people select into (if they are given the choice), which in turn alters the environment that others experience. Consequently, predispositions can reinforce environmental effects.

We suspect that an interactionist model of reflection would reach similar insights. As we have already mentioned, political and social contexts likely create incentives and disincentives for people to engage in reflection. People likely vary in how sensitive they are to those contextual cues. Individual differences in reflection may provide part of the explanation here. After all, individuals who are strongly motivated to be reflective do not need much incentive to do so, while those who lack motivation to be reflective require a healthy nudge to do so. Yet we would not rule out the possibility that other personality characteristics may shape how contextual cues push and pull at people's motivation to be reflective. For instance, threatening environments may induce highly anxious people who lack a strong motivation to be reflective to engage in reflection more quickly than these environments induce unreflective individuals who are comparably less anxious. Furthermore, in a free society, we fully anticipate that the predisposition to be reflective may also cause people to seek out environments that either allow them to avoid the need to interrogate their intuitions or frequently engage in self-critique and reflection.

We also intentionally focused on an area of political reasoning where people's intuitions are an unreliable guide. As we elaborated in Chapter 2, partisan identities frustrate an essential pathway to democratic accountability because they cause people to instinctively be harsher on politicians from the opposing party than they are on ones from their own party. It is in this context that reflection should be most helpful in directing people to make decisions in line with their values. Yet other types of politically relevant decisions may be ably guided by intuitions and vulnerable to "overthinking" (see Kruglanski and Gigerenzer, 2011; Tetlock, 2005). Paradoxically, the potential deleterious effects of reflection may happen in those domains where people possess a great deal of expertise and thus have the tendency to be overconfident about their ability to think through a problem. Likewise, it is possible to consume too much information when attempting to make a decision. Low-salience, nonpartisan issues that map well onto adaptive solutions, for instance, are likely ripe for overthinking by highly reflective individuals.

Finally, the Intuitionist Model we present in Figure 2.5 implies that the causal chain runs from intuitions to reflection, while the dual-process model on which we built ours (i.e., Figure 2.1) allows for the interplay between intuitive and reflective processes. We made this simplifying move because, for the purpose of this book, we were interested in explaining how people generate a single judgment (e.g., political opinion or vote choice) at a snapshot in time. In doing so, we treated people's intuitive responses as given. If the goal were to generate a dynamic model of attitude formation and change, however, it would become important to specify the ways in which reflection (or unreflective "rationalization") shapes people's downstream intuitions. For instance, it is plausible (and entirely consistent with the dual-process model) that patterns of System 1 forcefulness and System 2 engagement may create a self-reinforcing cycle. Individuals with strong System 1 intuitions and weak System 2 engagement may reinforce the power of their gut reactions through consistent reliance on intuitions. Likewise, individuals with less forceful intuitions and high levels of System 2 engagement may maintain weak intuitions by consistently second-guessing themselves.

7.4 BROADER IMPLICATIONS AND PATHWAYS FOR FUTURE RESEARCH

We believe that the Intuitionist Model of Political Reasoning, along with the empirical evidence reported in the foregoing chapters, have a number of implications that go beyond the specific research questions that we focused on here, opening pathways for future research. In this section, we highlight what we see as the most pressing implications, and we offer some speculations about how future research can further explicate and explore them.

7.4.1 Psychological Foundations of Motivated Reasoning

Our model provides a foundational framework that elaborates the classic model of motivated reasoning offered by Kunda (1990) and extended by Lodge and Taber (2013). The classic model conceptualizes motivated reasoning as arising from the interplay of two psychological motivations: a *directional motivation* that leads people to prefer a particular outcome (e.g., "my political party is right") and an *accuracy motivation* that leads people to seek out the "correct" response (e.g., the optimal strategy in a rational choice analysis). However, it is not entirely clear from this framework whether these motivations arise from situational or dispositional causes. A robust line of research investigates how situational characteristics can motivate people to prioritize an accurate response. For instance, informing people that they will be asked to provide reasons for their choices causes them to be less partisan (e.g., Bolsen, Druckman, and Cook, 2014; Redlawsk, 2002), as does paying them to provide accurate answers to factual questions that are often open to partisan interpretations (e.g., Bullock et al., 2015; Prior, Sood, and Khanna, 2015). Meanwhile, as we have already noted, influential models of motivated reasoning in the domain of politics focus almost exclusively on the power of directional motivations, implying that people as a general matter cannot escape being biased partisans (e.g., Kahan, 2012; Lodge and Taber, 2013).

Figure 7.3 refines Kunda's (1990) typology from the lens of our theoretical framework (see Nir, 2011 for a similar discussion). It offers dispositional antecedents for the directional and accuracy motivations.

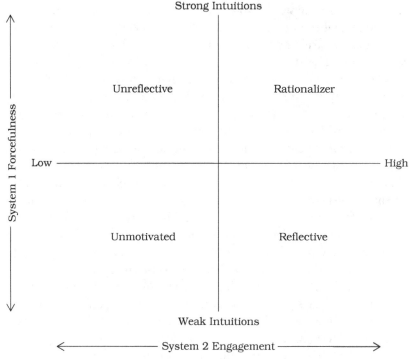

FIGURE 7.3. The Psychological Foundations of Motivated Reasoning

System 1 intuitions are directional by definition; they point in the direction of a particular decision. Consequently, System 1 forcefulness promotes directional motivations. Meanwhile, System 2 engagement provides the *ability*, but not necessarily the motivation, to arrive at accurate decisions when directional motivations push people toward inaccurate decisions. The motivation for accuracy, we contend, is a product of the interplay between System 1 and System 2. Our model's general prediction is that people are more likely to reflect on their intuitive responses in an effort to make a rational and reasonable decision when System 1 forcefulness is low and System 2 engagement is high (bottom right quadrant of Figure 7.3), and that people are more likely to reflexively go with their gut response when System 1 forcefulness is high and System 2 engagement is low (top left quadrant of Figure 7.3).

Yet as we telegraphed in Chapter 2, this prediction is merely the strongest one offered by the Intuitionist Model, providing a starting point for our initial empirical investigation. Additional research should explore other patterns of System 1 forcefulness and System 2 engagement. We surmise that when both are high, people are more likely to use conscious thought to construct rationalizations for going with their intuitions (top right quadrant of Figure 7.3). These individuals should behave like motivated reasoners in the sense that Kunda proposes, rather than the one implied by recent research in the political domain (e.g., Kahan, 2012; Lodge and Taber, 2013). These types of individuals attempt to form convincing explanations to justify intuition-based responses, and while they are willing to engage in mental gymnastics to do so, there are limits to how far they will go. From the standpoint of the Intuitionist Model of Political Reasoning, "rationalizers" are not entirely unreflective – they attempt to generate reasons for their decisions. They are simply more likely to fall prey to the kinds of cognitive biases that cloud human judgment than reflective individuals are. Nevertheless, when the facts overwhelmingly point in a particular direction, they are more likely to override their intuitive response than unreflective individuals.

Meanwhile, not only do individuals who are low in both System 1 forcefulness and System 2 engagement not have strong gut reactions, but they are also not inclined to think much about it, making them largely unmotivated to make consistent political decisions (bottom left quadrant of Figure 7.3). We suspect that these individuals are more likely to make political decisions that look like the "top-of-the-head" processing that Zaller's (1992) RAS model posits. "Unmotivated" individuals are more likely to accept considerations that are inconsistent with their political predispositions, and so if the balance of considerations available in the political environment runs against their partisan predispositions (e.g., a string of bad news about their party's candidate), they are more likely to make decisions that seem reflective at face value (e.g., negatively evaluate an inparty politician) but emerge from a path of least resistance rather than genuine reflection. For this reason, unmotivated individuals are likely to hold volatile and less coherent political attitudes.

Finally, we focused on how people's partisan identities shape their political intuitions. Given the importance of political parties in electoral democracies, we believe that they offered the most sensible place to begin. However, future research should consider other factors that shape people's political intuitions. We all possess a variety of identities (race, gender, age, region, etc.) that sometimes intersect with politics. When social identities beyond partisanship intersect with politics, we suspect that they will play an important role in shaping people's political attitudes. Moreover, we believe that the Intuitionist Model may be useful for theorizing about how people sort out competing identities, particularly when political controversies pit social and partisan identities against one another (e.g., Klar, 2013). For instance, we expect that the differential strength of affective attachments between competing social and partisan identities will influence which identity one's political intuitions reflect; to the extent that competing identities generate an ambivalent gut reaction and people feel torn between the two, reflection may help people sort out a sensible response.

7.4.2 Strategies to Motivate Reflection (or Minimize Its Importance)

If reflection is as useful for the health of democracy as we think it is, then is it possible to get people to be more reflective? One approach would be to train people to be more open-minded thinkers. Evidence from psychology suggests that training can hone people's critical thinking skills (Baron, 1993), and a liberal arts college education is often touted as serving this function for a democratic society. Yet we remain skeptical that education is a panacea. In our own data, levels of education correlate with reflection, but the relationship is weak and we cannot be certain about the causal direction. After all, individuals predisposed to be reflective are likely to seek out experiences that satisfy their motivation to be reflective. Moreover, we are less optimistic that training can overcome the tribal inclinations that animate partisanship. It is important to remember that reflection is not synonymous with being smart. Smart people, in fact, can be the best motivated reasoners. As we have discovered in our own classrooms, even our smartest students vary a great deal in their willingness to be open-minded!

Consequently, we suspect that a more pragmatic solution lies not in making people more reflective but in constructing political institutions that either motivate people to be more reflective *or* minimize the need to be reflective. With respect to motivating reflection, as we noted above, extant research shows that the situational context can motivate individuals to be more or less reflective (e.g., Bolsen, Druckman, and Cook, 2014; Bullock et al., 2015; Prior, Sood, and Khanna, 2015; Redlawsk, 2002). So, in principle, it seems that one could select institutional arrangements that nudge people to be more reflective than they normally would be. Some scholars contend that institutional settings that induce a diverse group of individuals to deliberate promote decisions that are well-informed, inclusive, and reflective in the sense we have defined here (e.g., Cohen, 1997; Fishkin, 2011; Gutmann and Thompson,

2005; Habermas, 1994). When people deliberate, they must provide reasons that justify their positions (Rawls, 1996), and doing so in a heterogenous social setting may encourage people to reconsider their gut responses and, thus, be less partisan (Klar, 2014).

Whether deliberative institutions work in practice hinges on participants' willingness to be open-minded, hear out the other side, and accord people with whom they disagree mutual respect (Gutmann and Thompson, 2005; Mansbridge et al., 2012). We worry that people's partisan identities in the context of an adversarial party system may frustrate attempts to achieve genuine deliberation in practice. As Ian Shapiro (2003) points out, deliberative institutions – such as a "Deliberation Day" in which people deliberate with members in their community before casting their votes on Election Day (Ackerman and Fishkin, 2002) – do not guarantee that people are willing to extend mutual respect to people with whom they virulently disagree. In an ideal setting, people would patiently listen with an open mind while others make their case and respond respectfully if they continue to disagree. In the real world, things are not always ideal. When uncompromising individuals are present, deliberation could devolve into heated conflict and hurled insults, which if anything would diminish other participants' motivation to be reflective.

Moreover, once we consider the possibility that political parties and partisan elites would likely take a keen interest in achieving particular outcomes from deliberative institutions, we are concerned that if deliberative institutions were to become a regular feature of the political system (as opposed to one-off affairs organized by academics), they would likely be overwhelmed by the same partisan impulses that one observes in contested electoral campaigns. For instance, we could easily imagine the Republican and Democratic parties arming ardent rank-and-file partisans with talking points that undercut deliberation and serve to dampen critical reflection rather than promote it. Indeed, one can easily observe something akin to this in online political discussions where meaningful deliberation is difficult to find amid the invective and rehearsed lines of attack that emanate from partisan sources.[7]

With respect to minimizing the need for voters to be reflective, the evidence that we offer in Chapter 6 suggests that reducing partisan polarization may lessen the degree to which partisan attachments influence the political decisions made by less reflective individuals. The two-party system may be particularly ill-designed from this perspective. Although reducing voting decisions to a choice between two distinct parties makes it easier for less informed voters to pick a side (Levendusky, 2010;

Sniderman, 2000), it also encourages partisans to view elections as a Manichean battle between good and evil. In contrast, multiparty systems do a better job of representing a broader set of issues (Dunn, Orellana, and Singh, 2009) and appear to increase voters' knowledge about the issue positions taken by the various parties (Gordon and Segura, 1997). As a result, multiparty systems may minimize the prevalence of unreflective partisanship by giving voters choices that are more clearly tied to their ideological values as opposed to social identities. Moreover, because multiparty systems often make it difficult (if not impossible) for a single party to possess a legislative majority, competing parties must form governing coalitions. This feature, in turn, may encourage competing parties to be more cooperative within the government and to lower the level of partisan rancor. Yet it should be noted that the quality of cross-national data on partisanship "is a mess" (Johnston, 2006, 348), making it difficult to empirically evaluate these claims.

In essence, we see a great deal of uncharted territory when it comes to designing institutions with reflection in mind. There are no easy or straightforward answers here. We also urge scholars to be mindful of the unintended consequences created by institutional design. If we focus narrowly on what will increase reflection (or minimize its importance), we may risk introducing new biases into the system that are more pernicious than the ones we wish to address.

7.4.3 A Call for Better Measurement

As we explained in Chapter 3, we took a pragmatic approach to measuring System 1 forcefulness and System 2 engagement. We believe that the evidence reported in the previous chapters demonstrates that need for affect and need for cognition do an adequate job capturing individual differences in reflection. Nonetheless, we are the first to admit that they are imperfect measures. These measures tap individual differences in how people attend to information, and our decision to use them in our analyses is in line with the intellectual tradition in which we are working. We are not the first scholars to connect political reasoning to information processing. Nonetheless, another approach would be to try to directly measure the operative forces involved in individual-level decision making. For instance, one such approach tries to capture individual differences in reflection by asking study participants to provide "meta-cognitions" about how much they rely on their intuitions to make decisions (Haran, Ritov, and Mellers, 2013; Heintzelman and King, 2016). We believe our measurement approach offers advantages compared to this measure, and some others, because it creates a wide range of possible states of reflection as opposed to blunt categorization schemes (see Figure 7.3), and our approach does not rely on subjects to self-report pertinent information regarding their decision-making processes, which strikes us as susceptible to bias.

Our first inclination to improve the measurement of reflection in the context of our framework would be to develop domain-specific, unobtrusive measures of System 1 forcefulness and System 2 engagement. We purposely began with domain-general measures of how people attend to information because we wanted to avoid confounding our operationalization of System 1 forcefulness and System 2 engagement with political attributes, such as ideology. However, taking this pathway entailed a tradeoff: less potential for bias but more potential for measurement error. After all, people have limited cognitive resources and varied interests. Some individuals with high levels of need for cognition, for instance, may really enjoy solving mental puzzles but detest thinking much about politics. We used obtrusive, explicit measures because they were validated and time-tested by psychologists, and this represents our first cut at operationalizing the important concepts in our theoretical model. Consequently, we close this chapter with a call for better measurement.

7.5 CONCLUSION

Our theoretical model enabled us to make what we believe to be two important contributions to the study of political attitude formation. First, even though every democrat and republican may be predisposed to be a motivated reasoner, some individuals are capable of harnessing thought to reach reasonable and rational decisions. Our model identifies the mechanism – the interplay between System 1 and System 2 processes – responsible for this variation in individuals' propensity for reflection. Second, partisan identities should not be considered either inherently good, because they facilitate low-rationality heuristics, or inherently bad, because they can induce a form of political tribalism. Political parties are not the enemy of democratic accountability, nor are they its guardians. Like all multifaceted political institutions, they are complicated and nuanced. Sound theoretical models should reflect that, and we believe that ours does.

In addition to contributing to the studies of partisanship, motivated reasoning, and democratic accountability, we hope our theoretical model opens new avenues of research for the study of attitude formation more generally. We join a growing field of scholars, largely in psychology and neuroscience but increasingly in the field of political psychology, to note that people's decisions are shaped in crucial and consequential ways by pre-conscious intuitions. Many people do not reason about politics so much as they intuit it. The degree to which people employ reasoning – in the sense of using their conscious mind to think and process their intuitions – and the extent to which they do so in ways that can be called "reasonable" from a normative standpoint depends on their motivational disposition to be reflective. We believe that this insight will help us push past artificial debates about rationality that populate the social sciences, especially the study of political behavior, and to focus instead on the development and refinement of theoretical models of (political) decision making that incorporate more descriptively accurate accounts of human cognition.

Appendix

Details of Empirical Studies and Statistical Analyses

2012 Campaign Study. These data came from a module placed on the 2012 Cooperative Campaign Analysis Project. The module consisted of 1,000 panelists living in the United States recruited by YouGov and interviewed in December 2011, the week just before the 2012 elections, and then again in the four weeks after the election. YouGov maintains a Census-matched Internet panel that generates nationally representative samples. We measured need for affect, need for cognition, and Big Five personality traits on the second wave of the panel. Demographics were measured on the first wave. Partisan identities were measured in the first and second waves. Voting decisions were measured in the post-election wave.

Governor Evaluation Study. In the spring of 2013, we fielded a web-based survey using Amazon's Mechanical Turk (MTurk). MTurk is an opt-in Internet survey in which participants complete brief surveys in return for monetary compensation ($0.50 in our study). Reasonable variation in the compensation rates for MTurk does not meaningfully affect the quality of the data (Buhrmester, Kwang, and Gosling, 2011). Although we cannot claim that this sample is representative of the United States, MTurk samples have not been found to differ from nationally representative samples in terms of psychological or political characteristics (Clifford, Jewell, and Waggoner, 2015), and they tend to be more diverse than student-based convenience samples (Berinsky, Huber, and Lenz, 2012; Buhrmester, Kwang, and Gosling, 2011). Our sample consisted of 661 adults living in the United States who identified with the party of their state's governor. Participants were first asked to answer a series of demographic and background questions, and then they were asked to complete the full need for affect and need for cognition batteries presented in Chapter 3. Participants were then randomly assigned to one of the conditions in the belief perseverance experiment described in Chapter 5. Of the 661 participants, 336 were randomly assigned to the shirking treatment and 325 were randomly assigned to the loyal treatment.

Emotion Processing Study. In the fall of 2014, we recruited 105 Temple University students to participate in a "visual processing study" in the Behavioral Foundations Lab, which is housed on campus. We make no claims about the representativeness of our sample but note that it is adequate for the narrow purpose we had: investigating whether need for affect and need for cognition correlate with fundamental differences in how individuals pre-consciously process emotional stimuli and the strength of affective attachments to partisan identities. With respect to the first goal, we can think of no reason why pre-conscious emotional processing would differ substantially for college students. With respect to our second goal, because college-aged students tend to have less well-formed partisan identities, we believe that using the sample works against our hypothesized associations. As we described in Chapter 3, after answering demographic questions as well as need for affect and need for cognition batteries, participants were asked to complete the partisan Implicit Attitude Test. At the end of the study, we collected participants' electrodermal activity (EDA) while they viewed a series of emotionally charged photos curated by the Center for the Study of Emotion and Attention (Lang, 1995). We measured EDA by recording participants' skin conductance level (i.e., tonic electrical conductivity) while they viewed the images using the BIOPAC MP150 data acquisition system and the AcqKnowledge 4.1 software package.

Party Cues Study. In the spring of 2015, we hired the Internet survey firm Qaultrics to administer a survey to 1,258 panelists living in the United States. Qualtrics maintains a panel and uses quota sampling methods to collect samples that approximate the national population. Participants completed demographic questions, need for affect and need for cognition batteries, and a series of questions that tap risk and loss aversion, and then they were randomly assigned to one of the conditions in the Party Cue experiments described in Chapter 4. Of the 1,088 participants who identified with (or leaned toward) one of the two major political parties, 537 were randomly assigned to participate in the low salience party cue experiment (inparty cue/proattitudinal treatment = 83, outparty cue/proattitudinal = 91, inparty/counterattitudinal = 90, outparty/counterattitudinal = 92, no cue/proattitudinal = 79, no cue/counterattitudinal = 102) and 551 were randomly assigned to participate in the high salience party cue experiment (inparty cue/proattitudinal treatment = 86, outparty cue/proattitudinal = 85, inparty/counterattitudinal = 88, outparty/counterattitudinal = 79, no cue/proattitudinal = 109, no cue/counterattitudinal = 104). Participants concluded the survey by answering questions about the two major parties and the traits of people who identify with them. Two weeks later, we recontacted 840 participants and administered the polarized rhetoric experiment described in Chapter 6. Of the 719 participants who identified with (or leaned toward) one of the two major political parties, 345 were randomly assigned to the polarized rhetoric treatment and 374 were assigned to the bipartisan rhetoric group.

Issue Polarization Study. In the summer of 2015, we hired Qualtrics to administer a survey to 1,302 panelists living in the United States. Participants answered demographics questions, need for affect and need for cognition batteries, and then a series of questions probing their opinions about political issues.

Table A.1 shows summary statistics for demographics, cognitive style measures, personality traits (where available), and political awareness (where available) for all five studies. Tables A.2, A.3, and A.4 show balance tests for the experimental studies.

TABLE A.1. *Summary Statistics for Studies*

Variable	2012 Campaign Study	Governor Study	Emotion Processing	Party Cues	Issue Polarization
Age	53.148 (14.396)	34.841 (12.478)	19.904 (2.296)	53.329 (13.851)	44.809 (16.855)
Female	0.516	0.572	0.600	0.586	0.504
White	0.742	0.802	0.581	0.866	0.816
Education	3.532 (1.504)	4.165 (1.278)	3.552 (0.930)	3.895 (1.455)	3.647 (1.389)
Income	5.319 (3.544)	4.495 (2.229)	5.524 (2.477)	4.885 (2.390)	4.273 (2.241)
Partisan Identification	3.725 (2.303)	4.851 (2.375)	2.825 (1.876)	3.755 (2.299)	3.861 (2.002)
Partisan	2.060 (1.064)	2.471 (0.500)	1.959 (1.020)	2.051 (1.066)	1.658 (1.129)
Conservatism	3.246 (1.144)	2.621 (1.263)	3.010 (1.522)	3.516 (1.569)	3.541 (1.321)
Political Awareness	0.693 (0.281)			2.692 (1.121)	
Openness	0.000 (0.568)		3.833 (0.616)		
Neuroticism	0.000 (0.735)		2.764 (0.827)		
Extroversion	0.000 (0.658)		3.393 (0.803)		
Conscientiousness	0.000 (0.613)		3.440 (0.690)		
Agreeableness	0.000 (0.531)		4.031 (0.731)		
Need for Affect	0.350 (0.811)	-0.022 (0.460)	-0.433 (0.739)	-0.168 (0.635)	-0.019 (0.532)
Need for Cognition	0.312 (0.851)	0.209 (0.584)	-0.272 (0.756)	0.064 (0.596)	0.152 (0.528)
N	1000	661	105	1258	1302

Means (proportions in the case of *female* and *white*) in cells and standard deviations in parentheses.

TABLE A.2. *Balance Tests for the Belief Preservation and Polarized Rhetoric Experiments*

	Belief Preservation Experiment Shirking Treatment	Polarized Rhetoric Experiment Polarized Prime Treatment
Age	0.000	−0.001
	(0.002)	(0.001)
Female	0.076	0.014
	(0.042)	(0.036)
White	−0.069	0.036
	(0.052)	(0.056)
Education	−0.013	0.000
	(0.016)	(0.013)
Income	−0.004	−0.033
	(0.009)	(0.008)
Party Identification	0.011	−0.013
	(0.016)	(0.011)
Partisan	0.001	0.004
	(0.041)	(0.016)
Conservatism	0.036	0.020
	(0.030)	(0.016)
Need for Affect	0.072	0.024
	(0.046)	(0.030)
Need for Cognition	−0.021	0.045
	(0.037)	(0.032)
Political Awareness		0.020
		(0.017)
Constant	0.448	0.549
	(0.204)	(0.114)
N	645	840
F	1.19	2.4
Adjusted R^2	0.003	0.018

OLS coefficients in cells and standard errors in parentheses.

TABLE A.3. *Balance Tests for the Low Salience Issue Party Cue Experiment*

	Inparty Cue Proattitudinal	Outparty Cue Proattitudinal	Inparty Cue Counterattitudinal	Outparty Cue Counterattitudinal	No Cue Proattitudinal
Age	-0.016	0.006	-0.005	-0.011	0.009
	(0.012)	(0.012)	(0.011)	(0.011)	(0.012)
Female	-0.308	-0.110	-0.330	-0.360	-0.032
	(0.321)	(0.318)	(0.316)	(0.310)	(0.333)
White	0.602	0.558	0.496	0.252	0.242
	(0.455)	(0.469)	(0.436)	(0.424)	(0.461)
Education	0.029	0.094	0.005	0.013	-0.063
	(0.117)	(0.114)	(0.115)	(0.113)	(0.117)
Income	0.023	0.047	-0.048	-0.047	0.020
	(0.068)	(0.067)	(0.067)	(0.066)	(0.070)
Party Identification	-0.095	-0.089	-0.013	-0.053	0.007
	(0.099)	(0.096)	(0.095)	(0.095)	(0.098)
Partisan	-0.058	-0.062	-0.354	0.106	-0.008
	(0.202)	(0.196)	(0.196)	(0.200)	(0.207)
Conservatism	0.221	0.350	-0.020	0.282	0.160
	(0.152)	(0.149)	(0.144)	(0.147)	(0.152)

Need for Affect	−0.168	−0.204	−0.312	−0.089	−0.181
	(0.145)	(0.142)	(0.139)	(0.142)	(0.146)
Need for Cognition	−0.237	−0.193	0.004	−0.201	0.218
	(0.245)	(0.246)	(0.247)	(0.242)	(0.256)
Political Awareness	0.446	0.076	−0.192	0.096	−0.161
	(0.282)	(0.275)	(0.277)	(0.273)	(0.285)
Constant	0.172	−1.679	1.875	−0.190	−0.861
	(1.081)	(1.093)	(1.045)	(1.052)	(1.120)
N	536				
$\chi^2(55)$	59.01				
Pseudo-R^2	0.03				

Multinomial logit estimates in cells and standard errors in parentheses. No cue/counterattitudinal treatment is the excluded category.

TABLE A.4. *Balance Tests for the High Salience Issue Party Cue Experiment*

	Inparty Cue Proattitudinal	Outparty Cue Proattitudinal	Inparty Cue Counterattitudinal	Outparty Cue Counterattitudinal	No Cue Proattitudinal
Age	0.003	−0.005	−0.005	−0.027	−0.014
	(0.011)	(0.011)	(0.011)	(0.012)	(0.010)
Female	0.192	−0.288	−0.523	−1.020	−0.120
	(0.319)	(0.312)	(0.309)	(0.323)	(0.296)
White	0.466	0.491	0.840	0.537	−0.025
	(0.466)	(0.454)	(0.479)	(0.453)	(0.391)
Education	0.026	−0.067	0.004	−0.305	−0.071
	(0.114)	(0.115)	(0.115)	(0.122)	(0.108)
Income	−0.010	0.025	−0.003	0.050	0.030
	(0.067)	(0.068)	(0.067)	(0.070)	(0.063)
Party Identification	0.083	−0.082	−0.057	−0.126	0.016
	(0.093)	(0.095)	(0.094)	(0.098)	(0.088)
Partisan	0.171	−0.081	−0.113	−0.104	−0.020
	(0.209)	(0.204)	(0.203)	(0.215)	(0.193)
Conservatism	−0.051	0.075	0.045	0.088	−0.034
	(0.140)	(0.139)	(0.139)	(0.142)	(0.130)

	(1)	(2)	(3)	(4)
Need for Affect	-0.029	-0.105	-0.088	0.089
	(0.152)	(0.149)	(0.155)	(0.144)
Need for Cognition	0.024	0.088	0.270	0.156
	(0.256)	(0.253)	(0.260)	(0.240)
Political Awareness	0.034	0.395	0.540	0.200
	(0.274)	(0.273)	(0.287)	(0.260)
Constant	-1.409	0.254	2.771	0.910
	(1.101)	(1.074)	(1.080)	(0.997)
N	552			
$\chi^2(55)$	54.81			
Pseudo-R^2	0.03			

Multinomial logit estimates in cells and standard errors in parentheses. No cue/counterattitudinal treatment is the excluded category.

A.2 MEASURING NEED FOR AFFECT AND NEED FOR COGNITION AND MODEL ESTIMATION STRATEGY

We use the Bayesian ordinal factor analysis model proposed by (Martin, Quinn, and Park, 2013) to estimate scores for each respondent along separate need for affect and need for cognition scales. This approach accounts for the internal consistency of the response items by explicitly accounting for error in both estimating the latent variables and in modeling their effects. The method simulates from the joint posterior distribution of the ordinal factor analysis model shown in Equation A.1, where y_i^* is the k-vector of latent responses belonging to respondent i, Λ is the k-vector of factor loadings, ϕ_i is a single real-valued factor score, and ϵ_i is a k-vector of disturbances.[8] In this application, the value of k is equal to the number of items included in the NFC and NFA batteries (sixteen and twenty-six for the complete batteries, respectively). Factor loadings and factor scores are assumed to have independent normal priors, and the cutpoints are assumed to have improper uniform priors (Quinn, 2004). For the sake of having comparable NFC and NFA scales, we constrain the posterior means for both scales to the $[-2, 2]$ interval. The simulation relies on a Gibbs sampling algorithm and is implemented as part of the MCMCpack package (Martin, Quinn, and Park, 2013) in R (R Development Core Team, 2013).[9] This method is closely related to unidimensional Bayesian ordinal item response theory (IRT) models (Quinn, 2004; Zheng and Rabe-Hesketh, 2007; van Schuur, 2011), and we note that either method of estimating NFC and NFA scores produces substantively similar results throughout. Importantly, these methods of estimating NFC and NFA scores make full use of the ordered, polytomous responses, and therefore we do not unnecessarily discard information.

$$y_i^* = \Lambda\phi_i + \epsilon_i, \text{ with } \epsilon_i \sim \mathcal{N}(0, I) \qquad (A.1)$$

To generate the need for affect and need for cognition estimates, we set the number of discarded (i.e., burn-in) iterations at 50,000 and the number of Markov chain Monte Carlo (MCMC) iterations at 5,000,000. We store (i.e., thin) every 500th iteration to produce a total of 10,000 posterior factor score estimates for each respondent for each of the NFC and NFA scales separately. Using various diagnostics (e.g., the Geweke [1992] and Heidelberger and Welch [1983] convergence diagnostics), we confirm that each chain achieved stationarity and was well mixed.

Throughout the manuscript, we introduce various models that estimate the effect of individual differences in reflection on the dependent variable. The basic structure of the equations is shown in Equation A.2. We offer more specific details regarding the model specification for each statistical test in the results appearing in Section 6 of the Appendix.

$$\text{DepVar} = \alpha + \beta_1 \text{NFC}_j + \beta_2 \text{NFA}_j + \beta_3 \text{NFC}_j \times \text{NFA}_j + [\delta z'] + \epsilon \quad (A.2)$$

NFC_j denotes the respondent's score on the need for cognition scale randomly drawn from his or her posterior distribution on the jth iteration of model estimation, NFA_j is similarly the respondent's score on the need for affect scale randomly drawn from his or her posterior distribution on the jth iteration, and $\text{NFC}_j \times \text{NFA}_j$ is the interaction of these terms constructed on the jth iteration. We include the interaction of the NFC and NFA measures to account for the possibility that the scales are correlated with one another (Maio and Esses, 2001). We also include in the models a number of socio-demographic, partisan, and ideological characteristics (represented by the vector of variables **z** with corresponding vector of coefficients δ in Equation A.2). Specifically, we include variables that account for the respondent's partisan affiliation, age, education, gender, income, race, level of conservatism, Big Five personality traits (when available), and political awareness (when available).

Where theoretically appropriate, we also interact NFC_j, NFA_j, and $\text{NFC}_j \times \text{NFA}_j$ with other variables (e.g., partisanship, treatment, etc.) to examine how those factors moderate the effect of reflection. In order to get a sense of how we model the interaction between experimental treatments and measures of reflection, we offer an example that comes from the Governor Evaluation study, shown in Equation A.3. We estimate this particular model using a multilevel linear model, where the dependent variable measures the real change in a respondent's likelihood of voting for his or her governor, measured as the post-disclosure value less the pre-disclosure value. Positive values for the dependent variable represent an increase in assessments from pre- to post-disclosure. The PD indicator identifies those respondents who were randomly assigned the positive disclosure treatment. This variable is then interacted with the aforementioned variables to capture any differences in the effects of NFC and NFA (individually and jointly) on changes in assessments across the treatments. In this model, we include random intercepts for states to account for differences in political environments and gubernatorial personalities.

$$\Delta \text{Attitude} = \alpha_m + \beta_1 \text{PD} + \beta_2 \text{NFC}_j + \beta_3 \text{NFA}_j + \beta_4 \text{NFC}_j \times \text{NFA}_j \quad (\text{A.3})$$
$$+ \beta_5 \text{NFC}_j \times \text{PD} + \beta_6 \text{NFA}_j \times \text{PD} + \beta_7 \text{NFC}_j$$
$$\times \text{NFA}_j \times \text{PD} + [\delta z'] + \epsilon$$
$$\alpha_m \sim N(\mu_\alpha, \sigma_\alpha^2) \text{ for } m \in \{1, \ldots, 50\} \text{ states}$$
$$\text{for } j \in \{1, 2, \ldots, 10000\} \text{ iterations}$$

To estimate the models, with general structure shown in Equation A.2, we adapt the Monte Carlo procedure detailed by Treier and Jackman (2008).[10] Specifically, we estimate the model 10,000 times, each time randomly sampling a factor score estimate from each respondent's NFC and NFA posterior distributions. After each iteration, we store the coefficient estimates for the NFC and NFA variables (and their interactions) and sample all other coefficients (for variables without posterior densities) from the multivariate normal distribution with mean equal to the vector of all estimated coefficients and variance equal to the estimated variance-covariance matrix. By randomly sampling from the NFC and NFA posterior distributions in each iteration of the model estimation, this modeling approach accounts for the uncertainty that we capture in the estimation of the latent NFC and NFA traits. Therefore, this modeling technique overcomes the errors-in-variables problem that results from assuming that latent traits are measured with perfect certainty. We note that using a frequentist specification of the models, in which NFC and NFA are measured using deterministic factor scores, generally yields substantively similar results to those using the approach detailed above. Even though the results of the Bayesian and frequentist models are usually substantively similar, the Bayesian specification is more appropriate given the empirical demands of the analysis. Although it surely has its merits, model simplicity should not lead us to favor a simple model to a more complex one when the latter is, indeed, more appropriate for the problem at hand (Neal, 1996; Gelman, 2009).

A.3 QUESTION WORDING FOR COVARIATES

TABLE A.5. *Question Wording for Big Five Traits*

Extraversion

- I am the life of the party.
- I feel comfortable around people.
- I don't talk a lot. (Inverse Scale)
- I keep in the background. (Inverse Scale)

Agreeableness

- I sympathize with others' feelings.
- I am interested in people.
- I insult people. (Inverse Scale)
- I am not really interested in others. (Inverse Scale)

Conscientiousness

- I am always prepared.
- I pay attention to details.
- I make a mess of things. (Inverse Scale)
- I leave my belongings around. (Inverse Scale)

Neuroticism

- I am relaxed most of the time.
- I seldom feel blue.
- I get stressed out easily. (Inverse Scale)
- I worry about things. (Inverse Scale)

Openness

- I have a rich vocabulary.
- I have a vivid imagination.
- I have difficulty understanding abstract ideas. (Inverse Scale)
- I am not interested in abstract ideas. (Inverse Scale)

TABLE A.6. *Question Wording for Demographic Controls*

Democrat
- Generally speaking, do you usually think of yourself as a …
  Options: "Republican," "Democrat," "Independent," "Libertarian," and "Other. Please describe in the space below"
  Note: If respondents selected a "Republican" or "Democrat," they were asked a follow-up question regarding the strength of their partisanship. If respondents selected "Independent" or "Libertarian," they were asked whether they considered themselves to be closer to one of the two majority parties (or neither).

Age
- In what year were you born?
  Options: Every year after 1914

Education
- What was the last level of schooling you completed?
  Options: "Less than high school graduate," "High school graduate," "Some college," "Currently a college student," "College graduate," and "Post college degree"

Female
- What is your gender?
  Options: "Male" and "Female"

Income
- We want to classify people into broad income groups only. This information is completely confidential.
  Please indicate the category that corresponds to your family's situation.
  Options: "Under $15,000," "Between $15,000 and $24,999," "Between $25,000 and $34,999," "Between $35,000 and $49,999," "Between $50,000 and $64,999," "Between $65,000 and $79,999," "Between $80,000 and $99,999," "Between $100,000 and $149,999," "Between $150,000 and $199,999," and "Over $200,000"

White
- What general racial or ethnic category do you consider yourself?
  Options: "Black," "White," "Latino/a or 'Hispanic,'" "Asian," "Native American," and "Other"

Conservatism
- Do you consider yourself …
  Options: "Very Liberal," "Liberal," "Somewhat Liberal," "Moderate," "Somewhat Conservative," "Conservative," and "Very Conservative"

A.4 IMAGE-LEVEL CORRELATIONS WITH NFC/NFA AND DISTRIBUTIONAL ANALYSIS

TABLE A.7. *Image-Level Correlations with Need for Affect and Need for Cognition*

	Need for Cognition (NFC)	Need for Affect (NFA)
Mundane:		
Image 1 (Spoon)	[−0.215,0.182]	[−0.210,0.187]
Image 2 (Basket)	[−0.231,0.165]	[−0.109,0.285]
Exciting:		
Image 1 (Ski Jump)	[−0.098,0.296]	[−0.257,0.140]
Image 2 (Sky Diving)	[−0.376,0.007]	[−0.184,0.213]
Happy:		
Image 1 (Cute Puppies)	[−0.322,0.068]	[−0.403,−0.025]
Image 2 (Island Paradise)	[−0.127,0.267]	[−0.124,0.271]
Sad:		
Image 1 (Cemetery)	[−0.333,0.056]	[−0.334,0.055]
Image 2 (Crying Child)	[−0.214,0.183]	[−0.185,0.212]
Image 3 (Disabled Child)	[−0.132,0.263]	[−0.235,0.161]
Threatening:		
Image 1 (9/11 Attacks)	[−0.225,0.171]	[−0.261,0.134]
Image 2 (Ferocious Dog)	[−0.354,0.032]	[−0.133,0.263]
Image 3 (Snake)	[−0.300,0.092]	[−0.333,0.056]

Note: 95 Percent Confidence Intervals for Image-Level Correlations with NFC and NFA.

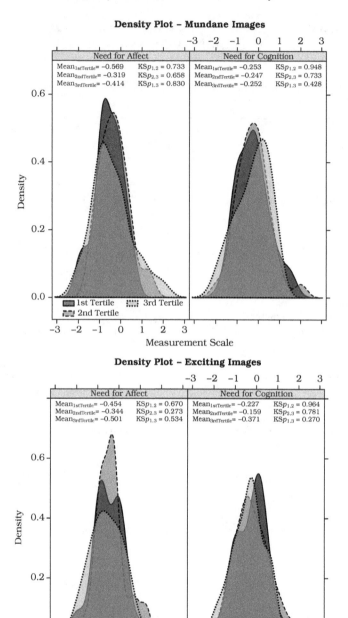

FIGURE A.1. Distributional Comparison of NFC/NFA across Tertiles of Emotional Respones

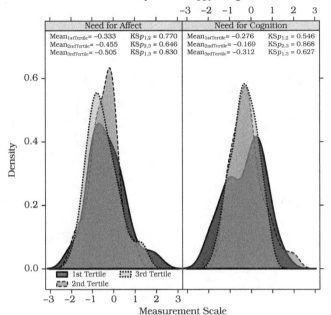

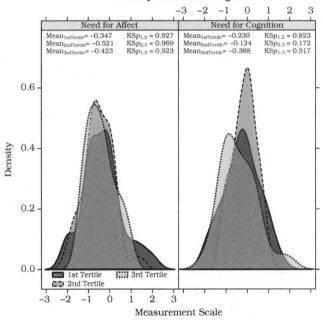

FIGURE A.1. *continued*

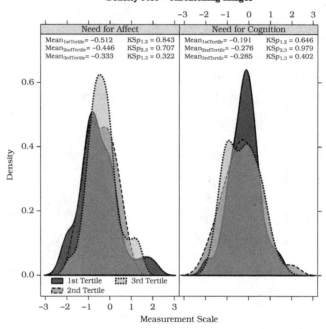

FIGURE A.1. *continued*

A.5 IMPLICIT PARTISAN AFFECT TEST PREDICTIONS

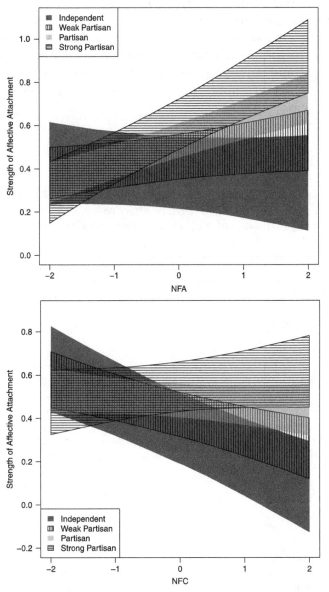

FIGURE A.2. Associations between Need for Affect, Need for Cognition, and Implicit Partisan Affective Attachment for Strong Partisans, Leaning Partisans, Weak Partisans, and Independents, Emotion Processing Study

A.6 STATISTICAL TABLES

The following tables provide the model results that generate the corresponding predictions appearing in the text. For more detail on the estimation process, refer to Section 2 of the Appendix. Note that trivial (i.e., nonsubstantive) variation in results is expected across successive estimations of the models since model estimates are simulated using a Gibbs sampling algorithm. Throughout the tables, the standard deviations of the posterior coefficient distributions are shown in parentheses, which are analogous to standard errors.

A.6.1 Chapter 3 Tables

TABLE A.8. *Associations between Need for Affect, Need for Cognition, and Implicit Partisan Affective Attachment for Strong Partisans and Independents, Emotion Processing Study*

	Coefficient (S.D.)
Need for Cognition (NFC)	−0.0809
	(0.0453)
Need for Affect (NFA)	0.0130
	(0.0437)
NFC × NFA	0.1284
	(0.0601)
Strength of Party ID (SPID)	0.0832
	(0.0559)
NFC × SPID	0.0301
	(0.0219)
NFA × SPID	0.0426
	(0.0238)
NFC × NFA × SPID	0.0624
	(0.0328)
Democrat	0.0739
	(0.1400)
Age	−0.0109
	(0.0211)
Education	0.0374
	(0.0502)
Female	−0.1195
	(0.0906)

TABLE A.8. *continued*

	Coefficient (S.D.)
Income	−0.0162
	(0.0205)
White	0.0651
	(0.0923)
Conservatism	0.0289
	(0.0379)
Extraversion	0.0002
	(0.0609)
Agreeableness	−0.0020
	(0.0655)
Conscientiousness	0.0020
	(0.0607)
Neuroticism	0.0763
	(0.0554)
Openness	−0.0016
	(0.0909)
Constant	0.6457
	(0.7851)
Number of Respondents	96
Iterations	10,000
Model	OLS

TABLE A.9. *Need for Affect and Need for Cognition Predict Performance on the Cognitive Reflection Task, Party Cues Study*

	Coefficient (S.D.)
Need for Cognition (NFC)	0.2434
	(0.0212)
Need for Affect (NFA)	−0.0471
	(0.0234)
NFC × NFA	−0.0721
	(0.0327)
Democrat	−0.3294
	(0.1073)
Age	−0.0058
	(0.0028)

TABLE A.9. *continued*

	Coefficient (S.D.)
Education	0.1052
	(0.0295)
Female	−0.2586
	(0.0766)
Income	0.0480
	(0.0165)
White	0.1363
	(0.1212)
Conservatism	−0.0387
	(0.0337)
Political Awareness	0.2027
	(0.0393)
Constant	−1.0102
	(0.2774)
Number of Respondents	1,258
Iterations	10,000
Model	Negative Binomial

TABLE A.10. *Associations between Need for Affect, Need for Cognition, and Risk Optimization, Party Cues Study*

	Prefer Certainty	Risk Seeking	Payout Maximizing
	Coefficient (S.D.)		
Need for Cognition (NFC)	0.1261	0.0364	0.4466
	(0.0372)	(0.0593)	(0.0917)
Need for Affect (NFA)	−0.0526	−0.0187	−0.2297
	(0.0360)	(0.0577)	(0.0865)
NFC × NFA	−0.0147	−0.4218	−0.5009
	(0.0491)	(0.0958)	(0.1384)
Democrat	0.0350	−0.2477	−0.1975
	(0.1651)	(0.2753)	(0.3947)
Age	−0.0086	−0.0191	−0.0184
	(0.0046)	(0.0077)	(0.0112)
Education	−0.0017	0.1228	0.6176
	(0.1349)	(0.2263)	(0.3313)
Female	0.4200	−0.0278	−0.3555
	(0.1320)	(0.2120)	(0.3150)

TABLE A.10. *continued*

	Prefer Certainty	Risk Seeking	Payout Maximizing
	Coefficient (S.D.)		
Income	0.0008	0.2443	0.1091
	(0.1330)	(0.2168)	(0.3183)
White	0.4105	−0.1937	0.9679
	(0.1931)	(0.2852)	(0.5549)
Conservatism	0.0112	−0.0903	−0.1213
	(0.0506)	(0.0847)	(0.1238)
Political Awareness	0.0846	0.1442	−0.7525
	(0.1365)	(0.2292)	(0.3303)
Cognitive Reflection	−0.1997	0.1300	−0.2475
Test Accuracy	(0.0694)	(0.1025)	(0.1683)
Constant	−0.1278	−0.2477	−1.4694
	(0.3883)	(0.6051)	(0.9597)
Number of Respondents	1,256		
Iterations	10,000		
Model	Multinomial Logit		

Note: The baseline outcome category used is "Loss Averse."

A.6.2 Chapter 4 Tables

TABLE A.11. *The Effects of Party Cues versus Policy Information on Low (Environmental Policy) and High (Medicaid Policy) Salience Issues, Party Cues Study*

	Environmental Policy (Low Salience)	Medicaid Policy (High Salience)
	Coefficient (S.D.)	
Need for Cognition (NFC)	0.3640	−0.0354
	(0.1239)	(0.1010)
Need for Affect (NFA)	0.0432	0.0665
	(0.1179)	(0.1053)
NFC × NFA	−0.4703	−0.7346
	(0.1873)	(0.1563)

TABLE A.11. *continued*

	Environmental Policy (Low Salience)	Medicaid Policy (High Salience)
Proattitudinal Treatment (PT)	0.6511	0.4447
	(0.3137)	(0.2498)
NFC × PT	−0.2727	0.2692
	(0.1663)	(0.1262)
NFA × PT	0.1300	0.1515
	(0.1599)	(0.1278)
NFC × NFA × PT	0.1285	0.3813
	(0.2590)	(0.1986)
Inparty Cue (InParty)	−0.6804	−0.0269
	(0.3199)	(0.2729)
OutParty Cue (OutParty)	−0.1529	−0.2081
	(0.3214)	(0.2814)
NFC × InParty	−0.3225	0.4414
	(0.1669)	(0.1442)
NFA × InParty	−0.5705	0.1106
	(0.1771)	(0.1455)
NFC × NFA × InParty	0.6922	0.0876
	(0.2583)	(0.2288)
PT × InParty	0.7841	−0.3197
	(0.4772)	(0.3821)
NFC × PT × InParty	0.7691	−0.5279
	(0.2483)	(0.2078)
NFA × PT × InParty	0.4825	0.2665
	(0.2640)	(0.2004)
NFC × NFA × PT × InParty	−0.8480	0.5607
	(0.3831)	(0.2899)
NFC × OutParty	−0.0050	0.8743
	(0.1949)	(0.1448)
NFA × OutParty	0.3380	−0.4467
	(0.1694)	(0.1495)
NFC × NFA × OutParty	0.9771	0.1371
	(0.3123)	(0.2067)
PT × OutParty	0.2929	0.1322
	(0.4525)	(0.3772)
NFC × PT × OutParty	0.5182	−0.6083
	(0.2453)	(0.2023)
NFA × PT × OutParty	−1.0928	0.1511
	(0.2406)	(0.2043)

TABLE A.11. *continued*

	Environmental Policy (Low Salience)	Medicaid Policy (High Salience)
NFC × NFA × PT × OutParty	−1.1056	−0.7440
	(0.4252)	(0.3629)
Controls	Yes	Yes
Constant	3.2180	4.4728
	(0.5741)	(0.4867)
Number of Respondents	534	551
Iterations	10,000	10,000
Model	OLS	OLS

Note: Control variables are included in the model estimation, but suppressed here to conserve space. Control variables are consistent with other models, and include Democrat, Age, Education, Female, Income, White, Conservatism, and Political Awareness.

TABLE A.12. *The Relationship between Weakening Partisan Identity and Need for Affect and Need for Cognition, 2012 Campaign Study*

	Coefficient (S.D.)
Need for Cognition (NFC)	0.3385
	(0.0964)
Need for Affect (NFA)	−0.2759
	(0.1258)
NFC × NFA	0.1189
	(0.0970)
Democrat$_{t+1}$	0.5937
	(0.4629)
Age	−0.0121
	(0.0121)
Education	−0.0147
	(0.1201)
Female	0.4833
	(0.3467)
Income	0.0546
	(0.0483)

TABLE A.12. *continued*

	Coefficient (S.D.)
White	−0.1653
	(0.3576)
Conservatism$_{t+1}$	0.2708
	(0.1816)
Political Awareness	−0.7510
	(0.6727)
Extraversion	−0.0902
	(0.2450)
Agreeableness	0.0550
	(0.3477)
Conscientiousness	0.0356
	(0.2928)
Neuroticism	0.0604
	(0.2478)
Openness	0.2130
	(0.3196)
Constant	−3.4478
	(1.1962)
Number of Respondents	844
Iterations	10,000
Model	Logit

A.6.3 Chapter 5 Tables

TABLE A.13. *Predicted Change in Evaluation of Governor by Low-NFC/High-NFA and High-NFC/Low-NFA Participants, Governor Evaluation Study*

	Coefficient (S.D.)	
Positive Disclosure [PD]	9.4599	9.3717
	(1.4500)	(1.4654)
Need for Cognition [NFC]	−0.4778	−0.3807
	(0.3418)	(0.3598)
Need for Affect [NFA]	2.9943	2.5158
	(0.7370)	(0.7565)
NFC × NFA	−1.3030	−0.8508
	(0.8866)	(0.8925)

TABLE A.13. *continued*

	Coefficient (S.D.)	
NFC × PD	3.3110	3.0869
	(0.6736)	(0.6894)
NFA × PD	−1.8430	−1.6203
	(1.0448)	(1.0661)
NFC × NFA × PD	2.0302	2.0320
	(1.2672)	(1.2831)
Democrat		−1.0331
		(2.4818)
Age		−0.0372
		(0.0568)
Education		−0.0513
		(0.5594)
Female		1.6038
		(1.4294)
Income		0.3113
		(0.3147)
White		1.3469
		(1.7749)
Conservatism		0.0876
		(0.9442)
Constant	−1.5232	−3.2892
	(1.1004)	(5.5538)
State Random Intercepts	Yes	Yes
Number of Respondents	658	645
Iterations	10,000	10,000
Model	Mixed Effects	Mixed Effects

TABLE A.14. *Shifts in Economic Perceptions from 2000 to 2004 with Covariates, American National Election Panel Study*

	Got Worse	Stayed Bad	Stayed Good	Got Better
	Coefficient (S.D.)			
Democrats	*Omitted (Baseline)*			
Independents	−1.3590	0.2912	−0.7441	−0.1505
	(0.3329)	(0.4282)	(0.5929)	(0.5512)
Republicans	−1.6430	−0.0109	−0.1808	1.6188
	(0.2341)	(0.3462)	(0.3334)	(0.3049)

TABLE A.14. *continued*

	Got Worse	Stayed Bad	Stayed Good	Got Better
	Coefficient (S.D.)			
Age	0.0040	−0.0135	−0.0018	0.0031
	(0.0064)	(0.0106)	(0.0105)	(0.0079)
Education	−0.0289	−0.0150	0.1518	0.2579
	(0.0715)	(0.1150)	(0.1105)	(0.0811)
Female	0.3388	0.7116	0.5269	0.1479
	(02151)	(0.3387)	(0.3435)	(0.2491)
Income	0.0610	−0.0166	0.0637	0.0561
	(0.0401)	(0.0689)	(0.0587)	(0.0420)
White	−0.8713	−0.8288	−0.0950	−0.3936
	(0.2512)	(0.3676)	(0.4689)	(0.3464)
Political Knowledge F.E.	Yes	Yes	Yes	Yes
Constant	0.8863	−0.6251	−2.9284	−3.1487
	(0.5114)	(0.8273)	(0.8944)	(0.6855)
Number of Respondents	723			
Model	Multinomial Logit			

Note: The baseline outcome category used is "Stayed Same."

TABLE A.15. *The Effect of Shifts in Monthly Unemployment on Change in Approval of President Obama, The American Panel Survey 2011–2015*

	Democrats		Republicans	
	High NFC/Low NFA	High NFA/Low NFC	High NFC/Low NFA	High NFA/Low NFC
	Coefficient (S.D.)		Coefficient (S.D.)	
Change in Unemployment	−0.6545	−1.0315	−0.4598	1.4310
	(0.3878)	(0.5190)	(0.3233)	(0.7183)
Change in Afghanistan Casualties	−0.0039	0.0026	−0.0009	−0.0031
	(0.0076)	(0.0102)	(0.0064)	(0.0142)
Obama's Duration in Office	0.0054	0.0035	0.0050	0.0007
	(0.0071)	(0.0094)	(0.0059)	(0.0131)
Election Year	−0.0245	−0.0630	−0.0450	0.1722
	(0.1354)	(0.1812)	(0.1129)	(0.2508)
Second Year	−0.2655	−0.1749	−0.2231	0.0247
	(0.2281)	(0.3053)	(0.1902)	(0.4226)
Constant	−0.1585	−0.1286	−0.1373	−0.0429
	(0.3201)	(0.4284)	(0.2668)	(0.5930)
Number of Respondents	39		39	
Model	OLS		OLS	

TABLE A.16. *The Relationship between Straight-Ticket Voting and Need for Affect and Need for Cognition, 2012 Campaign Study*

	Coefficient (S.D.)
Need for Cognition (NFC)	−0.3949
	(0.1325)
Need for Affect (NFA)	−0.0149
	(0.1618)
NFC × NFA	0.0828
	(0.1455)
Democrat$_{t+1}$	1.4441
	(0.5839)
Age	−0.0054
	(0.0151)
Education	−0.1772
	(0.1495)
Female	0.1229
	(0.4428)
Income	−0.0637
	(0.0597)
White	−0.3178
	(0.5513)
Conservatism$_{t+1}$	0.3169
	(0.2373)
Political Awareness	3.5292
	(0.8312)
Extraversion	0.1579
	(0.3055)
Agreeableness	0.4928
	(0.4225)
Conscientiousness	0.2990
	(0.3760)
Neuroticism	−0.2763
	(0.2960)
Openness	0.0835
	(0.3966)
Constant	0.1238
	(1.5499)
Number of Respondents	474
Iterations	10,000
Model	Logit

A.6.4 Chapter 6 Tables

TABLE A.17. *Reflection and Issue Polarization, 2012 Campaign Study and Issue Polarization Study*

	2012 Campaign Study		Issue Polarization Study
		Coefficient (S.D.)	
Need for Cognition (NFC)	0.0100	0.0058	0.0187
	(0.0039)	(0.0041)	(0.0035)
Need for Affect (NFA)	−0.0003	−0.0026	0.0113
	(0.0046)	(0.0048)	(0.0039)
NFC × NFA	−0.0004	−0.0002	−0.0178
	(0.0044)	(0.0044)	(0.0048)
Age	0.0012	0.0011	0.0010
	(0.0005)	(0.0005)	(0.0003)
Education	0.0035	0.0036	0.0076
	(0.0051)	(0.0052)	(0.0035)
Female	−0.0067	−0.0081	−0.0234
	(0.0144)	(0.0148)	(0.0091)
Income	0.0025	0.0019	0.0031
	(0.0020)	(0.0021)	(0.0021)
White	−0.0051	0.0033	0.0164
	(0.0158)	(0.0164)	(0.0117)
Conservatism	−0.0123	−0.0125	−0.0107
	(0.0059)	(0.0060)	(0.0033)
Political Awareness	0.2745	0.2595	
	(0.0289)	(0.0293)	
Extraversion		−0.0050	
		(0.0107)	
Agreeableness		0.0119	
		(0.0151)	
Conscientiousness		0.0045	
		(0.0127)	
Neuroticism		−0.0238	
		(0.0108)	
Openness		0.0100	
		(0.0134)	
Constant	0.5620	0.5757	0.5661
	(0.0403)	(0.0422)	(0.0230)
Number of Respondents	825	849	1,006
Iterations	10,000	10,000	10,000
Model	OLS	OLS	OLS

TABLE A.18. *Reflection and Affective Polarization, Party Cues Study*

	InParty Equation	OutParty Equation
	Coefficient (S.D.)	
Need for Cognition (NFC)	1.2557	−0.6985
	(0.4143)	(0.3661)
Need for Affect (NFA)	3.3683	−2.7789
	(0.4087)	(0.3683)
NFC × NFA	−0.4838	3.9149
	(0.5530)	(0.5236)
Democrat	−0.2479	1.1653
	(2.1553)	(1.8579)
Age	0.0990	−0.1661
	(0.0533)	(0.0457)
Education	−0.4993	0.0450
	(0.5460)	(0.4615)
Female	1.2597	1.4598
	(1.4926)	(1.2462)
Income	−0.0901	0.0033
	(0.3213)	(0.2738)
White	−6.6478	−0.7362
	(2.1487)	(1.8547)
Conservatism	−1.9109	0.3452
	(0.6615)	(0.5695)
Political Awareness	−1.8542	
	(0.6943)	
Constant	78.6468	22.7987
	(5.4642)	(4.6115)
Number of Respondents	1,085	1,083
Iterations	10,000	10,000
Model	SUR	SUR

Note: Political awareness is suppressed in the second equation to improve efficiency in the seemingly unrelated regression model. Estimating the equations as separate (independent) regression models does not substantively effect the results.

TABLE A.19. *Reflection and Attribution of Personality Traits to Inparty and Outparty Members, Party Cues Study*

	InParty Model		OutParty Model	
	Positive Equation	Negative Equation	Positive Equation	Negative Equation
	Coefficient (S.D.)			
Need for Cognition (NFC)	0.0200	0.0038	0.0163	0.0133
	(0.0052)	(0.0028)	(0.0031)	(0.0058)
Need for Affect (NFA)	0.0452	−0.0031	−0.0007	0.0357
	(0.0051)	(0.0027)	(0.0029)	(0.0056)
NFC × NFA	−0.0218	−0.0059	0.0089	−0.0392
	(0.0072)	(0.0039)	(0.0044)	(0.0078)
Democrat	0.0771	−0.0455	−0.0249	0.1199
	(0.0267)	(0.0147)	(0.0153)	(0.0294)
Age	0.0021	−0.0005	−0.0002	0.0016
	(0.0007)	(0.0004)	(0.0004)	(0.0007)
Education	−0.0090	0.0036	0.0069	−0.0152
	(0.0069)	(0.0037)	(0.0040)	(0.0073)
Female	−0.0015	−0.0156	0.0054	−0.0473
	(0.0185)	(0.0101)	(0.0106)	(0.0200)
Income	−0.0011	0.0014	0.0002	0.0012
	(0.0040)	(0.0022)	(0.0023)	(0.0044)

(continued)

TABLE A.19. *continued*

	InParty Model		OutParty Model	
	Positive Equation	Negative Equation	Positive Equation	Negative Equation
	Coefficient (S.D.)			
White	-0.0381	-0.0397	-0.0033	-0.0633
	(0.0268)	(0.0147)	(0.0155)	(0.0298)
Conservatism	-0.0005	0.0002	-0.0008	-0.0005
	(0.0081)	(0.0045)	(0.0047)	(0.0091)
Political Awareness	-0.0009		-0.0129	
	(0.0086)		(0.0049)	
Constant	0.4278	0.1344	0.1218	0.5264
	(0.0682)	(0.0373)	(0.0394)	(0.0746)
Number of Respondents	1,088	1,088	1,088	1,088
Iterations	10,000	10,000	10,000	10,000
Model	SUR	SUR	SUR	SUR

Note: Political awareness is suppressed in the second equation to improve efficiency in the seemingly unrelated regression model. Estimating the equations as separate (independent) regression models does not substantively effect the results.

TABLE A.20. *Reflection and the Effect of Polarized Rhetoric on Anger, Party Cues Study*

	Coefficient (S.D.)
Need for Cognition (NFC)	−1.8366
	(0.6280)
Need for Affect (NFA)	−4.2579
	(0.6660)
NFC × NFA	3.0267
	(1.1392)
Polarized Rhetoric Treatment (PRT)	43.3870
	(2.4257)
NFC × PRT	1.5559
	(1.1718)
NFA × PRT	6.8235
	(1.2603)
NFC × NFA × PRT	−4.1988
	(2.0030)
Democrat	−8.5145
	(3.2431)
Age	0.0950
	(0.0859)
Education	−0.5710
	(0.8456)
Female	−5.5280
	(2.3107)
Income	0.0629
	(0.4983)
White	3.7667
	(3.4840)
Conservatism	1.0196
	(1.0021)
Political Awareness	−2.3256
	(1.0920)
Constant	17.3912
	(8.5274)
Number of Respondents	710
Iterations	10,000
Model	OLS

A.6.5 Chapter 7 Tables

TABLE A.21. *Relationship between House District-Level Need for Affect and Need for Cognition and Punishment for Member Shirking, Party Cues Study*

	Coefficient (S.D.)
District Need for Cognition (NFC)	0.2003
	(0.0842)
District Need for Affect (NFA)	−0.2750
	(0.0711)
NFC × NFA	−0.0012
	(0.1046)
Member Shirking Level (Shirking)	−0.0849
	(0.0339)
NFC × Shirking	−0.0600
	(0.0255)
NFA × Shirking	0.0582
	(0.0187)
NFC × NFA × Shirking	−0.0250
	(0.0312)
Support for Democratic Presidential Candidate	0.0110
	(0.0067)
Median Age	−0.0079
	(0.0317)
Percent High School Graduate and Above	−0.0091
	(0.0211)
Percent Male	−0.1748
	(0.1066)
Median Household Income	−8.76e-06
	(6.99e-06)
Percent White	0.0099
	(0.0084)
Constant	10.8489
	(5.9509)
Number of Respondents	1,217
Iterations	10,000
Model	Logit

Notes

CHAPTER 1 DEMOCRATIC ACCOUNTABILITY AND THE "RATIONAL" CITIZEN

1. Franklin did not use the term "electoral democracy," preferring "republican government." We would also concede that an elitist impulse runs through the original design of governmental institutions in the United States (Hofstadter, 1989). The framers of the US Constitution were not wild-eyed, power-to-the-people democrats, after all. Nonetheless, social evolution over the nineteenth and twentieth centuries made democratic principles central to the American ethos (Aldrich, 1995), making it both relevant and essential to ask whether republican institutions are compatible with democratic ideals.

2. Although we do not think it is an accident that Thomas Hobbes shared this sentiment.

3. For the sake of clarity, when we refer to the two major political parties as organizational entities or to the political elites who affiliate with them, we capitalize the party label. For example, we write about the Democratic Party and Republican members of Congress. When we refer to ordinary citizens who choose to identify with one the major parties, we opt for lowercasing the labels democrats and republicans.

4. Rumsfeld's quote, made at a December 8, 2004, meeting with US troops stationed in the Middle East, was, "As you know, you go to war with the army you have, not the army you might want or wish to have at a later time."

5. Early on, psychologists treated predispositions and environmental factors as independent and additive, leading some to emphasize the importance of predispositions (e.g., Allport, 1937) and others to emphasize the importance of the environment (e.g., Mischel, 1968; see Kihlstrom, 2013, for a more comprehensive review). The debate petered out as psychologists began taking an "interactionist" view, which does not presume that either predisposition or the environment is more important than the other. Instead, both forces work in concert, with the effects of predispositions moderated by environmental

factors (Bowers, 1973; Dworkin and Kihlstrom, 1978). The interactionist's view framework fits well in Lewin's model, since it simply specifies the function by which P and E influence B,

$$f(P,E) = \alpha P + \beta E + \gamma PE.$$

CHAPTER 2 A THEORY OF INDIVIDUAL DIFFERENCES IN REFLECTION AND THE INTUITIONIST MODEL OF POLITICAL REASONING

1. The human mind works much more in line with David Hume's theory of human nature, which posited that reason springs from emotion (Hume, 2007). However, as we discuss later in this section, humans are more capable of regulating emotions through thought than Hume appreciated.
2. From the perspective of cognitive psychology, the mind is a product of the physical brain – one that is responsible for processing information – rather than a metaphysical entity (see Barkow, Cosmides, and Tooby, 1992, 8).
3. Camerer (2005, 31) succinctly describes a classic split-brain study that illustrates our conscious mind's ability to make up false narratives:

   The patient's right hemisphere was instructed to wave his hand (by showing the word "wave" on the left part of the visual screen, which only the right hemisphere processed). The left hemisphere saw the right hand waving but was unaware of the instructions that had been given to the right hemisphere (because the cross-hemisphere connections were severed). When the patient was asked why he waved, the left hemisphere (acting as spokesperson for the entire body) invariably came up with a plausible explanation, like "I saw somebody I knew and waved at them."

4. Stanovich (2009, 56) notes that it is more accurate to think of System 1 processes as a "*set* of systems" or mental modules that were added incrementally over the course of evolution (emphasis in the original). Moreover, some System 2 processes can operate outside of conscious awareness (Evans, 2010). Evans and Stanovich (2013) now advocate using the terms "Type 1 processing" and "Type 2 processing" to clarify that their dual-process model makes a distinction in how the mind processes information rather than the precise system that carries it out. We appreciate the desire for precision but opt to use the older System 1/System 2 terminology because it serves our aims well. We are less interested in contributing to knowledge about how the mind processes information than to knowledge about how qualitative differences in information processing influence political reasoning. We believe that conceptualizing these different processes as arising from two interconnected systems is a more useful analogy and that this simplification does not materially affect the hypotheses we draw from the theoretical framework.
5. We should note here that Gigerenzer and his colleagues (Gigerenzer, 2007; Gigerenzer and Goldstein, 1996; Kruglanski and Gigerenzer, 2011) reject dual-process theories of information processing (see discussion in the previous

section). Nonetheless, the System 1/System 2 framework is not incompatible with the notion that intuitions can lead to optimal decisions, however defined, as well as suboptimal ones (see Evans and Stanovich, 2013, 229).

6. We want to emphasize that, like all theoretical models, this dual-process model of information processing is an abstraction. While it is useful to think about two discrete systems with three discrete sets of processes, it is important to keep in mind that these are fundamentally fluid and dynamic processes. System 1, for instance, is always operating in the background, even when System 2 is at work, such that there could be interplay between the two. Moreover, as Figure 2.1 makes clear, System 2 action can push down into System 1 processes. A decision to override one's intuitions, for instance, can have downstream consequences by altering people's future gut reactions. It is beyond the scope of our project to model fully this dynamic process – although we do explore the downstream effects of reflection in Chapter 4. Nonetheless, we do believe that this simplified model of information processing offers useful insights about what people do when they are presented with new evidence and need to arrive at a decision. In these situations, we feel comfortable treating System 1 intuitions as exogenous to System 2 processes, even though we recognize that System 1 intuitions likely reflect previous instances of System 2 processing.

7. The quote is, "All models are wrong, but some are useful" (Box, 1979, 202).

8. We borrow the term "intuitionist" from Jonathan Haidt, who uses it to describe how central people's intuitions are to making moral judgments (Haidt, 2001).

9. In fact, one of us has contributed to this stream of research (Aarøe, Petersen, and Arceneaux, 2017; Arceneaux, 2012).

CHAPTER 3 MEASURING INDIVIDUAL DIFFERENCES IN REFLECTION

1. Holbrook (2006) and Kam (2005) employ the two-item measure of need for cognition placed on the American National Election Study. Bakker and Lelkes (2016) demonstrate that these null results are likely caused by the low reliability of the two-item measure.

2. A sixth study (The American Panel Survey), conducted independently of us by scholars at Washington University in Saint Louis, included measures of need for affect and need for cognition. We analyze these data in a separate study with Professor Daniel Butler and present some of these findings in Chapter 5. The American National Election Study also included a few items from the need for affect and need for cognition batteries on the 2013 recontact survey. Unfortunately, the researchers only included two items from the need for cognition battery and asked them in a nonstandard way. Consequently, the need for cognition measure fails to attain standard levels of reliability, which precludes us from including this data source in this project (see Bakker and Lelkes, 2016).

3. Nonetheless, and despite existing criticisms of doing so (e.g., Hollander, Sauerbrei, and Schumacher, 2004), we examined whether the data evince

natural cut points by conducting an optimal cut point analysis using the OptimalCutpoints package in R (Lopez-Raton et al., 2015). We find that the cut points identified in this analysis are highly sensitive to the selection criterion used in the optimization process (e.g., minimizing the absolute difference between sensitivity and specificity, the Youden index, etc.), and the resulting accuracy is unsatisfactory (i.e., the area under the receiver operating characteristic [ROC] curve is consistently below 0.6). These results bolster our decision to use the continuous need for affect and need for cognition scales in our analyses.

4. In the analytical models appearing in the following pages, we include a set of control variables to tap political, demographic, and, when possible, personality characteristics. The political variables used account for subjects' party affiliation, ideology, and, when available, political awareness. The demographic variables used account for subjects' age, education, gender, income, and race. Finally, when available, we account for subjects' Big Five personality traits – measures of agreeableness, conscientiousness, extroversion, neuroticism, and openness. These control variables are included in the analytical models whenever available.

5. To the extent that there are individual differences in how people experience emotions, they are often associated with a brain injury or neurodevelopment disorder (e.g., autism).

6. It does not affect the results if we keep the directional measure of the d score and estimate a more complicated statistical model.

7. We calculated the 83.5 percent credible intervals as opposed to the more standard 95 percent credible intervals because it allows us to use the overlap in credible intervals as a two-tailed test of statistical significance at the standard 0.05 alpha level (see, e.g., Goldstein and Healy, 1995; Maghsoodloo and Huang, 2010). We use this approach throughout this project when similarly comparing credible intervals.

8. As we do in all but the analysis of the effect of shifts in monthly unemployment on change in approval of President Obama (shown in Figure 5.3), we generate predictions for types of subjects by using the first percentile of the need for affect and need for cognition posterior means to represent low levels and the ninety-ninth percentile to represent high levels. We note that using percentiles of the distributions of the posterior means is a relatively conservative assessment of low and high attributes considering that posterior means, by definition, capture the central tendencies of the individual posterior densities. Using equivalent percentiles when incorporating more of the posterior distributions only exaggerates these values. We deviate from these percentiles in the one study noted above because of the limited sample size for that analysis and the decision to estimate the model separately for each party-type combination.

9. We note that the choice pair B and D yields the same expected utility as the choice pair B and C, and so can be considered equally "optimal" from an expected utility viewpoint. However, arriving at the choice pair B and C requires individuals to engage in the most reflection of any of the other choice pairs, since this pair is contrary to people's instincts to be risk averse with gains

and risk accepting with losses. Therefore, we are particularly interested, from a theoretical perspective, in how need for affect and need for cognition influence one's likelihood of selecting this nonintuitive choice pair. Nonetheless, we estimate a separate model to examine the likelihood of individuals selecting any optimal outcome in terms of expected utility (either choice pairs B and C or B and D), and we find substantively similar results.

CHAPTER 4   TOEING THE LINE: PARTISAN IDENTITIES AND POLICY ATTITUDES

1. A technical qualification is in order. Random assignment ensures that participants across treatment groups are equivalent when we average over an infinite number of randomized experiments. In any given experiment, there could be important differences across treatment groups by random chance. Of course, we cannot run an infinite number of experiments, but we can estimate the probability that the experiment we did run was a fluke. The lower that probability, the more confident we are that differences across treatment groups reflect the effect of the treatments as opposed to random chance.
2. We could also make comparisons to the nonpartisan cue, but this would involve comparing the partisan cues to a different counterfactual. It would tell us whether people find a partisan cue more (or less) trustworthy than a nonpartisan cue. That is an interesting question, but it is different from the one we are asking here, which is about the relative effects of inparty and outparty cues. Nonetheless, we included the nonpartisan cue group in the analysis, and interested readers can find the full results in the Appendix.
3. Readers interested in comparing the effects of the partisan cues to the nonpartisan cue can find the full results in the Appendix.
4. Given the observational research design, it is not possible to identify the specific mechanism by which need for affect and need for cognition generate the observed effects. In addition to being more defensive toward negative information about their party, it is also possible that those high in need for affect are less motivated to seek out negative information than are those high in need for cognition. Both mechanisms – defensiveness and selective exposure – generate the same observable implications regarding the effects of need for affect and need for cognition.

CHAPTER 5   THROWING THE RASCALS OUT: PARTISAN IDENTITIES AND POLITICAL EVALUATIONS

1. Achen and Bartels (2016) point out that voters often reward and punish incumbents for policy outcomes that they observe near the election, neglecting how incumbents have performed over their time in office. This kind of myopic voting can lead to a perverse logic in which incumbents are sanctioned on the basis of random fluctuations. Moreover, if incumbents know that voters are myopic, it also could allow politicians to ignore constituents' desires up until a

few months before the election (Healy and Lenz, 2014; Lindstädt and Vander Wielen, 2013). While these are worthy considerations, our focus here is about whether partisanship makes it difficult for voters to even evaluate politicians based on the present, much less over a longer time frame.

2. We excluded potential participants from the District of Columbia, since it does not have a governor, and from Rhode Island, since its governor did not affiliate with either the Democratic or Republican Party at the time of the study.

3. We use 90 percent credible intervals here to test whether the point estimates are statistically discernible from zero, as opposed to comparing credible intervals for overlap, as we do elsewhere.

4. The following results are robust to reasonable variation in these percentiles.

5. Because we do not possess data from a period in American history under Republican presidents or periods where the economy worsened under a Democratic president, we cannot say with certainty that less reflective democrats would behave like less reflective republicans if the shoe were on the other foot. Nonetheless, the data we observed in the ANES 2000-2002-2004 panel series suggests that democrats can be just as partisan in their reasoning as republicans can when it comes to evaluating economic performance.

CHAPTER 6   CAN'T WE DISAGREE WITHOUT BEING DISAGREEABLE? THE ROLE OF REFLECTION IN A POLARIZED POLITY

1. While there is disagreement over the degree to which the American electorate has become more ideologically extreme (e.g., Abramowitz and Saunders, 2008; Fiorina, Abrams, and Pope, 2008), there is a scholarly consensus that democrats and republicans have become more ideologically consistent.

2. We regressed these variables on an indicator for participation in the follow-up survey. The coefficients on all three variables were close to zero, and p-values were all above 0.4. A joint test also failed to reject the null hypothesis that all three coefficients are jointly zero ($F_{3,1249} = 0.31, p = 0.82$).

3. At the 0.05 α level using a two-tailed test.

CHAPTER 7   REFLECTIONS ON THE ROLE OF REFLECTION IN DEMOCRACIES

1. To simplify matters, we exclusively consider partisan voters in this analysis. However, if we were to incorporate nonpartisans, we would presumably observe similar overall trends in behavior across more and less reflective voters as a function of shirking.

2. While it is logical to assume that G is functionally related to shirking – as shirking increases, we might expect the effect of government policies to worsen – the precise nature of this relationship is unknown. Therefore, we adopt the conservative approach of assuming that G is constant and neutral (i.e., $G = 0$).

3. We hold α constant and assume $\epsilon \sim N(0,\theta)$ for all voters in order to focus on the effects of β and γ. Had we increased α and ϵ for less reflective voters, as our

theoretical model predicts, we would find that the baseline levels of support would be higher for less reflective voters and their error bounds wider.

4. Assuming that G is constant but negative (i.e., $G < 0$) would shift the predictions for more reflective individuals downward, and assuming that G decreases with shirking would exaggerate the marginal effects.

5. In particular, we explore the likelihood that an incumbent is reelected in 2014 as a function of his or her levels of shirking, districtwide levels of reflection, and the district-level analogues to the control variables used in previous analyses. The dependent variable for this model places retirements and electoral defeats in the same category (i.e., members who were not reelected). There is sound theoretical reason for doing this, since it has been argued elsewhere that electorally vulnerable members tend to voluntarily exit office to avoid defeat (see Jacobson and Kernell, 1981). Nonetheless, it is important to note that an alternative specification that separates out retirements and electoral defeats (using a multinomial logit specification) finds that need for affect and need for cognition, and their interaction, have similar consequences for both of these categories separately, thus offering an empirical justification for the decision to collapse the two categories into one.

6. Our analysis included controls for age, gender, education, and income. Contact the authors for details of this analysis.

7. We thank Chloé Bakalar for pointing out the effects of partisan talking points on deliberation in online social settings (personal communication).

APPENDIX   DETAILS OF EMPIRICAL STUDIES AND STATISTICAL ANALYSES

1. For a more detailed discussion of this method, see Martin, Quinn, and Park (2013).

2. We use the MCMCordfactanal function in MCMCpack. Documentation is available at the Comprehensive R Archive Network (CRAN) website.

3. We are grateful to Shawn Treier and Simon Jackman for sharing their model code.

References

Aarøe, Lene, Michael Bang Petersen, and Kevin Arceneaux. 2017. "The Behavioral Immune System Shapes Political Intuitions: Why and How Differences in Disgust Sensitivity Underlie Opposition to Immigration." *American Political Science Review*, 111(2): 277–94.

Abelson, R. 1963. Computer simulation of "hot" cognition. In *Computer Simulation of Personality*, ed. S. Tomkins and D. Messick. New York: Wiley pp. 277–298.

Abelson, Robert P. 1986. "Beliefs Are Like Possessions." *Journal for the Theory of Social Behaviour* 16(3):223–250.

Abramowitz, Alan I., and Kyle L. Saunders. 2008. "Is Polarization a Myth?" *Journal of Politics* 70(2):542–555.

Achen, Christopher H. 1992. "Social Psychology, Demographic Variables, and Linear Regression: Breaking the Iron Triangle in Voting Research." *Political Behavior* 14:195–211.

Achen, Christopher H., and Larry M. Bartels. 2016. *Democracy for Realists: Why Elections Do Not Produce Responsive Government*. Princeton, NJ: Princeton University Press.

Ackerman, Bruce, and James S. Fishkin. 2002. "Deliberation Day." *Journal of Political Philosophy* 10(2):129–152.

Adams, Greg D. 1997. "Abortion: Evidence of an Issue Evolution." *American Journal of Political Science* 41(3):718–737.

Ahler, Douglas J., and David E. Broockman. 2016. "Does Elite Polarization Imply Poor Representation? A New Perspective on the 'Disconnect' Between Politicians and Voters." Working Paper. URL: https://people.stanford.edu/dbroock/sites/default/files/ahler_broockman_ideological_innocence.pdf

Ahlering, Robert F. 1987. "Need for Cognition, Attitudes, and the 1984 Presidential Election." *Journal of Research in Personality* 21:100–102.

Ahuja, Sunil. 2008. *Congress Behaving Badly: The rise of Partisanship and Incivility and the Death of Public Trust*. Westport, CT: Praeger Publishers.

Aldrich, John H. 1995. *Why Parties?: The Origin and Transformation of Political Parties in America*. Chicago: University of Chicago Press.

Alford, John R., Carolyn L. Funk, and John R. Hibbing. 2005. "Are Political Orientations Genetically Transmitted?" *American Political Science Review* 99(2):153–168.

Alford, John R., Peter K. Hatemi, John R. Hibbing, Nicholas G. Martin, and Lindon J. Eaves. 2011. "The Politics of Mate Choice." *Journal of Politics* 73(2):362–379.

Allport, Gordon W. 1937. *Personality: A Psychological Interpretation*. New York: Holt, Rinehart, and Winston.

Althaus, Scott L. 2003. *Collective Preferences in Democratic Politics: Opinion Surveys and the Will of the People*. Cambridge: Cambridge University Press.

Anderson, Christopher J. 2000. "Economic Voting and Political Context: A Comparative Perspective." *Electoral Studies* 19:151–170.

Annenberg Public Policy Center. 2011. Civility in Congress (1935–2011) as Reflected in the Taking Down Process. Technical Report 2011-1 University of Pennsylvania.

Ansolabehere, Stephen, Jonathan Rodden, and James M. Snyder, Jr. 2008. "The Strength of Issues: Using Multiple Measures to Gauge Preference Stability, Ideological Constraint, and Issue Voting." *American Political Science Review* 102(2):215–232.

Anson, Ian G. Forthcoming. "'That's Not How It Works': Economic Indicators and the Construction of Partisan Economic Narratives." *Journal of Elections, Public Opinion & Parties* 1–22.

Arceneaux, Kevin. 2008. "Can Partisan Cues Diminish Democratic Accountability?" *Political Behavior* 30(2):139–160.

2012. "Cognitive Biases and the Strength of Political Arguments." *American Journal of Political Science* 56(2):271–285.

Arceneaux, Kevin, Martin Johnson, and John Cryderman. 2013. "Communication, Persuasion, and the Conditioning Value of Selective Exposure: Like Minds May Unite and Divide but They Mostly Tune Out." *Political Communication* 30(2):213–231.

Arceneaux, Kevin, and Robin Kolodny. 2009a. "Educating the Least Informed: Group Endorsements in a Grassroots Campaign." *American Journal of Political Science* 53(4):755–770.

2009b. "The Effect of Grassroots Campaigning on Issue Preferences and Issue Salience." *Journal of Elections, Public Opinion & Parties* 19(3):235–249.

Arceneaux, Kevin, and Ryan Vander Wielen. 2013. "The Effects of Need for Cognition and Need for Affect on Partisan Evaluations." *Political Psychology* 34:23–42.

Ashworth, Scott, and Ethan Bueno de Mesquita. 2014. "Is Voter Competence Good for Voters?: Information, Rationality, and Democratic Performance." *American Political Science Review* 108(3):565–587.

Bakker, Bert N., and Yphtach Lelkes. 2016. Selling Ourselves Short? How Abbreviated Measures of Personality Change the Way We Think About Personality and Politics. Technical report University of Amsterdam. Working Paper.

Bargh, John A., and Tanya L. Chartrand. 1999. "The Unbearable Automaticity of Being." *American Psychologist* 54(7):462–479.

Barkley, Alben William. 1954. *That Reminds Me.* New York: Doubleday.

Barkow, Jerome H., Leda Cosmides, and John Tooby. 1992. *The Adapted Mind: Evolutionary Psychology and the Generation of Culture.* Oxford: Oxford University Press.

Baron, Jonathan. 1993. "Why Teach Thinking? An Essay." *Applied Psychology* 42(3):191–214.

Bartels, Larry M. 1996. "Uninformed Votes: Information Effects in Presidential Elections." *American Journal of Political Science* 40(1):194–230.

    2000. "Partisanship and Voting Behavior, 1952–1996." *American Journal of Political Science* 44(1):35–50.

    2002. "Beyond the Running Tally: Partisan Bias in Political Perceptions." *Political Behavior* 24:117–150.

    2003. Democracy with Attitudes. In *Electoral Democracy*, ed. Michael MacKuen and George Rabinowitz. Ann Arbor, MI: University of Michigan Press pp. 48–82.

Bechara, Antoine. 2004. "The Role of Emotion in Decision-Making: Evidence from Neurological Patients with Orbitofrontal Damage." *Brain and Cognition* 55(1):30–40.

Bechara, Antoine, Hana Damasio, Daniel Tranel, and Antonio R. Damasio. 1997. "Deciding Advantageously before Knowing the Advantageous Strategy." *Science* 275:1293–1295.

Bechtel, Michael M., Jens Hainmueller, Dominik Hangartner, and Marc Helbling. 2015. "Reality Bites: The Limits of Framing Effects for Salient and Contested Policy Issues." *Political Science Research and Methods* 3(3):683–695.

Beck, Nathaniel. 1991. The Economy and Presidential Approval: An Information Theoretic Perspective. In *Economics and Politics: The Calculus of Support*, ed. Helmut Norpoth, Michael S. Lewis-Beck, and Jean-Dominique Lafay. Anne Arbor, MI: University of Michigan Press pp. 85–101.

Berelson, Bernard R., Paul F. Lazarsfeld, and William N. McPhee. 1954. *Voting: A Study of Opinion Formation in a Presidential Campaign.* Chicago: University of Chicago Press.

Berinsky, Adam J. 2009. *In Time of War: Understanding American Public Opinion from World War II to Iraq.* Chicago: University of Chicago Press.

Berinsky, Adam J., Gregory A. Huber, and Gabriel S. Lenz. 2012. "Evaluating Online Labor Markets for Experimental Research: Amazon.com's Mechanical Turk." *Political Analysis* 20:351–368.

Bisgaard, Martin. 2015. "Bias Will Find a Way: Economic Perceptions, Attributions of Blame, and Partisan-Motivated Reasoning during Crisis." *Journal of Politics* 77(3):849–860.

Bishop, George F. 2004. *The Illusion of Public Opinion: Fact and Artifact in American Public Opinion Polls.* New York: Rowman & Littlefield Publishers.

Bizer, George Y., Jon A. Krosnick, Allyson L. Holbrook, S. Christian Wheeler, Derek D. Rucker, and Richard E. Petty. 2004. "The Impact of Personality on

Cognitive, Behavioral, and Affective Political Processes: The Effects of Need to Evaluate." *Journal of Personality* 72(5):995–1027.

Bolsen, Toby, James N. Druckman, and Fay Lomax Cook. 2014. "The Influence of Partisan Motivated Reasoning on Public Opinion." *Political Behavior* 36(2):235–262.

Boudreau, Cheryl, and Scott A. MacKenzie. 2014. "Informing the Electorate? How Party Cues and Policy Information Affect Public Opinion about Initiatives." *American Journal of Political Science* 58(1):48–62.

Bowers, Kenneth S. 1973. "Situationism in Psychology: An Analysis and a Critique." *Psychological Review* 80(5):307.

Box, G. E. P. 1979. Robustness in the Strategy of Scientific Model Building. In *Robustness in Statistics*, ed. Robert L. Launer and Graham N. Wilkinson. New York: Academic Press pp. 201–236.

Brace, Paul, and Barbara Hinckley. 1991. "The Structure of Presidential Approval: Constraints within and across Presidencies." *Journal of Politics* 53(4):993–1017.

Brader, Ted. 2006. *Campaigning for Hearts and Minds: How Emotional Appeals in Political Ads Work*. Chicago: University of Chicago Press.

Brady, Henry E., and Paul M. Sniderman. 1985. "Attitude Attribution: A Group Basis for Political Reasoning." *The American Political Science Review* 79(4):1061–1078.

Brewer, Marilynn B. 2007. "The Importance of Being We: Human Nature and Intergroup Relations." *American Psychologist* 62(8):728–738.

Britt, Thomas W., Matthew R. Millard, Preetha T. Sundareswaran, and DeWayne Moore. 2009. "Personality Variables Predict Strength-Related Attitude Dimensions across Objects." *Journal of Personality* 77:859–882.

Broockman, David E., and Daniel M. Butler. 2015. "The Causal Effects of Elite Position-Taking on Voter Attitudes: Field Experiments with Elite Communication." *American Journal of Political Science* DOI: 10.1111/ajps.12243.

Brown, Adam R. 2010. "Are Governors Responsible for the State Economy? Partisanship, Blame, and Divided Federalism." *Journal of Politics* 72(3):605–615.

Buhrmester, Michael D., Tracy Kwang, and Samuel D. Gosling. 2011. "Amazon's Mechanical Turk: A New Source of Inexpensive, Yet High-Quality, Data?" *Perspectives on Psychological Science* 6:3–5.

Bullock, John G. 2007. Experiments on Partisanship and Public Opinion: Party Cues, False Beliefs, and Bayesian Updating PhD thesis Ph.D. dissertation, Stanford University.

2009. "Partisan Bias and the Bayesian Ideal in the Study of Public Opinion." *Journal of Politics* 71:1109–1124.

2011. "Elite Influence on Public Opinion in an Informed Electorate." *American Political Science Review* 105:496–515.

Bullock, John G., Alan S. Gerber, Seth J. Hill, and Gregory A. Huber. 2015. "Partisan Bias in Factual Beliefs about Politics." *Quarterly Journal of Political Science* 10(4):519–578.

Burden, Barry C., and Casey A. Klofstad. 2005. "Affect and Cognition in Party Identification." *Political Psychology* 26(6):869–886.

Burnham, Walter Dean. 2013. The Reagan Heritage. In *The Election of 1988: Reports and Interpretations*, ed. Gerald M. Pomper. New York: Chatham House.

Buss, David M. 1987. "Selection, Evocation, and Manipulation." *Journal of Personality and Social Psychology* 53(6):1214.

Butler, Daniel M., and David W. Nickerson. 2011. "Can Learning Constituency Opinion Affect How Legislators Vote? Results from a Field Experiment." *Quarterly Journal of Political Science* 6(1):55–83.

Cacioppo, John T., and Richard E. Petty. 1982. "The Need for Cognition." *Journal of Personality and Social Psychology* 42:116–131.

Cacioppo, John T., Richard E. Petty, and Chaun F. Kao. 1984. "The Efficient Assessment of Need for Cognition." *Journal of Personality Assessment* 48(3):306–307.

Cacioppo, John T., Richard E. Petty, Chaun F. Kao, and Regina Rodriguez. 1986. "Central and Peripheral Routes to Persuasion: An Individual Difference Perspective." *Journal of Personality* 51(5):1032–1043.

Cacioppo, John T., Richard E. Petty, Jeffrey A. Feinstein, and W. Blair G. Jarvis. 1996. "Dispositional Differences in Cognitive Motivation: The Life and Times of Individuals Varying in Need for Cognition." *Psychological Bulletin* 119(2):197–253.

Camerer, Colin, George Loewenstein, and Drazen Prelec. 2005. "Neuroeconomics: How Neuroscience Can Inform Economics." *Journal of Economic Literature* 43(3):9–64.

Campbell, Angus, Philip E. Converse, Warren E. Miller, and Donald E. Stokes. 1960. *The American Voter*. New York: Wiley.

Canes-Wrone, Brandice. 2005. *Who Leads Whom?: Presidents, Policy, and the Public*. Chicago: University of Chicago Press.

Canes-Wrone, Brandice, David W. Brady, and John F. Cogan. 2002. "Out of Step, Out of Office: Electoral Accountability and House Members' Voting." *American Political Science Review* 96:127–140.

Carlin, Ryan E., and Gregory J. Love. 2016. "Political Competition, Partisanship and Interpersonal Trust in Electoral Democracies." *British Journal of Political Science* 1–25.

Carmines, Edward G., and James A. Stimson. 1980. "The Two Faces of Issue Voting." *American Political Science Review* 74(1):78–91.

1989. *Issue Evolution: Race and the Transformation of American Politics*. Princeton, NJ: Princeton University Press.

Caspi, Avshalom, Karen Sugden, Terrie E. Moffitt, Alan Taylor, Ian W. Craig, HonaLee Harrington, Joseph McClay, Jonathan Mill, Judy Martin, Antony Braithwaite et al. 2003. "Influence of Life Stress on Depression: Moderation by a Polymorphism in the 5-HTT Gene." *Science* 301(5631): 386–389.

Chaiken, Shelly, Akiva Liberman, and Alice H. Eagly. 1989. Heuristic and Systematic Information Processing within and beyond the Persuasion Context. In *Unintended Thought*, ed. James S. Uleman and John A. Bargh. New York: The Guilford Press pp. 212–252.

Chong, Dennis. 2013. Degrees of Rationality in Politics. In *The Oxford Handbook of Political Psychology*, ed. Leonie Huddy, Sears David O., and Levy Jacck S. New York: Oxford University Press pp. 96–129.

Chong, Dennis, and James N. Druckman. 2007. "Framing Theory." *Annual Review of Political Science* 10(1):103–126.

2010. "Dynamic Public Opinion: Communication Effects over Time." *American Political Science Review* 104(4):663–680.

Cikara, Mina, Matthew M. Botvinick, and Susan T. Fiske. 2011. "Us Versus Them: Social Identity Shapes Neural Responses to Intergroup Competition and Harm." *Psychological Science* 22(3):306–313.

Ciuk, David J., and Berwood A. Yost. 2016. "The Effects of Issue Salience, Elite Influence, and Policy Content on Public Opinion." *Political Communication* 33(2):328–345.

Clifford, Scott, Ryan M. Jewell, and Philip D. Waggoner. 2015. "Are Samples Drawn from Mechanical Turk Valid for Research on Political Ideology?" *Research & Politics* 2(4):1–9.

Clinton, Joshua D., and Simon Jackman. 2009. "To Simulate or NOMINATE?" *Legislative Studies Quarterly* 34(4):593–621.

Clinton, Joshua D., Simon Jackman, and Douglas Rivers. 2004. "The Statistical Analysis of Roll Call Data." *American Political Science Review* 98(2):355–370.

Cobb, Michael D., Brendan Nyhan, and Jason Reifler. 2013. "Beliefs Don't Always Persevere: How Political Figures Are Punished When Positive Information about Them Is Discredited." *Political Psychology* 34(3):307–326.

Cobb, Michael D., and James H. Kuklinski. 1997. "Changing Minds: Political Arguments and Political Persuasion." *American Journal of Political Science* 41(1):88–121.

Coe, Kevin, Kate Kenski, and Stephen A. Rains. 2014. "Online and Uncivil? Patterns and Determinants of Incivility in Newspaper Website Comments." *Journal of Communication* 64(4):658–679.

Cohen, Arthur R., Ezra Stotland, and Donald M. Wolfe. 1955. "An Experimental Investigation of Need for Cognition." *The Journal of Abnormal and Social Psychology* 51(2):291–294.

Cohen, Geoffrey L. 2003. "Party over Policy: The Dominating Impact of Group Influence on Political Beliefs." *Journal of Personality and Social Psychology* 85(5):808–822.

Cohen, Jacob. 1983. "The Cost of Dichotomization." *Applied Psychological Measurement* 7(3):249–253.

Cohen, Joshua. 1997. Deliberation and Democratic Legitimacy. In *Deliberative Democracy: Essays on Reason and Politics*, ed. James Bobman and William Rehg. Cambridge, MA: MIT Press.

Condra, Mollie B. 1992. "Link between Need for Cognition and Political Interest, Involvement, and Media Use." *Psychology* 29:13–17.

Confer, Jaime C., Judith A. Easton, Diana S. Fleischman, Cari D. Goetz, David M. G. Lewis, Carin Perilloux, and David M. Buss. 2010. "Evolutionary Psychology: Controversies, Questions, Prospects, and Limitations." *American Psychologist* 65(2):110–126.

Conover, Pamela Johnston, Stanley Feldman, and Kathleen Knight. 1986. "Judging Inflation and Unemployment: The Origins of Retrospective Evaluations." *The Journal of Politics* 48(3):565–588.

Converse, Philip E. 1964. The Nature of Belief Systems in Mass Publics. In *Ideology and Discontent*, ed. David E. Apter. New York: Free Press pp. 206–261.

Conway, III, Lucian Gideon, Laura Janelle Gornick, Shannon C. Houck, Christopher Anderson, Jennifer Stockert, Diana Sessoms, and Kevin McCue. 2016. "Are Conservatives Really More Simple-Minded than Liberals? The Domain Specificity of Complex Thinking." *Political Psychology* 37(6): 777–798.

Cooper, Michael. 2012. "Conservatives Sowed Idea of Health Care Mandate, Only to Spurn It Later." *New York Times* February 15:A15.

Cosmides, Leda, and John Tooby. 2004. Evolutionary Psychology and the Emotions. In *Handbook of Emotions*, ed. Michael Lewis and Jeannette M. Haviland-Jones. New York: Guilford Press.

Craig, Stephen C. 1985. "The Decline of Partisanship in the United States: A Reexamination of the Neutrality Hypothesis." *Political Behavior* 7(1):57–78.

Dahl, Robert A. 1956. *A Preface to Democratic Theory*. Chicago: University of Chicago Press.

Dahl, Robert Alan. 1989. *Democracy and Its Critics*. New Haven, CT: Yale University Press.

Dawes, Christopher T., and James H. Fowler. 2009. "Partisanship, Voting, and the Dopamine D2 Receptor Gene." *Journal of Politics* 71(3):1157–1171.

Dawson, Michael E, Anne M. Schell, and Diane L. Filion. 2001. The Electrodermal System. In *Handbook of Psychophysiology*, Second Edition, ed. John T. Cacioppo, Louis G. Tassinary, and Gary G. Berntson. Cambridge: Cambridge University Press pp. 200–223.

De Neys, Wim. 2006. "Dual Processing in Reasoning Two Systems but One Reasoner." *Psychological Science* 17(5):428–433.

Dickson, Eric S. 2006. "Rational Choice Epistemology and Belief Formation in Mass Politics." *Journal of Theoretical Politics* 18(4):454–497.

Dickson, Eric S., and Kenneth Scheve. 2006. "Social Identity, Political Speech, and Electoral Competition." *Journal of Theoretical Politics* 18:5–39.

Dimberg, Ulf, Monika Thunberg, and Kurt Elmehed. 2000. "Unconscious Facial Reactions to Emotional Facial Expressions." *Psychological Science* 11(1):86–89.

Downs, Anthoy. 1957. *An Economic Theory of Democracy*. New York: Harper Collins.

Druckman, James N. 2001. "Using Credible Advice to Overcome Framing Effects." *Journal of Law, Economics, and Organization* 17(1):62–82.

Druckman, James N., Erik Peterson, and Rune Slothuus. 2013. "How Elite Partisan Polarization Affects Public Opinion Formation." *American Political Science Review* 107(1):57–79.

Duch, Raymond M., Harvey D. Palmer, and Christopher J. Anderson. 2000. "Heterogeneity in Perceptions of National Economic Conditions." *American Journal of Political Science* 44:635–652.

Dunn, Kris, Salomon Orellana, and Shane Singh. 2009. "Legislative Diversity and Social Tolerance: How Multiparty Systems Lead to Tolerant Citizens." *Journal of Elections, Public Opinion & Parties* 19(3):283–312.

Durr, Robert H. 1993. "What Moves Policy Sentiment?" *American Political Science Review* 87(1):158–170.

Dworkin, Robert H., and John F. Kihlstrom. 1978. "An S-R Inventory of Dominance for Research on the Nature of Person-Situation Interactions." *Journal of Personality* 46(1):43–56.

Egan, Patrick J. 2014. "'Do Something' Politics and Double-Peaked Policy Preferences." *Journal of Politics* 76(2):333–349.

Evans, Jonathan St. B. T. 2010. *Thinking Twice: Two Minds in One Brain.* Oxford: Oxford University Press.

Evans, Jonathan St. B. T., and Keith E. Stanovich. 2013. "Dual-Process Theories of Higher Cognition: Advancing the Debate." *Perspectives on Psychological Science* 8(3):223–241.

Fair, Ray C. 2009. "Presidential and Congressional Vote-Share Equations." *American Journal of Political Science* 53(1):55–72.

Feldman, Stanley. 1988. "Structure and Consistency in Public Opinion: The Role of Core Beliefs and Values." *American Journal of Political Science* 32(2):416–440.

Feldman, Stanley, and Christopher Johnston. 2014. "Understanding the Determinants of Political Ideology: Implications of Structural Complexity." *Political Psychology* 35(3):337–358.

Ferejohn, John. 1986. "Incumbent Performance and Electoral Control." *Public Choice* 50:5–25.

Fiorina, Morris P. 1978. "Economic Retrospective Voting in American National Elections: A Micro-Analysis." *American Journal of Political Science* 22(2):426–443.

1981. *Retrospective Voting in American Elections.* New Haven: Yale University Press.

Fiorina, Morris P., Samuel A. Abrams, and Jeremy C. Pope. 2008. "Polarization in the American Public: Misconceptions and Misreadings." *Journal of Politics* 70(2):556–560.

Fishkin, James S. 2011. *When the People Speak: Deliberative Democracy and Public Consultation.* Oxford: Oxford University Press.

Franklin, Benjamin. 2003/1787. Excerpt from Speech to the Constitutional Convention, July 26, 1787. In *The Political Thought of Benjamin Franklin*, ed. Ralph Ketcham. Indianapolis, IN: Hackett Publishing Company p. 398.

Franklin, Charles H., and John E. Jackson. 1983. "The Dynamics of Party Identification." *American Political Science Review* 77:957–973.

Frederick, Shane. 2005. "Cognitive Reflection and Decision Making." *Journal of Economic Perspectives* 19(4):25–42.

Furnham, Adrian, and Jeremy D. Thorne. 2013. "Need for Cognition." *Journal of Individual Differences* 34(4):230–240.

Gaines, Brian, James H. Kuklinski, Paul J. Quirk, Buddy Peyton, and Jay Verkuilen. 2007. "Same Facts, Different Interpretations: Partisan Motivation and Opinion on Iraq." *Journal of Politics* 69:957–974.

Gazzaniga, Michael S. 2011. *Who's in Charge? Free Will and the Science of the Brain.* New York: Harper Collins.

Geer, John G. 2006. *In Defense of Negativity: Attack Ads in Presidential Campaigns.* Chicago: University of Chicago Press.

Gelman, Andrew. 2009. "Bayes, Jeffreys, Prior Distributions and the Philosophy of Statistics." *Statistical Science* 24:176–178.

Gerber, Alan S., and Donald P. Green. 1998. "Rational Learning and Partisan Attitudes." *American Journal of Political Science* 42:794–818.

   1999. "Misperceptions about Perceptual Bias." *Annual Review of Political Science* 2(1):189–210.

Gerber, Alan S., and Gregory A. Huber. 2009. "Partisanship and Economic Behavior: Do Partisan Differences in Economic Forecasts Predict Real Economic Behavior?" *American Political Science Review* 103(3):407–426.

Gerber, Alan S., Gregory A. Huber, David Doherty, Conor M. Dowling, and Shang E. Ha. 2010. "Personality and Political Attitudes: Relationships across Issue Domains and Political Contexts." *American Political Science Review* 104(1):111–133.

Geweke, John. 1992. Evaluating the Accuracy of Sampling-Based Approaches to Calculating Posterior Moments. In *Bayesian Statistics*, ed. J. M. Bernardo, J. O. Berger, A. P. Dawid, and A. F. M. Smith. Vol. 4 Oxford: Clarendon pp. 169–194.

Gigerenzer, Gerd. 2007. *Gut Feelings: The Intelligence of the Unconscious.* New York: Penguin.

Gigerenzer, Gerd, and Donald G. Goldstein. 1996. "Reasoning the Fast and Frugal Way: Models of Bounded Rationality." *Psychological Review* 103(4):650–669.

Goldberg, Lewis R. 1990. "An Alternative Description of Personality': The Big-Five Factor Structure." *Journal of Personality and Social Psychology* 59(6):1216–1229.

Goldstein, Harvey and Michael J.R. Healy. 1995. "The Graphical Presentation of a Collection of Means." *Journal of the Royal Statistical Society* 158(1): 175–177.

Gordon, Stacy B., and Gary M. Segura. 1997. "Cross–National Variation in the Political Sophistication of Individuals: Capability or Choice?" *Journal of Politics* 59(1):126–147.

Goren, Paul. 2001. "Core Principles and Policy Reasoning in Mass Publics: A Test of Two Theories." *British Journal of Political Science* 31(01).

Gray, Jeffrey Alan. 1987. *The Psychology of Fear and Stress.* Cambridge: Cambridge University Press.

Green, Donald, Bradley Palmquist, and Eric Schickler. 2002. *Partisan Hearts and Minds: Political Parties and the Social Identities of Voters.* New Haven, CT: Yale University Press.

Green, Donald P., and Ian Shapiro. 1994. *Pathologies of Rational Choice Theory: A Critique of Applications in Political Science.* New Haven, CT: Yale University Press.

Greenwald, Anthony G., Brian A. Nosek, and Mahzarin R. Banaji. 2003. "Understanding and using the Implicit Association Test: I. An Improved Scoring Algorithm." *Journal of Personality and Social Psychology* 85(2):197–216.

Greenwald, Anthony G., Debbie E. McGhee, and Jordan L. K. Schwartz. 1998. "Measuring Individual Differences in Implicit Cognition: The Implicit Association Test." *Journal of Personality and Social Psychology* 74(6):1464–1480.

Greenwald, Anthony G., Mahzarin R. Banaji, Laurie A. Rudman, Shelly D. Farnham, Brian A. Nosek, and Deborah S. Mellott. 2002. "A Unified Theory of Implicit Attitudes, Stereotypes, Self-Esteem, and Self-Concept." *Psychological Review* 109(1):3–25.

Groenendyk, Eric. 2013. *Competing Motives in the Partisan Mind: How Loyalty and Responsiveness Shape Party Identification and Democracy.* Oxford: Oxford University Press.

Gross, J. J. 1998. "The Emerging Field of Emotion Regulation: An Integrative Review." *Review of General Psychology* 2(3):271–299.

Grynaviski, Jeffrey D. 2006. "A Bayesian Learning Model with Applications to Party Identification." *Journal of Theoretical Politics* 18:323–346.

Gutmann, Amy, and Dennis Thompson. 2005. *Why Deliberative Democracy?* Princeton, NJ: Princeton University Press.

Gvirsman, Shira Dvir. 2015. "Testing Our Quasi-Statistical Sense: News Use, Political Knowledge, and False Projection." *Political Psychology* 36(6):729–747.

Habermas, Jürgen. 1994. "Three Normative Models of Democracy." *Constellations* 1(1):1–10.

Haddock, Geoffrey, Gregory R. Maio, Karin Arnold, and Thomas Huskinson. 2008. "Should Persuasion Be Affective or Cognitive? The Moderating Effects of Need for Affect and Need for Cognition." *Personality and Social Psychology Bulletin* 34:769–778.

Haidt, J., and C. Joseph. 2004. "Intuitive Ethics: How Innately Prepared Intuitions Generate Culturally Variable Virtues." *Daedalus* 133(4): 55–66.

Haidt, Jonatahn. 2001. "The Emotional Dog and Its Rational Tail: A Social Intuitionist Approach to Moral Judgment." *Psychological Review* 108(4):814–834.

2012. *The Righteous Mind: Why Good People Are Divided by Politics and Religion.* New York: Pantheon Books.

Haran, Uriel, Ilana Ritov, and Barbara A. Mellers. 2013. "The Role of Actively Open-Minded Thinking in Information Acquisition, Accuracy, and Calibration." *Judgment & Decision Making* 8(3):188–201.

Haselton, Martie G., Gregory A. Bryant, Andreas Wilke, David A. Frederick, Andrew Galperin, Willem E. Frankenhuis, and Tyler Moore. 2009. "Adaptive Rationality: An Evolutionary Perspective on Cognitive Bias." *Social Cognition* 27(5):733–763.

Hatemi, Peter K., Rose McDermott, Lindon J. Eaves, Kenneth S. Kendler, and Michael C. Neale. 2013. "Fear as a Disposition and an Emotional State: A Genetic and Environmental Approach to Out-Group Political Preferences." *American Journal of Political Science* 57(2):279–293.

Healy, Andrew, and Gabriel S. Lenz. 2014. "Substituting the End for the Whole: Why Voters Respond Primarily to the Election-Year Economy." *American Journal of Political Science* 58(1):31–47.

Healy, Andrew J., Neil Malhotra, and Cecilia Hyunjung Mo. 2010. Irrelevant Events Affect Voters' Evaluations of Government Performance. *Proceedings of the National Academy of Sciences* 107(29):12804–12809.

Heidelberger, Philip, and Peter D. Welch. 1983. "Simulation Run Length Control in the Presence of an Initial Transient." *Operations Research* 31:1109–1144.

Heintzelman, Samantha J., and Laura A. King. 2016. "Meaning in Life and Intuition." *Journal of Personality and Social Psychology* 110(3):477–492.

Henry, Patrick J., and David O. Sears. 2002. "The Symbolic Racism 2000 Scale." *Political Psychology* 23(2):253–283.

Herszenhorn, David M., and Robert Pear. 2010. "Final Votes in Congress Cap Battle on Health Bill." *New York Times* p. A1.

Hetherington, Marc J. 2001. "Resurgent Mass Partisanship: The Role of Elite Polarization." *American Political Science Review* 95(3):619–631.

Hetherington, Marc J., and Jonathan D. Weiler. 2009. *Authoritarianism and Polarization in American Politics*. Cambridge: Cambridge University Press.

Hibbing, John R., Kevin B. Smith, and John R. Alford. 2013. *Predisposed: Liberals, Conservatives, and the Biology of Political Differences*. New York: Routledge.

Hibbs, Douglas A., Douglas Rivers, and Nicholas Vasilatos. 1982. "On the Demand for Economic Outcomes: Macroeconomic Performance and Mass Political Support in the United States, Great Britain, and Germany" *Journal of Politics* 44(2):426–462.

Hill, Seth. Forthcoming. "Learning Together Slowly: Bayesian Learning about Political Facts." *Journal of Politics*.

Hoadley, John F. 1986. *Origins of American Political Parties: 1789–1803*. Lexington, KY: University Press of Kentucky.

Hofstadter, Richard. 1989. *The American Political Tradition and the Men Who Made It*. New York: Vintage.

Holbrook, Thomas M. 2006. "Cognitive Style and Political Learning during the 2000 Presidential Campaign." *Political Research Quarterly* 59:343–352.

Hollander, Norbert, Will Sauerbrei, and Martin Schumacher. 2004. "Confidence Intervals for the Effect of a Prognostic Factor after Selection of an 'Optimal' Cutpoint." *Statistics in Medicine* 23(11):1701–1713.

Hovland, Carl I., and Walter Weiss. 1951. "The Influence of Source Credibility on Communication Effectiveness." *Public Opinion Quarterly* 15(4):635–650.

Huddy, Leonie, Lilliana Mason, and Lene Aarøe. 2015. "Expressive Partisanship: Campaign Involvement, Political Emotion, and Partisan Identity." *American Political Science Review* 109(1):1–17.

Huddy, Leonie, Stanley Feldman, and Christopher Weber. 2007. "The Political Consequences of Perceived Threat and Felt Insecurity." *Annals of the American Academy of Political and Social Science* 614(11):131–153.

Hume, David. 2007. *A Treatise of Human Nature: A Critical Edition*, edited by David Fate Norton, and Mary J Norton. Oxford: Clarendon Press.

Huskinson, Thomas L. H., and Geoff Haddock. 2004. "Assessing Individual Differences in Attitude Structure: Variance in the Chronic Reliance on Affective and Cognitive Information." *Journal of Experimental Social Psychology* 40:82–90.

Iyengar, Shanto, and Donald R. Kinder. 1987. *News That Matters: Television and American Opinion*. Chicago: University of Chicago Press.

Iyengar, Shanto, Gaurav Sood, and Yphtach Lelkes. 2012. "Affect, Not Ideology: A Social Identity Perspective on Polarization." *Public Opinion Quarterly* 76(3):405–431.

Iyengar, Shanto, and Sean J. Westwood. 2015. "Fear and Loathing across Party Lines: New Evidence on Group Polarization." *American Journal of Political Science* 59(3):690–707.

Jacobs, Lawrence R., and Robert Y. Shapiro. 2000. *Politicians Don't Pander*. Chicago: University of Chicago Press.

Jacobson, Gary C., and Samuel Kernell. 1981. *Strategy and Choice in Congressional Elections*. New Haven: Yale University Press.

Jarvis, W. Blair G., and Richard E. Petty. 1996. "The Need to Evaluate." *Journal of Personality and Social Psychology* 70(1):172–194.

Jerit, Jennifer, and Jason Barabas. 2012. "Partisan Perceptual Bias and the Information Environment." *Journal of Politics* 74(3):672–684.

Johnston, Richard. 2006. "Party Identification: Unmoved Mover or Sum of Preferences?" *Annual Review of Political Science* 9(1):329–351.

Jost, John T., Jack Glaser, Arie W. Kruglanski, and Frank J. Sulloway. 2003. "Political Conservatism and Motivated Social Cognition." *Psychological Bulletin* 129:339–375.

Kahan, Dan M. 2012. "Ideology, Motivated Reasoning, and Cognitive Reflection." *Judgment & Decision Making* 8(4):407–424.

Kahneman, Daniel. 2011. *Thinking, Fast and Slow*. New York: Macmillan.

Kam, Cindy D. 2005. "Who Toes the Party Line? Cues, Values, and Individual Differences." *Political Behavior* 27(2):163–182.

Kelman, Mark. 2011. *The Heuristics Debate*. Oxford: Oxford University Press.

Key, Valdimer Orlando. 1966. *The Responsible Electorate*. Boston: Belknap Press of Harvard University Press.

Key, V. O. Jr. 1964. "Politics, Parties, and Pressure Groups." New York: Thomas Y. Crowell Co.

Kihlstrom, John F. 2013. The Person–Situation Interaction. In *Oxford Handbook of Social Cognition*, ed. Donal E. Carlston. Oxford: Oxford University Press pp. 768–805.

Klar, Samara. 2013. "The Influence of Competing Identity Primes on Political Preferences." *Journal of Politics* 75(4):1108–1124.

2014. "Partisanship in a Social Setting." *American Journal of Political Science* 58(3):687–704.

Klein, Ezra. 2010. "Was Medicare Popular When It Passed?" *The Washington Post*. URL: *http://voices.washingtonpost.com/ezra-klein/2010/03/was_medicare_popular_when_it_p.html* Accessed February 10, 2016.

Konda, Thomas M., and Lee Sigelman. 1987. "Public Evaluations of the American Parties, 1952–1984." *Journal of Politics* 49(3):814–829.

Kramer, Gerald H. 1977. "A Dynamical Model of Political Equilibrium." *Journal of Economic Theory* 16(2):310–334.

1983. "The Ecological Fallacy Revisited: Aggregate versus Individual-Level Findings on Economics and Elections, and Sociotropic Voting." *American Political Science Review* 77(1):92–111.

Krosnick, Jon A., and Richard E. Petty. 1995. *Attitude Strength: Antecedents and Consequences*. New York: Psychology Press.

Kruglanski, Arie W. 1989. *Lay Epistemics and Human Knowledge: Cognitive and Motivational Bases*. New York: Plenum Press.

Kruglanski, Arie W., and Gerd Gigerenzer. 2011. "Intuitive and Deliberate Judgments Are Based on Common Principles." *Psychological Review* 118(1):97–109.

Ksiazkiewicz, Aleksander, Steven Ludeke, and Robert Krueger. Forthcoming. "The Role of Cognitive Style in the Link between Genes and Political Ideology." *Political Psychology* doi: 10.1111/pops.12318.

Kunda, Ziva. 1990. "The Case for Motivated Reasoning." *Psychological Bulletin* 108:480–498.

Lakatos, Imre. 1970. Falsification and the Methodology of Scientific Research Programmes. In *Criticism and the Growth of Knowledge*, ed. Imre Lakatos and Alan Musgrave. Cambridge: Cambridge University Press pp. 91–193.

Lang, Peter J. 1995. "The Emotion Probe." *American Psychologist* 50(5):372–385.

Lau, Richard R., and David P. Redlawsk. 2001. "Advantages and Disadvantages of Cognitive Heuristics in Political Decision Making." *American Journal of Political Science* 45(4):951–971.

2006. *How Voters Decide: Information Processing During Election Campaigns*. New York: Cambridge University Press.

Lavine, Howard G., Christopher D. Johnston, and Marco R. Steenbergen. 2012. *The Ambivalent Partisan: How Critical Loyalty Promotes Democracy*. Oxford: Oxford University Press.

LeBoeuf, Robyn A., and Eldar Shafir. 2003. "Deep Thoughts and Shallow Frames: On the Susceptibility to Framing Effects." *Journal of Behavioral Decision Making* 16(2):77–92.

Lee, Jayeon. 2014. "Are Some People Less Influenced by Others' Opinions? The Role of Internal Political Self-Efficacy and Need for Cognition in Impression Formation on Social Networking Sites." *Cyberpsychology, Behavior, and Social Networking* 17(9):571–577.

Lenz, Gabriel S. 2012. *Follow the Leader?: How Voters Respond to Politicians' Policies and Performance*. Chicago: University of Chicago Press.

Levendusky, Matthew. 2009. *The Partisan Sort: How Liberals Became Democrats and Conservatives Became Republicans*. Chicago: University of Chicago Press.

2010. "Clearer Cues, More Consistent Voters: A Benefit of Elite Polarization." *Political Behavior* 32(1):111–131.

Lewin, Kurt. 1935. *A Dynamic Theory of Personality: Selected Papers*. New York: McGraw-Hill Book Co.

Lewis-Beck, Michael S., William G. Jacoby, Helmut Norpoth, and Herbert F. Weisberg. 2009. *The American Voter Revisited*. Ann Arbor, MI: University of Michigan Press.

Lindstädt, René, and Ryan J. Vander Wielen. 2013. "Dynamic Elite Partisanship: Party Loyalty and Agenda Setting in the U.S. House." *British Journal of Political Science* 44(4):741–772.

Lodge, Milton, and Charles S. Taber. 2013. *The Rationalizing Voter*. Cambridge: Cambridge University Press.

Lopez-Raton, Monica, Maria Xose Rodriguez-Alvarez, Carmen Cardarso-Suarez, and Francisco Gude-Sampedro. 2015. "OptimalCutpoints: An R Package for Selecting Optimal Cutpoints in Diagnostic Tests." *Journal of Statistical Software* 61(1):1–36.

Lufityanto, G., C. Donkin, and J. Pearson. 2016. "Measuring Intuition: Nonconscious Emotional Information Boosts Decision Accuracy and Confidence." *Psychological Science* 27(5):622–634.

Lupia, Arthur. 1994. "Shortcuts versus Encyclopedias: Information and Voting Behavior in California Insurance Reform Elections." *American Political Science Review* 88(1):63–76.

Lupia, Arthur, and Mathew D. McCubbins. 1998. *The Democratic Dilemma: Can Citizens Learn What They Need to Know?* New York: Cambridge University Press.

MacKuen, Michael B., Robert S. Erikson, and James A. Stimson. 1989. "Macropartisanship." *American Political Science Review* 83:1125–1142.

MacKuen, Michael B., Robert S. Erikson, and James A. Stimson. 1992. "Peasants or Bankers? The American Electorate and the US Economy." *American Political Science Review* 86(3):597–611.

Madison, James. 2003/1787. "The Federalist No. 10." *The Federalist Papers*. New York: Penguin Putnam.

Maghsoodloo, Saeed and Ching-Ying Huang. 2010. "Comparing the Overlapping of Two Independent Confidence Intervals with a Single Confidence Interval for Two Normal Population Parameters." *Journal of Statistical Planning and Inference* 140(11): 3295–3305.

Maio, Gregory R., and Victoria M. Esses. 2001. "The Need for Affect: Individual Differences in the Motivation to Approach or Avoid Emotions." *Journal of Personality* 69(4):583–614.

Malka, Ariel, Christopher J. Soto, Michael Inzlicht, and Yphtach Lelkes. 2014. "Do Needs for Security and Certainty Predict Cultural and Economic Conservatism? A Cross-National Analysis." *Journal of Personality and Social Psychology* 106(6):1031–1051.

Manin, Bernard. 1997. *The Principles of Representative Government*. Cambridge: Cambridge University Press.

Mansbridge, Jane, James Bohman, Simone Chambers, Thomas Christiano, Archon Fung, John Parkinson, Dennis F. Thompson, and Mark E. Warren. 2012. A Systemic Approach to Deliberative Democracy. In *Deliberative Systems: Deliberative Democracy at the Large Scale*, ed. Jane Mansbridge and John Parkinson. Cambridge: Cambridge University Press Cambridge pp. 1–26.

Manza, J., and F. L. Cook. 2002. "A Democratic Polity?: Three Views of Policy Responsiveness to Public Opinion in the United States." *American Politics Research* 30(6):630–667.

Marcus, George E., W. Russell Neuman, and Michael MacKuen. 2000. *Affective Intelligence and Political Judgment.* Chicago: University of Chicago Press.

Margolis, Michele F. Forthcoming. From politics to the pews: How partisanship and the political environment shape religious identity. Chicago: University of Chicago Press.

Martin, Andrew D., Kevin M. Quinn, and Jong Hee Park. 2013. "Markov Chain Monte Carlo (MCMC) Package." http://mcmcpack.wustl.edu, Version 1.3-3.

Maslow, A. H. 1943. "A Theory of Human Motivation." *Psychological Review* 50(4):370–396.

Mayer, Nicole D., and Zakary L. Tormala. 2010. "'Think' Versus 'Feel' Framing Effects in Persuasion." *Personality and Social Psychology Bulletin* 36(4):443–454.

McAdams, Dan P., and Jennifer L. Pals. 2006. "A New Big Five: Fundamental Principles for an Integrative Science of Personality." *American Psychologist* 61(3):204–217.

McCarty, Nolan, Keith T. Poole, and Howard Rosenthal. 2006. *Polarized America: The Dance of Ideology and Unequal Riches.* Cambridge: MIT Press.

McCombs, M. E. and D. L. Shaw. 1972. "The Agenda-Setting Function of Mass Media." *Public Opinion Quarterly* 36(2):176–187.

McCrae, Robert R., and Paul T. Costa. 1987. "Validation of the Five-Factor Model of Personality across Instruments and Observers." *Journal of Personality and Social Psychology* 52(1):81–90.

McDermott, Rose, James H. Fowler, and Oleg Smirnov. 2008. "On the Evolutionary Origin of Prospect Theory Preferences." *Journal of Politics* 70(2):335–350.

McGraw, Kathleen M. 1990. "Avoiding Blame: An Experimental Investigation of Political Excuses and Justifications." *British Journal of Political Science* 20:119–131.

McKelvey, Richard D. 1975. "Policy-Related Voting and Electoral Equilibrium." *Econometrica: Journal of the Econometric Society* 43(5/6):815–843.

Mencken, Henry Louis. 1916. *A Little Book in C Major.* New York: John Lane Company.

Mischel, Walter. 1968. *Personality and Assessment.* New York: Wiley.

Mondak, Jeffery J., Matthew V. Hibbing, Damarys Canache, Mitchell A. Seligson, and Mary R. Anderson. 2010. "Personality and Civic Engagement: An Integrative Framework for the Study of Trait Effects on Political Behavior." *American Political Science Review* 104(1):85–110.

Monroe, Kristen R. 1978. "Economic Influences on Presidential Popularity." *Public Opinion Quarterly* 42(3):360–369.

Mooney, Chris. 2012. *The Republican Brain: The Science of Why They Deny Science – and Reality.* Hoboken, NJ: John Wiley & Sons.

Mueller, John E. 1970. "Presidential Popularity from Truman to Johnson." *American Political Science Review* 64(1):18–34.

Mutz, Diana C. 1998. *Impersonal Influence: How Perceptions of Mass Collectives Affect Political Attitudes.* Cambridge: Cambridge University Press.

Neal, Radford M. 1996. *Bayesian Learning for Neural Networks*. Lecture Notes in Statistics. New York: Springer.

Nelson, Thomas E., Rosalee A. Clawson, and Zoe M. Oxley. 1997. "Media Framing of a Civil Liberties Conflict and Its Effect on Tolerance." *American Political Science Review* 91(3):567–583.

New, Joshua J., and Tamsin C. German. 2015. "Evolution and Human Behavior." *Evolution and Human Behavior* 36(3):165–173.

News, NBC and the *Wall Street Journal*. 1993. NBC News/*Wall Street Journal* *Poll*. Technical report Hart-Teeter Research Companies.

   2011.   NBC News/*Wall Street Journal* Poll: 2012 Presidential Election/Economy/Federal Debt Ceiling/Health Care Reform. Technical report Hart and McInturff Research Companies.

Nicholson, Stephen P. 2011. "Dominating Cues and the Limits of Elite Influence." *Journal of Politics* 73(4):1165–1177.

   2012. "Polarizing Cues." *American Journal of Political Science* 56(1):52–66.

Nie, Norman H., Sidney Verba, and John R. Petrocik. 1976. *The Changing American Voter*. Cambridge, MA: Harvard University Press.

Nir, Lilach. 2011. "Motivated Reasoning and Public Opinion Perception." *Public Opinion Quarterly* 75(3):504–532.

Norpoth, Helmut. 1984. "Economics, Politics, and the Cycle of Presidential Popularity." *Political Behavior* 6(3):253–273.

Ohman, Arne, and Susan Mineka. 2003. "The Malicious Serpent: Snakes as a Prototypical Stimulus for an Evolved Module of Fear." *Current Directions in Psychological Science* 12(1):5–9.

Osman, Magda. 2004. "An Evaluation of Dual-Process Theories of Reasoning." *Psychonomic Bulletin and Review* 11(6):988–1010.

Oxley, D. R., K. B. Smith, J. R. Alford, M. V. Hibbing, J. L. Miller, M. Scalora, P. K. Hatemi, and J. R. Hibbing. 2008. "Political Attitudes Vary with Physiological Traits." *Science* 321(5896):1667–1670.

Page, Benjamin I., and Calvin C. Jones. 1979. "Reciprocal Effects of Policy Preferences, Party Loyalties and the Vote." *American Political Science Review* 73(4):1071–1089.

Page, Benjamin I., and Robert Y. Shapiro. 1992. *The Rational Public: Fifty Years of Trends in Americans' Policy Preferences*. Chicago: University of Chicago Press.

Petersen, Michael Bang. 2015. "Evolutionary Political Psychology: On the Origin and Structure of Heuristics and Biases in Politics." *Political Psychology* 36:45–78.

Petersen, Michael Bang, Ann Giessing, and Jesper Nielsen. 2015. "Physiological Responses and Partisan Bias: Beyond Self-Reported Measures of Party Identification." *PLoS ONE* 10(5):e0126922.

Petty, Richard E., and Duane T. Wegener. 1998. Attitude Change: Multiple Roles for Persuasion Variables. In *The Handbook of Social Psychology*, ed. Daniel T. Gilbert, Susan T. Fiske, and Gardner Lindzey. 4 ed. Vol. 1 New York: McGraw-Hill pp. 323–390.

Petty, Richard E., and John T. Cacioppo. 1981. *Attitudes and Persuasion: Classic and Contemporary Approaches*. Dubuque, IA: William C. Brown.

1986. "The Elaboration Likelihood Model of Persuasion." *Advances in Experimental Social Psychology* 19(123–205).

Petty, Richard E., and Pablo Brinol. 2002. Attitude Change: The Elaboration Likelihood Model of Persuasion. In *Marketing for Sustainability: Towards Transactional Policy Making*, ed. Gerard C. Bartels and Wil Nelissen. IOS Press pp. 176–190.

Popkin, Samuel L. 1994. *The Reasoning Voter: Communication and Persuasion in Presidential Campaigns*. Chicago: University of Chicago Press.

Prior, Markus, Gaurav Sood, and Kabir Khanna. 2015. "You Cannot Be Serious: The Impact of Accuracy Incentives on Partisan Bias in Reports of Economic Perceptions." *Quarterly Journal of Political Science* 10(4):489–518.

Quinn, Kevin M. 2004. "Bayesian Factor Analysis for Mixed Ordinal and Continuous Responses." *Political Analysis* 12:338–353.

R Development Core Team. 2013. "R: A Language and Environment for Statistical Computing." Vienna: R Foundation for Statistical Computing, Version 3.0.0.

Rabin, Matthew, and Richard H. Thaler. 2001. "Anomalies: Risk Aversion." *The Journal of Economic Perspectives* 15(1):219–232.

Rahn, Wendy M. 1993. "The Role of Partisan Stereotypes in Information Processing about Political Candidates." *American Journal of Political Science* 37(2):472–496.

Rand, David G. 2016. "Cooperation, Fast and Slow: Meta-Analytic Evidence for a Theory of Social Heuristics and Self-Interested Deliberation." *Psychological Science* 27(9):1192–1206.

Rawls, John. 1996. *Political Liberalism*. New York: Columbia University Press.

Redlawsk, David P. 2002. "Hot Cognition or Cool Consideration? Testing the Effects of Motivated Reasoning on Political Decision Making." *Journal of Politics* 64(4):1021–1044.

Riggle, Ellen D., Victor C. Ottati, Robert S. Wyer, Jr., James Kuklinski, and Norbert Schwarz. 1992. "Bases of Political Judgments: The Role of Stereotypic and Nonstereotypic Information." *Political Behavior* 14(1):67–87.

Rohde, David W. 1991. *Parties and Leaders in the Postreform House*. Chicago: University of Chicago Press.

Rokeach, Milton. 1960. *The Open and Closed Mind*. New York: Basic Books.

Ross, Lee, Mark R. Lepper, and Michael Hubbard. 1975. "Perseverance in Self-Perception and Social Perception: Biased Attributional Processes in the Debriefing Paradigm." *Journal of Personality and Social Psychology* 32(5):880–892.

Royston, Patrick, Douglas G. Altman, and Will Sauerbrei. 2006. "Dichotomizing Continuous Predictors in Multiple Regression: A Bad Idea." *Statistics in Medicine* 25(1):127–141.

Rucker, Derek D., Blakeley B. McShane, and Kristopher J. Preacher. 2015. "A Researcher's Guide to Regression, Discretization, and Median Splits of Continuous Variables." *Journal of Consumer Psychology* 25(4):666–678.

Rudolph, Thomas J. 2003. "Who's Responsible for the Economy? The Formation and Consequences of Responsibility Attributions." *American Journal of Political Science* 47(4):698–713.

Rudolph, Thomas J., and Elizabeth Popp. 2007. "An Information Processing Theory of Ambivalence." *Political Psychology* 28:563–585.

Ryan, Timothy, Matthew S. Wells, and Brice D. L. Acree. 2016. "Emotional Responses to Disturbing Political News: The Role of Personality." *Journal of Experimental Political Science* 3(2):174–184.

Schattschneider, E. E. 1942. *Party Government.* New York: Holt, Rinehart, and Winston.

Schooler, Jonathan W., Michael D. Mrazek, Benjamin Baird, and Piotr Winkielman. 2015. Minding the Mind: The Value of Distinguishing among Unconscious, Conscious, and Metaconscious Processes. In *American Psychological Association Handbook of Personality and Social Psychology: Volume 1. Attitudes and Social Cognition*, ed. M. Mikulincer and Phillip R. Shaver. Washington: American Psychological Association pp. 179–202.

Schwartz, Shalom H., Jan Cieciuch, Michele Vecchione, Eldad Davidov, Ronald Fischer, Constanze Beierlein, Alice Ramos, Markku Verkasalo, Jan-Erik Lönnqvist, Kursad Demirutku, Ozlem Dirilen-Gumus, and Mark Konty. 2012. "Refining the Theory of Basic Individual Values." *Journal of Personality and Social Psychology* 103(4):663–688.

Settle, Jaime E., Christopher T. Dawes, and James H. Fowler. 2009. "The Heritability of Partisan Attachment." *Political Research Quarterly* 62(3):601–613.

Shapiro, Ian. 2003. *The State of Democratic Theory.* Princeton, NJ: Princeton University Press.

Sides, John, and Lynn Vavreck. 2013. *The Gamble: Choice and Chance in the 2012 Presidential Election.* Princeton, NJ: Princeton University Press.

Simon, Herbert A. 1959. "Theories of Decision-Making in Economics and Behavioral Science." *The American Economic Review* 49(3):253–283.

Slothuus, Rune. 2010. "When Can Political Parties Lead Public Opinion? Evidence from a Natural Experiment." *Political Communication* 27(2):158–177.

Sniderman, Paul M. 2000. Taking Sides: A Fixed Choice Theory of Political Reasoning. In *Elements of Reason: Cognition, Choice, and the Bounds of Rationality*, ed. Arthur Lupia, Mathew D. McCubbins, and Samuel L. Popkin. Cambridge: Cambridge University Press pp. 67–84.

Sobieraj, Sarah, and Jeffrey M. Berry. 2011. "From Incivility to Outrage: Political Discourse in Blogs, Talk Radio, and Cable News." *Political Communication* 28(1):19–41.

Social Security History. 2014. "Legislative History." URL: *www.ssa.gov/history/tally65.html* Accessed February 10, 2016.

Sohlberg, Jacob. 2015. "Thinking Matters: The Validity and Political Relevance of Need for Cognition." *International Journal of Public Opinion Research* 28(3)428–439.

Soroka, Stuart N., and Christopher Wlezien. 2010. *Degrees of Democracy.* New York: Cambridge University Press.

Stanovich, Keith E. 2009. Distinguishing the Reflective, Algorithmic, and Autonomous Minds: Is It Time for a Tri-Process Theory? In *In Two Minds: Dual Processes and Beyond*, ed. Jonathan Evans and Keith Frankish. New York: Oxford University Press pp. 55–88.

2011. *Rationality and the Reflective Mind.* New York: Oxford University Press.

Stanovich, Keith E., and Richard F. West. 2000. "Individual Differences in Reasoning: Implications for the Rationality Debate." *Behavioral and Brain Sciences* 23:645–726.

Stimson, James A., Michael B. MacKuen, and Robert S. Erikson. 1995. "Dynamic Representation." *American Political Science Review* 89:543–565.

Stokes, Donald E. 1963. "Spatial Models of Party Competition." *American Political Science Review* 57(2):368–377.

Tesler, Michael, and John Sides. March 3, 2016. "How Political Science Helps Explain the Rise of Trump: The Role of White Identity and Grievances." *The Washington Post Monkey Cage Blog* https://www.washingtonpost.com/news/monkey-cage/wp/2016/03/03/how-political-science-helps-explain-the-rise-of-trump-the-role-of-white-identity-and-grievances/.

Tetlock, Philip. 2005. *Expert Political Judgment: How Good Is It? How Can We Know?* Princeton, NJ: Princeton University Press.

Theodoridis, Alexander G. Forthcoming. "Me, Myself, and (I), (D), or (R)? Partisanship and Political Cognition through the Lens of Implicit Identity." *Journal of Politics.*

Tilley, James, and Sara B. Hobolt. 2011. "Is the Government to Blame? An Experimental Test of How Partisanship Shapes Perceptions of Performance and Responsibility." *Journal of Politics* 73(2):316–330.

Tomz, Michael, and Robert P. Van Houweling. 2009. "The Electoral Implications of Candidate Ambiguity." *American Political Science Review* 103(1): 83–98.

Treier, Shawn, and Simon Jackman. 2008. "Democracy as a Latent Variable." *American Journal of Political Science* 52:201–217.

Tversky, Amos, and Daniel Kahneman. 1981. "The Framing of Decisions and the Psychology of Choice." *Science* 211(4481):453–458.

Valentino, Nicholas A., Ted Brader, Eric W. Groenendyk, Krysha Gregorowicz, and Vincent L. Hutchings. 2011. "Election Night's Alright for Fighting: The Role of Emotions in Political Participation." *Journal of Politics* 73(1):156–170.

Valentino, Nicholas A., Vincent L. Hutchings, Antoine J. Banks, and Anne K. Davis. 2008. "Is a Worried Citizen a Good Citizen? Emotions, Political Information Seeking, and Learning via the Internet." *Political Psychology* 29(2):247–273.

van Schuur, Wijbrandt H. 2011. *Ordinal Item Response Theory: Mokken Scale Analysis.* Los Angeles: Sage.

Vonnegut, Kurt. 1963. *Cat's Cradle.* New York: Bantam Doubleday Dell Publishing Group.

Washington, George. 1796. "Farewell Address." Philadelphia, PA.

Watson, David, and Lee Anna Clark. 1994. "The PANAS-X: Manual for the Positive and Negative Affect Schedule-Expanded Form." Iowa City, IA: University of Iowa. **URL:** http://ir.uiowa.edu/cgi/viewcontent.cgi?article=1011& context=psychology_pubs

Wattenberg, Martin P. 1998. *The Decline of American Political Parties, 1952–1996.* Cambridge, MA: Harvard University Press.

Weber, Christopher, and Christopher M. Federico. 2007. "Interpersonal Attachment and Patterns of Ideological Belief." *Political Psychology* 28(4):389–416.

Webster, Donna M., and Arie W. Kruglanski. 1994. "Individual Differences in Need for Cognitive Closure." *Journal of Personality and Social Psychology* 67(6):1049–1062.

Wegner, Daniel M. 2003. "The Mind's Best Trick: How We Experience Conscious Will." *Trends in Cognitive Sciences* 7(2):65–69.

Weinschenk, Aaron C. 2010. "Revisiting the Political Theory of Party Identification." *Political Behavior* 32(4):473–494.

Weisberg, Herbert F., and Steven P. Nawara. 2010. "How Sophistication Affected the 2000 Presidential Vote: Traditional Sophistication Measures versus Conceptualization." *Political Behavior* 32(4):547–565.

Westen, D., P. S. Blagov, K. Harenski, and C. Kilts. 2006. "Neural Bases of Motivated Reasoning: An fMRI Study of Emotional Constraints on Partisan Political Judgment in the 2004 US Presidential Election." *Journal of Cognitive Neuroscience* 18(11):1947–1958.

Wlezien, Christopher. 1995. "The Public as Thermostat: Dynamics of Preferences for Spending." *American Journal of Political Science* 39(4):981–1000.

Wlezien, Christopher, Mark Franklin, and Daniel Twiggs. 1997. "Economic Perceptions and Vote Choice: Disentangling the Endogeneity." *Political Behavior* 19(1):7–17.

Woon, Jonathan. 2012. "Democratic Accountability and Retrospective Voting: A Laboratory Experiment." *American Journal of Political Science* 56(4):913–930.

Zajonc, Robert B. 1980. "Feeling and Thinking: Preferences Need No Inferences." *American Psychologist* 33:151–175.

Zaller, John. 1992. *The Nature and Origins of Mass Opinion.* Cambridge: Cambridge University Press.

Zheng, Xiaohui, and Sophia Rabe-Hesketh. 2007. "Estimating Parameters of Dichotomous and Ordinal Item Response Models with gllamm." *The Stata Journal* 7:313–333.

Index